A Writer's AMERICA

ALFRED KAZIN

A Writer's AMERICA

Landscape in Literature

With 102 illustrations, 16 in color

ALFRED A. KNOPF · NEW YORK 1988

TITLE PAGE: *Wayside grave on the Oregon Trail; a reminder of the perils of "westering" (1872).*

THIS IS A BORZOI BOOK PUBLISHED BY ALFRED A. KNOPF, INC.

Copyright © 1988 by Alfred Kazin

Library of Congress Cataloging-in-Publication Data

Kazin, Alfred, 1915–
  A writer's America: landscape in literature / Alfred Kazin.
    p. cm.
    Bibliography: p.
    Includes index.
    ISBN 0-394-57142-8
    1. American literature – History and criticism. 2. Landscape in literature.   3. United States in literature.   4. Nature in literature.   5. Local color in literature.   I. Title.
  PS169.L35K39 1988
  810'.9'36 – dc19   88–1299
                                                                              CIP

First American Edition
Manufactured in the German Democratic Republic

CONTENTS

Introduction   7

CHAPTER ONE   *New Worlds*   9

CHAPTER TWO   *Romantic America*   45

CHAPTER THREE   *Westward I Go Free*   81

CHAPTER FOUR   *Local Color*   121

CHAPTER FIVE   *Power Centers*   152

CHAPTER SIX   *To California and Beyond:*   195
The Roving American

Acknowledgments   229

Bibliography   230

List of Illustrations   232

Index   236

FOR JUDITH

from sea to shining sea

The look of things, the look that conveys their meaning, to catch the colour, the relief, the expression, the surface, the substance of the human spectacle.

Henry James: *The Art of Fiction* (1884)

INTRODUCTION

Leopold Mozart was definitely not American when he warned his celebrated son: "Nature is the greatest enemy." From its beginning as the original creation, as pure "unstoried wilderness," Nature in America has dominated the imagination of Europeans exploring the place, of settlers hoping that so much available land really meant a "New World," of writers enraptured with this new divinity. America was the world's myth before there was actually a place that could be called "America"; the genuine substance of that myth was not just a new continent, abundant land, but the magic of its actuality, the consummation of a dream, a second chance for mankind. The "great circle" for which Columbus had started out was at last in sight; America made it possible for the world to be seen as one.

As "God's own country," however, this paradise was always getting lost. Was Nature just raw material, as likely as any to be defiled and exhausted? At the heart of American literature lies the continuing uncertainty. On the one hand Nature was the gift of gifts, "fresh from the Creator's hand." As late as 1925, in one of the most beautiful of American books, Scott Fitzgerald ended *The Great Gatsby* with undiminished longing for that fabled beginning. "For a transitory enchanted moment man must have held his breath in the presence of this continent, compelled into an esthetic contemplation he neither understood nor desired, face to face for the last time in history with something commensurate to his capacity for wonder."

But on the other hand! Nothing about American writing and writers is so well known as its passionate protest against every curtailment of national hope and individual will. In a country that once thought of itself as "Nature's Nation" but now proclaims itself one vast technological hookup, no subject is more pressing to many people than "conservation," the preservation of "wilderness areas." The constitution of the State of New York contains a commitment to keep the vast Adirondack State Preserve, the largest of national parks, "forever wild."

Nature not just *in* America but *as* America was a dream from the beginning. An unoccupied continent plus the young republic's good fortune in having for its "fathers" men of the Enlightenment combined—as is written in the Declaration of Independence— to give authority to "the laws of nature and to Nature's God." Two centuries later many Americans—by no means all of them mountain poets from the Northwest—see a betrayal of some early commitment to Nature in this most urbanized and "developed" of nations. The wilderness societies are so numerous and active that they have taken to buying up vast tracts of land in order to keep them unsullied.

The sense of loss, even of guilt, at the merest hint of defilement to Nature was routine in America when the eighteenth-century botanist William Bartram revisited a favorite cove in Indian-occupied East Florida and lamented some rudimentary attempts to make the place habitable. The legendary Daniel Boone is supposed to have indignantly removed himself when another settler appeared in Kentucky miles away.

Yet the literature of this notoriously rootless people is haunted by the sense of place that amazed D.H. Lawrence in the American classics. American writing is just as famous for Thoreau's fierce attachment to a pond in Massachusetts as it is for Melville's world wandering. No real American place lingered long in the mind of Edgar Allan Poe; he was never really at home there. Yet no reader of Nathaniel Hawthorne can forget the stockades of Puritan Boston in *The Scarlet Letter*, the very look of the decaying house in *The House of the Seven Gables*, even of the inhuman forest fit only for the Devil, who proclaims in Hawthorne's story "Young Goodman Brown" that "Evil is the nature of mankind. Evil must be your only happiness."

Some ingrained memory of mankind's eternal wandering, of the hardships of the terrible passage over, has lingered in American writing along with expressive gratitude for a place of one's own. America's "sacred places" were made so not by religion but by attachment to places that spelled safety. In the freezing, deserted North Woods country of the Adirondacks, an Irish family that had fled there from the famine refused to leave their hardscrabble farm even on Sundays; the priest had to come to them. Bit by bit, as among the English who built up the Connecticut River Valley and became its "River Gods," the Scotch-Irish who fled from Scotland upon the defeat of the Stuarts to cross the Appalachians into the wild Indian country of the Mississippi Delta, the ragged, often desperate, first arrivals became the first citizens of each little piece of new country.

And left the story of their rise, often enough of their decline, to be told by eccentric descendants—Ralph Waldo Emerson in Concord, Walt Whitman in Brooklyn, Emily Dickinson in Amherst, William Faulkner in Oxford, Mississippi. These were followed by the children of recent immigrants and the descendants of slaves—Saul Bellow from Chicago, Richard Wright from Mississippi, Ralph Ellison from Oklahoma. The enduring sense of place such writers created fills American writing with the sight and fury of a hundred different American settlements. And how different from each other, how often speechless with each other, these "Americas" remain. A nation composed of many nations, a people who often have nothing in common but their being Americans (this can become everything), have produced a literature united only by the sense of difference within the country itself.

Yet behind all these writers still lies some everlasting background that we call "Nature"—land, the land that was here before there was anything else. And what have the writers in this book not said about it, in amazement, in rapture, in frustration! From Jefferson exclaiming over the Blue Ridge to John McPhee describing the "bruises" in the ponds of great empty Maine, from Nathaniel Hawthorne in Concord laughing over the sluggishness of the local river to Huckleberry Finn bewitched by sunrise on the Mississippi, there is such a journey here into the face of Nature as has always filled out the world's insufficient sense of wonder.

ALFRED KAZIN
New Year's Day 1986

CHAPTER ONE

NEW WORLDS

By the end of 1781 the long-drawn-out war for American independence had finally come to an end on a battlefield in Virginia overlooking the Atlantic Ocean. "There is something absurd in supposing a continent to be governed by an island," Thomas Paine wrote. Thomas Jefferson, more aware than any other leader of the Revolution that his country was indeed a continent, would soon be going abroad for the young republic. But because a secretary to the French Legation in Philadelphia had passed a series of questions "relating to the laws, institutions, geography, climate, flora and fauna" of Mr. Jefferson's native state, he took time to write the one book he would publish in his tumultuously crowded life, *Notes on the State of Virginia*.

At Monticello, his "little mountain," the hilltop mansion he had designed and helped to build overlooking the Blue Ridge Mountains to the West, Jefferson now summed up all the knowledge available about a province that was believed in its founding charter (1609) to extend "from sea to sea." In 1781 it actually extended from the Atlantic to the Appalachians, and included what are now West Virginia and Kentucky, a roughly triangular area that Jefferson too generously thought a third larger than Great Britain plus Ireland. He proudly called it "My Country." In twenty-three chapters he described Virginia's boundaries, rivers, seaports, mountains, cascades, aborigines, laws, manners. Nor did he overlook "proceedings as to Tories." For him the war against England was a war against the old order prevailing everywhere in Europe.

Serenely neo-classical Monticello owes much to the Renaissance architect Palladio, more to Thomas Jefferson. It awes visitors as a triumph of taste, but it was built to serve the boundless curiosity and activity of Thomas Jefferson—architect, inventor and experimenter extraordinary, agriculturist, natural philosopher, political philosopher, bibliophile, musician, lawyer, wartime governor, soon to be Minister to France, Secretary of State, Vice-President and third President of the United States.

Monticello, stately as it looks, an eighteenth-century "picture" of a great landowner's benevolent authority, was a plantation seat that had to double as the workshop of a universal savant who lived in the middle of a great forest. Planning his own house, laying out its grounds, inventing appliances and creature comforts unthinkable to primitive Virginia, Jefferson on a grand scale was playing Adam, Prospero, Robinson Crusoe—owner and master of everything he surveyed, the first man on the place. This almost Biblical sense of authority was to lead him as President to send out Lewis and Clark on a "scientific" survey of the land from the Missouri River to the Pacific, preparing its inevitable absorption into the continental United States. He drew into tiers the map of new States in the Midwest and gave names to ten of them.

The great dome over the mansion at Monticello can make a visitor think that Jefferson's intellect is still presiding over the estate he laid out in every particular. He put a similar dome over his favorite creation, the University of Virginia, one even over his modest summer retreat at Poplar Forest. He was the proprietor of Monticello, 10,000 acres, and a hundred slaves; many were trained to carpentry, cabinet-making, house-building, weaving, tailoring, shoemaking. He imported the first threshing machine known in Virginia, invented the first scientific plough. Along the way he was a prime inventor of the United States. Of course it was Jefferson who wrote the Declaration of Independence. No country had deliberately created itself before. No such separation of church and state had been known in any country before Jefferson wrote the Virginia Statute of Religious Freedom. If Washington, the nation's capital, reflects the power of the United States in its solid mass of cold white Roman "temples," Monticello will always reflect the intoxicating sense of possibility on which the nation was founded.

Jefferson's biographer Dumas Malone notes that no one before Jefferson had thought of setting a plantation at such a height. The woods were thick, grading had to be done in stubborn soil, and everything had to be carried up a mountain. But Jefferson "had not disciplined his mind to the loss of imagination, . . . His eye, like his mind, sought an extended view. From this spot he could see to the eastward an expanse of forested country, rolling like the sea; and to the westward he could look across the treetops to a mountain wall of lavender and blue. . . . The country was little marred by the hand of man as yet and the prospect was majestic." On the estate, the open ground to the west seemed to call for shrubbery; Jefferson wanted it to remain an asylum for wild animals, excepting only beasts of prey. He thought of procuring a buck-elk to be monarch of the wood.

Notes on Virginia, written to satisfy the curiosity of the Old World, is alive with the glow Jefferson felt in reporting everything available about that new situation in the West, "My Country." He modified Palladio to make more window space and terraced roofs looking out to the Blue Ridge. Although he had studied at the College of William and Mary and had trained as a lawyer in the old colonial capital of Williamsburg on the coast, Jefferson was by birth and inclination a product of the Piedmont and what another Southern writer, William Faulkner, would call the "unstoried wilderness." Monticello was the creation of a patrician who was more a political visionary and a practical observer than any other Virginian of his class. Jefferson identified himself not with the English institutions at the tidewater but with the mountain country and beyond.

In *Notes on Virginia* he listed not only the great rivers of Virginia that rush down to Chesapeake Bay—the Rapphannock, the York, the James, the Potomac—but also the Ohio, "the most beautiful river on earth, the periodically flooded Mississippi, the muddy Missouri, the gentle Illinois, the lovely Wabash, and a dozen other streams." Much that went into the building of Monticello Jefferson devised and helped to manufacture himself, as was natural to pioneer country. His prime sense of being a new man in a new country imparted a certain rapture to the political argument behind the Declaration of Independence. It appealed to "self-evident" truths, such as are proclaimed by Nature. When it became necessary for one people to dissolve the political band connecting them with another, they could "assume among the powers of the earth the separate and equal station to which the Laws of Nature and of Nature's God entitle them." Abraham Lincoln formed his political philosophy around the Declaration of Independence. It was to encourage many an American visionary to find on the frontier "self-evident" justification for his political actions.

Monticello, Thomas Jefferson's Palladian mansion in Virginia, from which Jefferson could look out at "an expanse of forested country, rolling like the sea."

One of these visionaries was John Brown, who in 1859 tried to stir up a slave insurrection by attacking the United States arsenal at Harpers Ferry in the Blue Ridge Mountains at the confluence of the Potomac and Shenandoah Rivers. Long before this extraordinary site was called Harpers Ferry and before the slavery issue became "the fireball in the night" that frightened Jefferson into the realization that "this government, the world's best hope," might not last, *Notes on Virginia* described it as if no one had been there before Thomas Jefferson.

The passage of the Potomac through the Blue Ridge is, perhaps, one of the most stupendous scenes in nature. You stand in a very high point of land. On your right comes up the Shenandoah, having ranged along the foot of the mountain an hundred miles to seek a vent. On your left approaches the Potomac, in quest of a passage also. In the moment of their junction they rush together against the mountain, render it asunder and pass off to the sea. The first glance of this scene hurries our senses into the opinion, that this earth has been created in time, that the mountains were formed first, that the rivers began to flow afterwards, that in this place, particularly, they have been dammed up by the Blue Ridge of mountains, and have formed an ocean which filled the whole valley; that continuing to rise they have at length broken over at this spot, and have torn the mountain down from its summit to its base. . . .

The distinct finishing which nature has given to the picture is of a very different character. . . . For the mountain being cloven asunder, she presents to your eye, through the cleft, a small catch of smooth blue horizon, at an infinite distance in the plain country, inviting you, as it were, from the riot and tumult roaring around, to pass through the breach and participate of the calm below. Here the eye ultimately composes itself. . . . You cross the Potomac above the junction, pass along its side through the base of the mountain for three miles, its terrible precipices hanging in fragments over you, and within about twenty miles reach Frederictown and the fine country around that. This scene is worth a voyage across the Atlantic.

In "On the Prospect of Planting Arts and Learning in America" (1752) Bishop Berkeley described

> The Muse, disgusted at an Age and Clime,
>   Barren of every glorious Theme,
> In distant Lands now waits a better Time,
>   Producing Subjects worthy Fame:
>
> In happy Climes, where from the genial Sun
>   And virgin earth such Scenes ensue,
> The Force of Art by Nature seems outdone,
>   And fancied Beauties by the true.

In describing the confluence of the Potomac and the Shenandoah, Jefferson, like a good American, takes it for granted that "the Force of Art by Nature seems outdone." What excites him is Nature charging about, erupting and breaking through the expected, on land very near his own. Nothing could be less like the experience of an eighteenth-century Englishman on the Grand Tour. This is "Nature's Nation," and Jefferson's very own. Another wonder described in *Notes on Virginia*, the Natural Bridge, was actually on

The Natural Bridge, on Jefferson's vast property, was 270 feet deep. Jefferson found it frightening to climb, but from below "the rapture is really indescribable."

Jefferson's 10,000 acres—which does not restrain him from hailing "the most sublime of Nature's works. . . . It is impossible for the emotions arising from the sublime, to be felt beyond what they are here; so beautiful an arch, so elevated, so light, and springing as it were up to heaven, the rapture of the spectator is really indescribable!"

The characteristically American note in Jefferson's description of the rivers meeting at the Blue Ridge, rendering the mountain "asunder," is one that dominates all early descriptions of Western landscape. Astonishment, pride, "God's Own Country." But deeper and actually more lasting has been the sense of creation in the making. Jefferson exults in a sight for the eyes that is a continuous force. Jefferson the natural philosopher investigated Nature for his own survival as well as for curiosity's sake. But in recognizing from "the first glance of this scene . . . that this earth has been created in time, that the mountains were formed first, that the rivers began to flow afterwards," he offers us the process of creation made visible. Nothing about the New World was to put such a spell on writers, whether they saw America or not, as the fond belief that it represented the oldest world, pristine. It was the beginning of things, without man to sully the picture.

John Locke, who never saw it but needed the metaphor, roundly declared in 1690, "Thus in the beginning all the world was America, for nothing like money was known." America as perfect archaism, the world still showing its origins, was to haunt Europeans and Americans alike. "That naked country," as Charles II indifferently called it on the occasion of an early colony's rebellion against a royal governor, opened up sites for exploration that united geology to natural religion in a way especially pleasing to deism— God reduced to mere process. There was a myth about America before it had a name and was a definite place—it was what lay beyond the known world. It somehow remained beyond the known world to many who uneasily settled on its "nakedness." The Mexican writer Carlos Fuentes said that the Old World discovered the New but then had been unable to imagine it.

The world-transforming role Jefferson assigned to the "American experiment" was duplicated by the transformation in Nature he could see going on in the mountains of Virginia. *Notes on Virginia* breathes the excitement of some fabulous first encounter. This recurrent thrill of discovery was to be the secret of the prime American books, from *Walden* and *Leaves of Grass* and *Moby-Dick* to *Huckleberry Finn*. Thoreau, visiting Maine in 1846, saw "the raw materials of a planet."

Perhaps I most fully realized that this was primeval, untamed, and forever untamable *Nature*, or whatever else men call it, while coming down this part of the mountain. We were passing over "Burnt Lands," burnt by lightning, perchance, though they showed no recent marks of fire, hardly so much as a charred stump. . . . When I reflected what man, what brother or sister or kinsman of our race made it and claimed it, I expected the proprietor to rise up and dispute my passage. It is difficult to conceive of a region uninhabited by man. We habitually presume his presence and influence everywhere. And yet we have not seen pure Nature, unless we have seen her thus vast and drear and unhuman, though in the midst of cities. Nature was here something savage and awful, though beautiful. I looked with awe at the ground I trod on, to see what the Powers had made there. . . . This was that Earth of which we have heard, made out of Chaos and Old Night. . . . Man was not to be associated with it. It was Matter, vast, terrific—not this Mother Earth that we have heard of.

Nothing like this had ever been seen before! And Jefferson on his acres (all the time looking west to the Blue Ridge) was (as William Faulkner liked to say of his imaginary creation Yoknapatawpha County) the sole owner and proprietor. Jefferson's "own 'country'," says Dumas Malone, "was almost the only scene of his activity until he had entered into middle life, and if he did not know more about it than anybody else, he described it in his *Notes on Virginia* more fully than anyone else had ever done." He was happy to depend on a map of Virginia that his own father had drawn. The sober tone of the book (Jefferson had been invited to write the article on the United States for Diderot's great *Encyclopédie*) reveals a man who has become enamored of his subject by possessing it.

Whitman, unrolling the American scene before him in *Song of Myself*, was to say "*I am the man, I suffer'd, I was there.*" Jefferson describing Virginia is certainly "there." The book is full of Jefferson's glee in being able to describe a wholly new world no one before him has so thoroughly enumerated, classified, documented in the most systematic up-to-the-minute way, with all the scientific and statistical resources of the day open to him.

America as enduring myth, a second chance for mankind, was not lost on the President-philosopher who in his first inaugural address (1800) was to describe the United States as "the world's best hope. . . . Kindly separated by nature and a wide ocean from the exterminating havoc of one quarter of the globe . . . a chosen country, with room enough for our descendants to the thousandth and thousandth generation . . ." But Jefferson's belief that, in the New World, Nature gladly yielded its secrets transcended every myth; he incorporated the native landscape into his passion for science.

The world-famous French naturalist Count Buffon, keeper of the Jardin du Roi in Paris, was insufferably positive that animals on the American continent were smaller on the average than their European counterparts. "Science is more important in a republican than in any other government," Jefferson believed. "And in an infant country like ours we must depend for improvement on the science of other countries, longer established, possessing better means, and more advanced than ours." But the great Buffon, "the most learned of all others in the science of natural history," did not know America at first hand. He imbibed errors about America from English papers, and had curious notions. He believed, *inter alia*, that Indians as a race lacked virility and, Jefferson complained in his *Notes on Virginia*, made the "imputation of impotence in the conception and nourishment of animal life on a large scale."

Why did Buffon insist that the animals common to both the Old and New Worlds were smaller in the latter? That those peculiar to the New were on a smaller scale? That those which had been domesticated in both had degenerated in America? That on the whole America even exhibited fewer species? "And the reason he thinks is," Jefferson scornfully replied, "that the heats of America are less; that more waters are spread over its surface by nature, and fewer of these drained off by the hand of man. In other words, that *heat* is friendly, and *moisture* adverse to the production and development of large quadrupeds. . . . The truth of this is inscrutable to us by reasonings a priori. Nature has hidden from us her modus agendi. Our only appeal on such questions is to experience; and I think that experience is against the supposition."

Jefferson took particular satisfaction in proving that mammoths, looking like elephants but of another species, had once flourished in primitive America. With the insolent gift for tall tales that was to become common among American writers defending the New World against the Old, Jefferson made a point of mocking Buffon to his face when he was Minister to France. He explained that he had been unable to take it with him, but had picked up an uncommonly large panther skin in a Philadelphia shop for $16. He boasted about American deer with horns two feet long, claimed that the American moose stood so tall that reindeer could walk under his belly. He sent Buffon a large box containing the skin, horns, and skeleton of a moose, along with horns of the caribou, elk, deer, and spike-horned buck. The moose was seven feet tall and good enough to be stuffed, but Jefferson solemnly apologized that the creature had lost so much hair on the voyage. His disproof of Buffon seems poignant now in view of the erosion of Nature since his time. "Such is the economy of nature, that no instance can be produced of her having permitted any one race of her animals to become extinct; of her having formed any link in her great work so weak as to be broken."

Like so many investigators of the New World, European and American, Jefferson was haunted by the sense that parts of America had been occupied by aborigines unrelated to present Indian tribes. In his chapter on Indians in Virginia he described the barrows, the ancient burial grounds,

> of which many are to be found all over this country. These are of different sizes, some of them constructed of earth, and some of loose stones. That they were repositories of the dead, had been obvious to all; but on what particular occasion constructed, was matter of doubt. . . . Some . . . supposed them the general sepulchres for towns, conjectured to have been on or near these grounds; and this opinion was supported by the quality of the lands in which they are found (those constructed of earth being generally in the softest and most fertile meadow-grounds on riversides) and by a tradition, said to be handed down from the Aboriginal Indians, that, when they settled in a town, the first person who died was placed erect, and earth put about him, so as to cover and support him; that, when another died, a narrow passage was dug to the first, the second reclined against him, and the cover replaced, and so on. There being one of these in my neighbourhood, I wished to satisfy myself whether any, and which of these opinions were just. For this purpose I determined to open and examine it thoroughly.

Jefferson dissected some skeletons and with his usual regard for method enumerated anatomical details. He was determined to know "from whence come those aboriginal inhabitants of America." He must have been among the first to deduce that they had crossed over from Asia along a land bridge long disappeared into the Bering Strait. He professed himself saddened by the lack of attention given to Indian history and languages. "It is to be lamented, very much lamented, that we have suffered so many of the Indian tribes already to extinguish, without our having previously collected and deposited in the records of literature, the general rudiments at least of the languages they spoke . . . and hence to construct the best evidence of the derivation of this part of the human race."

So unsentimental an observer of America early in the next century as Alexis de Tocqueville tried to uncover in his *Democracy in America* "traces of an unknown people." Describing the "primitive Indians" he encountered in 1831, he added, "there can be no doubt that another people, more civilized and in all respects more advanced, preceded them in these same regions." He cited a "dim tradition" among Indian tribes on the Atlantic Coast about more ancient tribes that had lived west of the Mississippi.

In Nature's Wonderland (*Thomas Doughty, 1835, detail*).

"Frankliniana," botanical drawing by William Bartram.

Along the banks of the Ohio and throughout the central plain, man-made tumuli are continually coming to light. . . . There . . . thousands of our fellow men did live; we cannot doubt that.

When did they come there and what was their origin, history, and fate? No man can answer.

It is a strange thing that peoples should have so completely vanished from the earth, that even the memory of their name is lost; their languages are forgotten and their glory vanished like a sound without an echo; but I doubt that there is any which has not left some tomb as a memorial of its passage.

Even as the New World was being opened up, it became an amazing new chapter in the history of science. Its largely uninhabited surface fostered imaginings and longings for some fabulous past. What perplexed and fascinated the earliest explorers and settlers continues to fascinate the American writer to this day. What was behind the "naked country"? Tocqueville's book is particularly distinguished by accurate projections of the future in America. But he confessed that the very discovery of America seemed to him providential. It was as if the Deity had kept the New World in reserve all those centuries. There was some purpose to the unprecedented extension of human experience. This was a conviction shared by those severe and excellent minds in America, from the Puritans to Jefferson, Lincoln, Melville, Dickinson, who felt that with all the difficulties of living in a "half-savage country" (Ezra Pound), a "half-finished civilization" (John Cheever), Americans were privileged. They were witnessing a reissue of the world in its infancy. They were present at the creation.

Puritan settlers felt that by subjecting themselves for ten and even twelve weeks to the horrors of the North Atlantic crossing they were undergoing a *rite de passage* directly under the eye of God to His own country as set forth in the Bible. They were less sure when they were perched along Massachusetts Bay with "the vast and furious ocean" on one side of them, the ever "dark" unpenetrated forest on the other. In *History of Plymouth Plantation* the Puritan leader William Bradford described the first landing on Cape Cod:

what could they see but a hideous and desolate wilderness, full of wild beasts and wild men—and what multitudes there might be of them they knew not. Neither could they, as it were, go up to the top of Pisgah to view from this wilderness a more goodly country to feed their hopes; for which way soever they turned their eyes (save upward to the heavens) they could have little solace or content in respect of any outward objects. For summer being done, all things stand upon them with a weatherbeaten face, and the whole country, full of woods and thickets, represented a wild and savage hue.

In *The Scarlet Letter* (1850) Nathaniel Hawthorne suggested that Puritan Boston, narrow in every sense, may have suffered from physical imprisonment between sea and forest. The novel is suffused with physical darkness and claustrophobia as imprisoning as Puritan dogma. The only color in the narrow landscape is the scarlet letter that the heroine bravely wears as a token not of punishment for adultery but of inner liberation from these punitive surroundings. But the terrible Puritan magistrates and ministers actually took from their unfriendly surroundings renewed confidence in themselves as a chosen people. As Harvard's intellectual historian Perry Miller said, the fathers of New England "brought the land into an engagement with God." Boston was "a city upon a hill," Jerusalem revived. The Puritan divines trusted theology to explain their sufferings and to reveal their fate. The suspicion of witchcraft was justified by the forest all around them. Only the Devil could find his home there, and only the forest could explain the Devil. The forest was the one place on earth resistant to God. There it was, hovering over the children of God. Even Roger Williams, banished from Massachusetts and founder of Rhode Island, declared the wilderness of America "a clear resemblance of the world, where greedy and furious men persecute and devour the harmless and innocent as the wild beasts pursue and devour the hinds and roes." In Hawthorne's story "Young Goodman Brown," the Devil says to the townspeople seeking him out in the forest, "Welcome, my children, to the communion of your race. Ye have found, thus young, your nature and your destiny. . . . By the sympathy of your human hearts for sin, ye shall scent out all the places . . . where crime has been committed, and shall exult to behold the whole earth one stain of guilt, one mighty blood-spot."

As the fury against witchcraft died away, it became clear (in Miller's words) that "the onus of error lay heavy upon the land. . . . Out of sorrow and chagrin, out of dread, was born a new love for the land which had been desecrated, but somehow also consecrated, by the love of the innocents." A worldly, cheerful, and engaging Puritan, Samuel Sewall, was capable of a modern Nature lover's rapture. In his assiduous record of life in early Massachusetts, he enumerated the delights of Plum Island, now the Parker River National Wildlife Refuge, three miles from Newburyport.

> As long as *Plum Island* shall faithfully keep the commanded Post; notwithstanding all the hectoring Words, and hard Blows of the proud and boisterous Ocean; as long as any Salmon, or Sturgeon shall swim in the streams of *Merrimack*; or any Perch, or Pickeril, in Crane-Pound; as long as the Sea-Fowl shall know the Time of their coming, and not neglect seasonably to visit the Places of their Acquaintance: as long as any Cattel shall be fed with the Grass growing in the Medows, which do humbly bow themselves before Turkie-Hill; as long as any Sheep shall walk upon *Old Town Hills*, and shall from thence pleasantly look down upon the River *Parker*, and the fruitful *Marishes* lying beneath; as long as any free and harmless Does shall find a White Oak, or other Tree within the Township, to perch, or feed, or build a careless Nest upon; and shall voluntarily present themselves to perform the office of Gleaners after Barley-Harvest; as long as Nature shall not grow Old and dote; but shall constantly remember to give the rows of Indian corn their education, by Pairs; so long shall Christians be born there; and being first made meet, shall from thence be Translated, to be made partakers of the Inheritance of the Saints in Light.

"Place-names—the name." For Proust names were an essential part of the childhood landscape he loved. Sewall shows evident delight in the earliest names of American places. Naming newfound or newly made places was to become an American tradition—especially when it meant taking over Indian names for places from which Indians were driven. Whitman in *Leaves of Grass* was to compare himself to Adam "new naming" the animals and plants in Eden. To give a name was to appropriate a place, if only in imagination. As Robert Frost claimed in "The Gift Outright" (1942), the poem he read at John Kennedy's inauguration, "The land was ours before we were the land's."

To the Puritans the wilderness was a place of evil. To the Romantics it represented the Sublime, an attitude that produced paintings like Thomas Moran's Solitude *(1869).*

No one in the coming procession of American writers was to be more conscious than Herman Melville of how old, scripturally old, primordially old, the New World actually appeared. D.H. Lawrence was surprised to find that "your classic American literature is *older* than our English." Melville's particular achievement in *Moby-Dick* was to wrest his book, like the Eddas of old, out of ferocious depths. He gave his characters Old Testament names and presented the doomed whaling voyage as a murderous quest of the "mightiest animated mass that has survived the Flood." Melville said of *Moby-Dick*, "It is not a piece of fine feminine Spitalfields silk—but it is of the horrible texture of a fabric that should be woven of ships' cables & hawsers. A Polar wind blows through it, & birds of Prey hover over it." The harshness of all primitive Nature dominates the book through the prime features of great sea and great beast. In the struggle between man's effort to find a home for his mind in Nature and indifference of Nature itself, Nature in the shape of a whale first eludes man (after taking his leg off) and finally destroys ship and crew.

Is it possible, Melville asks over and again, that Nature must remain outside man, a great brute presiding over a world where an "intangible malignity has reigned from the beginning"? What made the book unpalatable to Melville's contemporaries was that he recurrently portrays the struggle from the side of Nature, not man. In the finale, when the exasperated beast downs the ship, the tremendous surge of Melville's prose brings home the ferocious indifference of the sea itself. We are back to the great unending gash of the Creation—indeed, we may never have left it. "Now small fowls flew screaming over the yet yawning gulf; a sullen white surf beat against its steep sides; then all collapsed, and the great shroud of the sea rolled on as it rolled five thousand years ago."

Finding one's way in Nature back to the legendary beginning of things was not always so severe in America. The joy Jefferson took in his native landscape was a tribute to his love of scientific inquiry and his contempt for religious fanaticism. Away from New England, religion could be mild, especially in the Quaker establishment of Pennsylvania. Natural history served better than theology to answer questions raised by the New World's constantly astonishing disclosures of the secrets hidden within Nature in the raw.

A self-educated Quaker farmer, John Bartram (1699–1777), planted the first botanical garden in America, now part of the Philadelphia park system. It contained both native and exotic species. Bartram had great English patrons, eventually became "Florida Botanist" to George III, and somehow managed to satisfy both Lord Petre, whose gardens and hothouses were the most extensive in the kingdom, and the English Quaker Peter Collinson, who demanded fossils, "evidence of the Deluge." Bartram was a sturdy, intensely religious, fiercely independent frontier type. In 1738 he made a five-weeks journey through Maryland and Virginia to Williamsburg, then up the James River and over the Blue Ridge Mountains, covering 1,100 miles without a single companion. "Our Americans have very little taste for these amusements. I can't find one that will bear the fatigue to accompany me in my peregrinations."

Bartram exchanged plants with the notable European botanists of the day, introduced American species into Europe and established many European species in the New World. The Swedish botanist Peter Kalm said, "I owe him many things, for he possessed that great quality of communicating everything he knew." Meticulous accounts of his journeys around the American continent in search of new plants were regularly sent abroad, and he left extraordinary records of Indian life in his *Journal of the Five Nations and Lake Ontario*. Unlike his more famous son Billy, he was not sentimental about Indians. After one of them chewed up his hat, John's advice to all and sundry was "to bang them stoutly."

William Bartram (1739–1823) began his legendary career by accompanying his father to Florida for specimens wanted by English patrons. He loved Florida, at one time set up as an indigo planter on the St. John's River, and was commissioned by the Duchess of Portland to draw shells "and all marine productions." The English physician and botanist Dr. John Fothergill paid William Bartram for five years to search out rare plants in the Floridas, Carolina, and Georgia. Along the way William was a mentor to the Scottish-born ornithologist Alexander Wilson and made the most complete and correct list of American birds before Wilson's *Ornithology*.

In 1791 William published *Travels through North & South Carolina, Georgia, East and West Florida, the Cherokee Country, the Extensive Territories of the Muscogulges or Creek Confederacy, and the Country of the Chactaws; Containing an Account of the Soil and Natural Productions of those Regions, together with Observations on the Manners of the Indians.* Bartram's *Travels* appeared in London the next year. The once radical Wordsworth was so pleased with the idyllic picture that he took the book with him to Germany in 1798. The *Travels* made its way into "She Was a Phantom of Delight" and "Ruth". One can see why.

> Proceeding on our return to town, continued through part of this high forest skirting on the meadows: began to ascend the hills of a ridge which we were under the necessity of crossing; and having gained its summit, enjoyed a most enchanting view; a vast expanse of green meadows and strawberry fields; a meandering river gliding through, saluting in its various turnings the swelling, green, turfy knolls, embellished with parterres of flowers and fruitful strawberry beds; flocks of turkeys strolling about them; herds of deer prancing in the meads or bounding over the hills; companies of young, innocent Cherokee virgins, some busy gathering the rich fragrant fruit, others having already filled their baskets, lay reclined under the shade of floriferous and fragrant native bowers of Magnolia, Azalea Philadelphus, perfumed Calycanthus, sweet Yellow Jessamine and cerulean Glycine frutescens, disclosing their beauties to the fluttering breeze, and bathing their limbs in the cool fleeting streams; whilst other parties, more gay and libertine, were yet collecting strawberries, or wantonly chasing their companions, tantalising them, staining their lips and cheeks with the rich fruit.
>
> The sylvan scene of primitive innocence was enchanting, and perhaps too enticing for hearty young men long to continue idle spectators.

Coleridge, only twenty-two in 1794 and at loose ends after having left Cambridge in a brief farcical attempt to be a cavalryman, was deeply influenced by Bartram's indications of so much space in America. With his friend Southey, Coleridge proposed to found a perfect society of equals, "Pantisocracy," on the banks of the Susquehanna. This was to consist of educated men and women who should withdraw from the world to some suitable spot (apparently available only in America). A few hours of work would provide them with the simple necessities of life, leaving the rest of their time free for high intellectual converse. Coleridge was so stirred by bookish images of landscape in America that he foresaw in the second generation of his utopian colony a combination of "the innocence of the patriarchal age with the knowledge and genuine refinements of European culture."

William Bartram's *Travels* supplied many of the images that later found their way into "The Ancient Mariner," "Kubla Khan," and lesser poems. Bartram also supplied noble Creek warriors, lovely Cherokee maidens, flowery savannahs, fragrant groves; as the naturalist David Rains Wallace has noted, "Fragments of their splendor still linger in today's condominium-laden Florida." William Bartram travelling with his collection of seeds, plants, notes, and drawings was a kind of Johnny Appleseed to the English Romantic poets, planting seeds in natural history that were to flower in Coleridge's visionary imagination.

Later in life Coleridge called Bartram's book the last book "written in the spirit of the old travellers." Bartram was not the first American and certainly not the last to describe his own country as if it had never been seen before. The *Travels* became famous because of the spell it exercised on English poets, but through Coleridge in particular one glimpses Bartram's guileless invocation of totally new scenes. Coleridge, in those mysterious and still elusive lines of "Kubla Khan: or a Vision in a Dream: A Fragment," described a place *where Alph, the sacred river, ran/Through caverns measureless to man/Down to a sunless sea*. Bartram in Part II, Chapter V:

I was however induced to deviate a little from my intended course, and touch at the inchanting little Isle of Palms. . . . What a beautiful retreat is here! blessed unviolated spot of earth, rising from the limpid waters of the lake: its fragrant groves and blooming lawns invested and protected by encircling ranks of the Yucca gloriosa. . . . I at last broke away from the enchanting spot, and stepped on board my boat, hoisted sail, and soon approached the coast of the main, . . .

I seated myself upon a swelling green knoll, at the head of the crystal bason. Near me, on the left, was a point or projection of an entire grove of the aromatic Illicium Floridanum; on my right, and all around behind me, was a fruitful Orange grove, with Palms and Magnolias interspersed; in front, just under my feet, was the inchanting and amazing crystal fountain, which incessantly threw up, from dark, rocky caverns below, tons of water every minute, forming a bason, capacious enough for large shallops to ride in, and a creek of four or five feet depth of water, and near twenty yards over, . . . About twenty yards from the upper edge of the bason, and directly opposite to the mouth or outlet of the creek, is a continual and amazing ebullition, where the waters are thrown up in such abundance and amazing force, as to jet and swell up two or three feet above the common surface: white sand and small particles of shells are thrown up with the waters, near to the top, when they diverge from the centre, subside with the expanding flood, and gently sink again, forming a large rim or funnel around about the aperture or mouth of the fountain. . . . Thus far I know to be matter of real fact, and I have related it as near as I could conceive or express myself. But there are yet remaining scenes inexpressibly admirable and pleasing.

Behold, for instance, a vast circular expanse before you, the waters of which are so extremely clear as to be absolutely diaphanous or transparent as the ether; . . .

At the same instant innumerable bands of fish are seen, some clothed in the most brilliant colours; the voracious crocodile stretched along at full length, as the great trunk of a tree in size; the devouring garfish, inimical trout, and all the varieties of gilded painted bream; the barbed catfish, dreaded sting-ray, skate, and flounder. . . .

But behold yet something far more admirable, see whole armies descending into an abyss, into the mouth of the bubbling fountain: they disappear! are they gone for ever? is it real? I raise my eyes with terror and astonishment; I look down again to the fountain with anxiety, when behold them as it were emerging from the blue ether of another world, apparently at a vast distance; at their first appearance, no bigger than flies or minnows; now gradually enlarging, their brilliant colours begin to paint the fluid.

Bartram's incessant activity extended the American imagination. He did this just by the example he presented of a naturalist going it alone on horseback and canoe in the wilderness, from the Carolinas to Louisiana and the Mississippi. There is something irresistible about the figure Bartram presents in his book, going about with his collection of seeds, plants, notes, and drawings. Dr. John Fothergill had instructed him to travel into the lands of the Cherokees and the Muscogulges. This journey led him at some points even west of the Mississippi. It is just as startling now to read his descriptions of Arcadian places, like Shell Bluff on the Georgia shore of the Savannah, just across the river from today's U.S. Atomic Energy Commission Savannah River Plant Reservation.

Henry David Thoreau, jealous of Bartram's amazing coverage, went out of his way in *his* Journal to laugh at Bartram's opening statement. "The Author sets sail from Philadelphia and arrives at Charleston, from Whence he Begins His Travels." Thoreau thought it unnecessary to go all the way from Philadelphia to the unfathomed interior of Florida:

A man must generally get away some hundreds or thousands of miles before he can be said to begin on his travels. Why not begin his travels at home? Would he have to go far or look very closely to discover novelties? . . . It takes a man of genius to travel in his own country, in his native village. . . . I am, perchance, most and most profitably interested in the things which I already know a little about; a mere and utter novelty is a mere monstrosity to me.

Thoreau was a *literary* genius, "Billy" Bartram perhaps no more than a dedicated student of natural history. Thoreau, in his famous self-confrontation on the shores of Walden Pond, disparaged anything extensive and ambitious in the use of American landscape. There was from the beginning an imperial cast of mind to explorations of this vast continent that violently disturbed Thoreau when he awoke to the Mexican War and the slave South's hunger for the vast new territories. Colonel George Washington, even before independence, had smacked his lips over "our rising empire."

The startling thing about Bartram in the Southern wilderness of the eighteenth century is that this pious Quaker-Deist botanist was surprised into becoming a Romantic ahead of his time. He describes his journeys and adventures on an enveloping tide of "amazement" at everything he sees. He comes up with a vocabulary of delight, for he feels himself living amid wonders that are also picturesque dangers.

Coleridge, Wordsworth (and later Carlyle) overlooked a practical purpose to Bartram's journey: he was scouting possible trading posts. But they certainly took Bartram at his word when he described the dangers, the predators, the by no means entirely noble or trustworthy Seminoles. Coleridge freely transcribed into his notebook Bartram's notice of that perennial Florida feature, the alligators or crocodiles (Bartram did not distinguish between them), and emphasized in his wonder at the "alligator's terrible roar . . . you can scarcely be persuaded but that the whole globe is dangerously agitated."

Bartram could be Quakerly benevolent about Nature to the point of being syrupy over the "harmony" that the Creator had managed to instill into the Florida scene. But just as the Seminoles at one point spoke half-seriously of wanting to bleed Bartram because they found him too "forward" and "heroic," so a modern reader cannot help trembling a little at the hazards and extremities Bartram encountered. He was one with polar explorers and deep sea divers. At one point, seeking to retrieve some fish from a lagoon, he watches alligators as

They suddenly dart upon each other. The boiling surface of the lake marks their rapid course, and a terrific conflict commences. They now sink to the bottom folded together in horrid wreaths. The water becomes thick and discoloured. Again they rise, their jaws clap together, re-echoing through the deep surrounding forests. Again they sink, when the contest ends at the muddy bottom of the lake, . . . Not thinking it prudent to take my fusee with me, lest I might lose it overboard in case of a battle, which I had every reason to dread before my return, I therefore furnished myself with a club for my defence, went on board, . . . I kept strictly on the watch, and paddled with all my might towards the entrance of the lagoon, hoping to be sheltered there from the multitude of my assailants; but ere I had half-way reached the place, I was attacked on all sides, several endeavouring to overset the canoe. My situation now became precarious to the last degree: two very large ones attacked me closely, at the same instant, rushing up with their heads and part of their bodies above the water, roaring terribly and belching floods of water over me. They struck their jaws together so close to my ears, as almost to stun me, and I expected at every moment to be dragged out of the boat and instantly devoured.

Bartram makes for the shore, "for, by keeping close to it, I should have my enemies on one side of me only," and thinks he may be able to jump out of the canoe on shore, "as it is easy to outwalk them on land, although comparatively as swift as lightning in the water." He makes good his entrance into the lagoon, "though not without opposition from the

William Bartram's sketch of bull alligators on the St. John's River in East Florida, 1773. He noted their "terrible roar."

alligators, who formed a line across the entrance." He finally gets back into the river out of the lagoon, "pursued near to my landing" by "an old daring one, about twelve feet in length."

On a journey to the little Tennessee River, Bartram

saw a scene, new and surprising, which at first threw my senses into such a tumult, that it was some time before I could comprehend what was the matter; however, I soon accounted for the prodigious assemblage of crocodiles at this place, which exceeded every thing of the kind I had ever heard of.

How shall I express myself so as to convey an adequate idea of it to the reader, and at the same time avoid raising suspicions of my veracity? Should I say, that the river (in this place) from shore to shore, and perhaps near half a mile above and below me, appeared to be one solid bank of fish, of various kinds, pushing through this narrow pass of St. Juan's into the little lake, on their return down the river, and that the alligators were in such incredible numbers, and so close together from shore to shore, that it would have been easy to have walked across on their heads, had the animals been harmless? What expressions can sufficiently declare the shocking scene that for some minutes continued, whilst this mighty army of fish were forcing the pass? During this attempt, thousands, I may say hundreds of thousands, of them were caught and swallowed by the devouring alligators. I have seen an alligator take up out of the water several great fish at a time, and just squeeze them betwixt his jaws, while the tails of the great trout flapped about his eyes and lips, ere he had swallowed them. The horrid noise of their closing jaws, their plunging amidst the broken banks of fish, and rising with their prey some feet upright above the water, the floods of water and blood rushing out of their mouths, and the clouds of vapour issuing from their wide nostrils, were truly frightful.

At another time a wolf leaped into a tree when Bartram was sleeping and ran off with the fish he had kept there for safety. Dangers alternate with delights and the astonishment at the amount of space procured by English aristocrats. One Mr. Rolle "obtained from the crown a grant of forty thousand acres, in any part of East Florida, where the land was unlocated." Rolle and the hundred families accompanying him sailed from England and found themselves on the St. John; they ascended the river in a boat,

and being struck with its majesty, the grand situations of its banks, and fertility of its lands, and at the same time considering the extensive navigation of the river, and its near vicinity to St. Augustine, . . . he altered his views on St. Mark's, and suddenly determined on this place, where he landed his first little colony.

Bartram's essential enduring note is of Florida as paradise, and therefore (the rueful American note) of a Paradise soon lost.

Neither nature nor art could any where present a more striking contrast, as you approached this savanna. The glittering water pond played on the sight, through the dark grove, like a brilliant diamond, on the bosom of the illumined savanna, bordered with various flowery shrubs and plants; and as we advanced into the plain, the sight was agreeably relieved by a distant view of the forests, which partly environed the green expanse on the left hand, whilst the imagination was still flattered and entertained by the far distant misty points of the surrounding forests, which projected into the plain, alternately appearing and disappearing; . . . But that venerable grove is now no more. All has been cleared away and planted with indigo, corn, and cotton, but since deserted: . . . It appeared like a desert to a great extent, and terminated, on the land side, by frightful thickets, and open pine forests.

Hector St. John de Crèvecoeur was a French soldier present at the fall of Quebec who settled in upper New York State. Adopting the persona of a simple American farmer, he wrote one of the most famous "emigrant letters" of the eighteenth century in *Letters from an American Farmer* (1782). Crèvecoeur's unqualified picture of primitive America as an egalitarian paradise was a literary version of the "peaceable kingdom" that the itinerant Quaker painter and preacher Edward Hicks was to portray in a hundred different versions. Hicks was ingenuous; Crèvecoeur more subtle but winningly enthusiastic. His book brought "joyful news out of the new world," as the Elizabethans used to say, to sophisticates in Belfast, Dublin, and London. This "American Farmer" rejoiced people even in Philadelphia. Bartram's *Travels* had fostered in England daydreams of the Florida jungle as an exotic land thick with crocodiles and dusky Indian maidens. Crèvecoeur's idealizations of rural life in the frontier country of western New York had traceable effects on the imaginations of Campbell, Byron, Southey, and encouraged others as well as Coleridge to dream of a literary colony in America as the perfect society. William Hazlitt thought Crèvecoeur one of the three notable writers the eighteenth century had produced in the American colonies. Crèvecoeur had caught "not only the objects but the feelings of a new country. The power to sympathize with nature, without thinking of ourselves or others, if it is not a definition of genius, comes very near to it."

Crèvecoeur was by no means as simple and universally benevolent as he sounds. He was a petty nobleman in Normandy before serving under Montcalm when the French lost Canada; he was eventually to return to America as a French diplomat. He had a distinct gift for mythologizing himself as well as the newborn American Republic when he presented his "Letters" as "a plain American farmer." But the New World had laid a spell on him, and in Crèvecoeur one can see eighteenth-century skepticism dissolving under the rays of the newfound belief that here sinful man could be born again. Crèvecoeur was delighted to make a new life for himself away from feudal Canada. He described benevolence and fair dealing everywhere—and this in a language that is a premonition of the effect that the American Revolution was to have in Paris.

Some few towns excepted, we are all tillers of the earth, from Nova Scotia to West Florida. . . . A pleasing uniformity of decent competence appears throughout our habitations. . . . We have no princes, for whom we toil, starve, and bleed; we are the most perfect society now existing in the world. Here man is free as he ought to be; nor is this pleasing equality so transitory as many others are. Many ages will not see the shores of our great lakes replenished with inland nations, nor the unknown bounds of North America entirely peopled. Who can tell how far it extends? Who can tell the millions of men whom it will feed and contain? For no European foot has yet travelled half the extent of this mighty continent!

Letters from an American Farmer (1782) by Hector St. John de Crèvecoeur presented an idyllic picture of the American countryside—a vision that still suffuses such paintings as Thomas Cole's River in the Catskills.

As for arrivals from Europe, "who owned not a single foot of the extensive surface of this planet,"

> Every thing has tended to regenerate them; new laws, a new mode of living, a new social system; here they are become men; in Europe they were as so many useless plants, wanting vegetative mold and refreshing showers; . . . but now by the power of transplantation, like all other plants they have taken root and flourished! . . . By what invisible power has this surprising metamorphosis been performed?

What follows is a classic passage quoted almost as often as the opening lines of the Declaration of Independence:

> What then is the American, this new man? . . . *He* is an American, who, leaving behind him all his ancient prejudices and manners, receives new ones from the new mode of life he has embraced, the new government he obeys, and the new rank he holds. He becomes an American by being received in the broad lap of our great *Alma Mater*. Here individuals of all nations are melted into a new race of men, whose labors and posterity will one day cause great changes in the world. Americans are the western pilgrims,who are carrying along with them that great mass of arts, sciences, vigor, and industry which began long since in the east; they will finish the great circle.

Crèvecoeur was not the first nor the last emigrant to persuade himself—and the folks back home—that he had found the Golden Age. What gives *Letters from an American Farmer* its lasting value is the consistency with which Crèvecoeur was able to bestow his enthusiasm on a landscape he had just encountered. He is the *philosophe* as farmer. The vast mountainous spaces of upper New York State somehow exist for him to feel benevolence. In a far-fetched, perhaps imaginary, interview with John Bartram inserted into the *Letters*, he turned that eminently practical botanist into another Gallic idealization of Franklin as Cincinnatus at the plow, the ideal plowman, full of civic genius. What is pleasing in Crèvecoeur is his adoption of the landscape as at once primordial and benevolent, Biblical in its promise, America as the greatest "find."

Jefferson, the Bartrams, Washington Irving and James Fenimore Cooper, Francis Parkman and other celebrators of the unsettled American landscape respond to something given. Crèvecoeur makes you feel that although he is writing from America, he is really living in his imagination. His America, like John Locke's or John Donne's, is still metaphor, a retrieval of Europe's bitterness and fatigue. All that the ages have called for in the redemption of humanity is here. He professes not to understand why anyone should visit Italy and "the town of Pompey under ground" when in *this* world may be found "what is not in books – the humble rudiments and embryos of society spreading everywhere, the recent foundations of our towns, and the settlements of so many rural districts. . . ."

Describing a midwinter landscape, he turns himself into St. Francis mothering the birds. Instead of trapping and "murthering" the quail, "often in the angles of the fences where the motion of the wind prevents the snow from settling, I carry them both chaff and grain; the one to feed them, the other to prevent their tender feet from freezing to the earth as I have frequently observed them to do."

Crèvecoeur (unlike his fellow Frenchman John James Audubon) in fact turned even his bestiary into a soothing version of the Golden Age. Nothing was more common in

Passenger pigeons in their thousands, darkening the sky. Audubon's description of their slaughter was far removed from Crèvecoeur's view of peaceable man and benevolent Nature.

"early" America than the slaughter of passenger pigeons, which once flew in such numbers that they literally blackened the sky for days on end with their astronomical numbers. Audubon described pigeons on the banks of the Green River in Kentucky passing over him like a current of air.

> Thousands of the pigeons were soon knocked down by the polemen, whilst more continued to pour in. The fires were lighted, then a magnificent, wonderful, almost terrifying sight presented itself. The pigeons, arriving by the thousands, alighted everywhere, one above another, until solid masses were formed on the branches all around. . . . The scene was one of uproar and confusion. I found it quite useless to speak or even to shout, to those persons nearest to me. . . . I was made aware of the firing only by seeing the shooters re-loading. . . . The uproar continued the whole night. . . . The howling of the wolves now reached our ears, and the foxes, the lynxes, cougars, bears, racoons, opossums and polecats were sneaking off. Eagles and hawks, accompanied by a crowd of vultures, took their place and enjoyed their share of the spoils.
>
> When each man had as many as he could possibly dispose of, the hogs were let loose on the remainder.

Crèvecoeur, on the other hand, wanted America fabulous. He cites an "unpublished study" on Bees—"Their government, their industry, their quarrels, their passions, always present me with something new." He loves to rest under the locust tree where his beehive stands. "By their movements I can predict the weather, and can tell the day of their swarming." When other men hunt game, he goes bee-hunting. What novelty he finds in nature—it is humble! He shoots a king bird and

immediately opened his maw, from which I took 171 bees; I laid them all on a blanket in the sun, and to my great surprise fifty-four returned to life, licked themselves clean and joyfully went back to the hive, where they probably informed their companions of such an adventure and escape.

Identifying himself with the most extreme "versions of pastoral," Crèvecoeur managed to find Arcadia by visiting places then remote indeed—Nantucket and Martha's Vineyard. Nantucket had been given under "patent" as early as 1571 to over twenty proprietors under the province of New York,

which then claimed all the islands from the Neway Sink to Cape Cod. They found it so universally barren and so unfit for cultivation that they mutually agreed not to divide it, as each could neither live on, nor improve, that lot which might fall to his share. They then cast their eyes on the sea, and finding themselves obliged to become fishermen, they looked for a harbor, and having found one, they determined to build a town in its neighbourhood and to dwell together. For that purpose they surveyed as much ground as would afford to each what is generally called here a home lot. Forty acres were thought sufficient to answer this double purpose; for to what end should they covet more land than they could improve, or even inclose; nor being possessed of a single tree, in the whole extent of their new dominion.

Crèvecoeur portrayed an island existence in which more than half the inhabitants were at sea, fishing in milder latitudes. The island itself

appears to be the summit of some huge sandy mountain, affording some acres of dry land for the habitation of man. . . . Other submarine ones lie to the southward of this . . . the Nantucket shoals . . . the bulwarks which so powerfully defend this island from the impulse of the mighty ocean, and repel the force of its waves; which, but for the accumulated barriers, would ere now have dissolved its foundations, and torn it in pieces.

Like so many early observers, he foresees the doom of the Indians. "They are hastening towards a total annihilation, and this may be perhaps the last compliment that will ever be paid them by any traveller." Still, in Quaker Nantucket "they were not extirpated by fraud, violence, or injustice, as hath been the case in so many provinces." There *were* snakes in paradise. The close descriptions that surprised and delighted Hazlitt come out in a passage on snakes. Unlike the rattlesnakes, so lethal that one had only to strike at a farmer's legs for poison to get into the man's shoes, endangering everyone who successively wore them, the black snake

always diverts me because it excites no idea of danger. Their swiftness is astonishing; they will sometimes equal that of a horse; at other times they will climb up trees in quest of our tree toads; or glide on the ground at full length. On some occasions they present themselves half in the reptile state, half erect; their eyes and their heads in the erect posture appear to great advantage; the former display a fire which I have often admired, and it is by these they are enabled to fascinate birds and squirrels. When they have fixed their eyes on an animal, they become immovable; only turning their head sometimes to the right and sometimes to the left, but still with their sight invariably directed to the object.

Sitting "solitary and pensive in my primitive arbor," Crèvecoeur hears a strange rustling noise he cannot account for, climbs one of his great hemp stalks, and observes the furious fight between a black snake and a water snake, each six feet long. They make a "scene uncommon and beautiful" as the water snake tries to escape to the ditch, is pursued by the "keen-eyed black one," which twists its tail twice around a stalk of hemp, seizing its adversary by the throat by twisting its own neck twice around that of the water snake, pulling it back from the ditch.

Crèvecoeur assumed a persona still new in history, "American farmer," in order to project America as regeneration. "The history of the earth! Does it present anything but crimes of the most heinous nature, committed from one end of the world to the other?" For Crèvecoeur America was more than the handy symbol that it had been to John Locke and so many other Old World thinkers bandying a name. It was the state of Nature where man could be brought back to his true nature.

Obviously Crèvecoeur was more French than American, a disciple of Rousseau. Nature as the primordial state had another meaning to Americans as the nineteenth century opened on the accession of the vast Louisiana Territory. From Canada to the Gulf, this was more than twice the size of the country at Jefferson's inauguration. As soon as Napoleon sold "Louisiana," President Jefferson and his private secretary Captain Meriwether Lewis of the United States Army (who called in Captain William Clark) organized an expedition from the Mississippi River up the Missouri to the Columbia River and the Pacific Ocean that would ultimately nail down the whole Northwest for the United States.

"Lewis and Clark" became the most significant transcontinental exploration in American history, the most decisive in securing American mastery over a continent. The two captains came back to St. Louis on September 23, 1806, after more than two years in the wilderness, with scientific and literary records that are as extraordinary as the great journey itself. In laying out the general route Jefferson had ordered careful observations of the Indian tribes and of the wild country. The almost daily journals that Lewis and Clark kept are in extent, closeness of detail, the recording of human exertions, far beyond anything else on primitive America. Certain pages cannot be read without awe and an equal sense of pride at what highly intelligent and infinitely resourceful human beings will endure if their quest is great enough.

Neither Lewis nor Clark had much formal education; their spelling was largely by ear. But their doggedness in keeping up for official eyes (Jefferson's first) the step-by-step record can make us still relive the *urgency* of their expedition.

Nowhere else is the wilderness so thick, the possible river routes so many and deceiving, the portages so brutal, the "buffaloe" herds so vast, the rapids and mountain cliffs so threatening, the rains (once they have reached the Pacific Coast) so devouring. Yet you are always conscious of the great goal before them, a continent to win, and of the

"Great White Father" back in Washington who has sent them there and in whose name they assure the often dubious Indians of the benevolence of the United States.

Living on the country, they endure the most monotonous diet from section to section; there are endless mishaps to their boats, stores, arms, and ammunition; there are frightful physical injuries; along the Pacific the local Indians, corrupted by the maritime trade with other white men, will not respect any agreement on the exchange of goods and are forever trying to rob them. But the sense we get almost anywhere in the Journals is not only of omnipresent peril, but of an almost unbearable excitement in the face of the unknown. "It added up to a strangeness," said Bernard De Voto, editing the journals, "for which nothing in the previous frontier culture was a preparation."

4 September 1804 "Great numbers of Buffaloe & Elk on the hill. . . . I saw Several foxes & Killed a Elk & 2 Deer & Squirrels   the men with me killed an Elk, 2 Deer & a Pelican . . . a great number of Grous & 3 Foxes . . . vast herds of Buffaloe deer Elk and Antilopes were seen feeding in every direction as far as the eye of the observer could reach . . . 8 fallow Deer 5 Common & 3 Buffaloe killed to day . . . Muskeetors verry troublesom.

They wintered in the Mandan villages (in the vicinity of Bismarck, North Dakota), seeking all the time information about the headwaters of the Missouri and possible connections to the Columbia. They learned a good deal about the local Indians; a squaw could be lawfully killed for running away. The 28th of November, 1804,

river full of floating ice, began to Snow at 7 oClock *am* and continued all day. at 8oClock the black Cat Came to See us,   after Showing those Chiefs many things which was Curiosities to them, and Giveing a fiew presents of Curious Handkerchiefs arm bans & paint with a twist of Tobacco they departed at 1 oclock much pleased,   at parting we had Some little talk on the Subject of the British Trader M. Le rock Giveing meadels & Flags, and told those Chiefs to impress it on the minds of their nations that those simbiles were not to be received by any from them, without they wished to [incur] the displeasure of their Great American Father, . . .

21 February 1805 Capt Lewis returned with 2 Slays loaded with meat, after finding that he could not overtake the Soues War party, (who had in their way distroyed all the meat at one Deposit which I had made & Burnt the Lodges) deturmined to proceed on to the lower Deposit which he found had not been observed by the Soues he hunted two day Killed 36 Deer & 14 Elk . . . the meet which he killed and that in the lower Deposit amounting to about 3000 lb . . . one Drawn by 16 men had about 2400 lb. on it

13 April 1805 . . . we found a number of carcases of the Buffaloe lying along shore, which had been drowned by falling through the ice in winter and lodged on shore by the high water when the river broke up about the first of this month we saw also many tracks of the white bear of enormous size . . . we have not as yet seen one of these anamals, tho' their tracks are so abaundant and recent . . . the Indians give a very formidable account of the strength and ferocity of this anamal which they never dare to attack but in parties of six eight or ten persons . . . this anamal is said more frequently to attack a man on meeting with him, than to flee from him. When the Indians are

St. John's River, Florida *(Hermann Herzog, 1832–1932), the river that was central to William Bartram's discoveries and adventures.*

about to go in quest of the white bear, previous to their departure, they paint themselves and perform all those supersticious rights commonly observed when they are about to make war uppon a neighbouring nation

22 April 1805 I ascended to the top of the cutt bluff this morning, from whence I had a most delightfull view of the country, the whole of which except the vally formed by the Missouri is void of timber or underbrush, exposing to the first glance of the spectator immence herds of Buffaloe, Elk, deer, & Antelopes feeding in one common and boundless pasture.

29 April 1805 . . . fell in with two brown or yellow bear; both of which we wounded; one of them made his escape, the other after my firing on him pursued me seventy or eighty yards, but fortunately had been so badly wounded that he was unable to pursue me so closely as to prevent my charging my gun . . . killed him. it was a male not fully grown, we estimated his weight at 300 lbs . . . this anamal appeared to me to differ from the black bear; it is a much more furious and formidable anamal, and will frequently pursue the hunter when wounded, it is asstonishing to see the wounds they will bear before they can be put to death. . . .
game is still very abundant we can scarcely cast our eyes in any direction without perceiving deer Elk Buffaloe or antelopes. The quanity of wolves appear to increase in the same proportion

13 June 1805 [The Great Falls of the Missouri] . . . the grandest sight I ever beheld, the hight of the fall is the same of the other but the irregular and somewhat projecting rocks below receives the water in it's passage down and brakes it into a perfect white foam which assumes a thousand forms in a moment sometimes flying up in jets of sparkling foam to the hight of fifteen feet and are scarcely formed before large roling bodies of the same beaten and foaming water is thrown over and conceals them.

14 June 1805 . . . a herd of at least a thousand buffaloe . . . a large white, reather brown bear, had perceived and crept on me within 20 steps before I discovered him; on the first moment I drew up my gun to shoot, but at the same time recolected that she was not loaded and that he was too near for me to hope to perform this opperation before he reached me, as he was then briskly advancing on me; it was an open level plain, not a bush within miles. . . . accordingly I ran haistily into the water about waist deep, and faced about and presented the point of my espontoon . . . the moment I put myself in this attitude of defence he sudenly wheeled about . . . and retreated with quite as great precipitation as he had just before pursued me . . .
It now seemed to me that all the beasts of the neighbourhood had made a league to destroy me, or that some fortune was disposed to amuse herself at my expense, for I had not proceeded more than three hundred yards from the burrow of [a] tyger cat, before three bull buffaloe, which wer feeding with a large herd about half a mile from me on my left, separated from the herd and ran full speed towards me. . .

On 16 October 1805 they sighted the Columbia River, the first white men who ever saw it east of the Cascade Mountains. On 7 November, "Great joy in camp we are in *view* of the *Ocean*, this great Pacific Ocean which we have been so long anxious to See." In the

Indians Hunting the Bison *(Karl Bodmer, c. 1844, detail).*

notebook which he kept on his knee to record courses and bearings, Clark had written *"Ocian in view*! O! the joy." The Pacific distinctly belied its name. The wet weather of the Northwest Coast besieged them constantly. Clark wrote that by December he was very glad to leave the Coast where "the sea which is imedeately in front roars like a repeeted roling thunder and have rored in that way ever since our arrival in its borders which is now 24 days since we arrived in sight of the Great Western Ocian, I cant say Pasific as since I have seen it, it has been the reverse." Before leaving he carved, on a large pine tree, the famous legend, "William Clark December 3rd 1805. By Land from the U States in 1804 & 1805." As they neared St. Louis on the journey back they were informed "that we had been long Since given out [up] by the people of the U S Generaly and almost forgotten, the President of the U. States had yet hopes of us . . ."

OPPOSITE: The Lewis and Clark
Expedition *(Thomas Mickell Burnham,
c. 1850), with the two leaders
romantically highlighted against the
bluffs of the Missouri River.* RIGHT:
"Canoe Striking a Tree," *frontispiece
of the journal of the Lewis and Clark
expedition.* BELOW: Buffalo Chase in
Winter, Indians on Snowshoes *(George
Catlin, c. 1832).*

One day railroads would follow the Lewis and Clark route up the Missouri Valley to the Pacific. Americans trembled to think of the wilderness receding. William Bartram in eighteenth-century Florida (which resembled Joseph Conrad's Africa more than it does today's condominium Florida), bemoaned the ruination of the landscape. As Proust was to say, "the only true paradise is the paradise we have lost." There was a melancholy pride in having so much space to lose. Ralph Waldo Emerson wrote while he was in England in 1833:

> On the way to Winchester, whither our host accompanied us in the afternoon, my friends asked many questions respecting American landscapes, forests, houses—my house, for example. . . . There, I thought, in America, lies nature sleeping, over-growing, almost conscious, too much by half for man in the picture, and so giving a certain *tristesse*, like the rank vegetation of swamps and forests seen at night, steeped in dews and rains, which it loves; and on it man seems not able to make much impression. There, in that great sloven continent, in high Allegheny pastures, in the sea-wide sky-skirted prairie, still sleeps and murmurs and hides the great mother, long since driven away from the trim hedge-rows and over-cultivated gardens of England.

Francis Parkman's many picturesque and aggressively eloquent volumes on the struggle between England and France for the American continent he liked to call his "History of the American Forest." It was the work of a neurasthenic, near-blind Boston patrician who despised the evolving democracy of his country and lived only to work out on such a large scale his obsession with the wilderness as the real national epic. In the teeth of physical and psychic handicaps that often made it impossible for him to work more than a few minutes a day, Parkman managed to complete the project he had formed as a youth. This was nothing less than to describe in full—with the great forest as background—the imperial struggle for the New World that began with the French exploration of the Mississippi Valley, the Jesuit missionaries and explorers, and the eventual resistance to and replacement of the French as the American colonists learned as soldiers of the Crown the tactics that were to win them independence. George Washington's ascent as military leader began in his early twenties when he displayed skills as a surveyor, topographer and scout guiding troops through the mountains and forests of western Virginia into the Ohio Valley.

Parkman was one of the classic American authors who inaugurated American literature in the nineteenth century by rebelling against a clerical background. Unlike the withdrawn transcendentalist tribe who thought of letters as a replacement for the church, Parkman was fanatical about the wilderness. It was the world Americans had lost. Reduced by his mysterious physical afflictions to an invalid and hermit existence, he expressed some essential fierceness and even fanaticism by attaching himself to the wars over the wilderness that marked the heroic age, the last true epic.

As a young man Parkman was convinced that his own period in American history was worthless. He thought democracy as "vicious an extreme as absolute authority. . . . I do not object to a good constitutional Monarchy, but prefer a conservative republic." He rejoiced in the Civil War. It transformed the ideal of "seeking adventure outside the confines of civilization" to the ideal of doing "one's duty in a strenuous way within society." The enormous loss of life would teach America, especially its well-to-do classes, the folly of self-fulfillment. He thought Lincoln too common to join Washington in the American Pantheon. Parkman determined very early to find his spiritual home in the still primitive world of prairies and Indians.

He did not like Indians at all, but he went out to Wyoming from St. Louis in 1846 "chiefly with a view of observing the Indian character," an important chapter for the work of a lifetime. Parkman went West because he was driven by the tutelary spirit of his age. He was convinced that the wilderness was on the edge of extinction. And though "a civilized white man can discover very few points of sympathy between his own nature and that of an Indian," he was fascinated by what he saw at the bottom of the Indian character, "a wild idea of liberty and utter intolerance of restraint." He was to say of himself that "his thoughts were always in the forest, whose features . . . possessed his waking and sleeping dreams, filling him with vague cravings impossible to satisfy."

The plains country was a challenge to a man of such uncertain health and temper; Parkman strained himself further by desperately keeping up on horseback with the Indians. He was a zealous Puritan out of his time, flogging his body mercilessly to show that the spirit must conquer. At one point he lived with a band of Sioux for weeks, sharing their food and shelter and participating in buffalo hunts and ceremonials. But with all his determined stoicism and many near-breakdowns, he presented his middle-class readers in the East with the still-novel freshness and exhilaration of the West.

The Oregon Trail (1849) was certainly not *The Journals of Lewis and Clark*. It was the memoir of a dude in rough country, disapproving of the primitive Indians and their "lawlessness," clinging to his saddle despite violent dysentery so as not to shame himself. He could never conceal his irritation with much that he lived with. The "majestic" bearing of the Indians fascinated him, but they were dangerous to every emigrant not carrying a rifle. Parkman traveling with his cousin Quincy Adams Shaw was always glad of company on the "trail," but apprehensive. He conveyed the immense emptiness of the prairies, the vague sense of disturbance from spectral figures on the plains. As in all the best American landscape writing, he triumphed especially in the blow-by-blow description of physical exertion that Mark Twain was to get into *Roughing It* and *Huckleberry Finn*, Hemingway in "Big Two-Hearted River."

Parkman's big subject in *The Oregon Trail* was the flatness of what early explorers and travelers all saw as "the great American desert."

A low, undulating line of sand-hills bounded the horizon before us. That day we rode ten hours, and it was dusk before we entered the hollows and gorges of these gloomy little hills. At length we gained the summit, and the long-expected valley of the Platte lay before us. We . . . sat joyfully looking down upon the prospect . . . strange, too, and striking to the imagination, and yet it had not one picturesque or beautiful feature; nor had it any of the features of grandeur, other than its vast extent, its solitude, and its wildness. For league after league, a plain as level as a lake was outspread beneath us . . . . an occasional clump of wood, rising in the midst like a shadowy island, relieved the monotony of the waste. No living thing was moving throughout the vast landscape, except the lizards that darted over the sand through the rank grass and prickly pears at our feet. . . .

Four hundred miles still intervened between us and Fort Laramie; and to reach that point cost us the travel of three more weeks. During the whole of this time we were passing up the middle of a long, narrow, sandy plain, reaching like an

Fort Laramie *(Alfred J. Miller, 1851). Laramie became a major stopping place on the Oregon Trail. Francis Parkman saw it as an oasis in "the great American desert." Parkman understood and trusted the Indians, but they remained a real threat to most travelers until late in the*

outstretched belt nearly to the Rocky Mountains. Two lines of sand-hills, broken often into the wildest and most fantastic forms, flanked the valley at the distance of a mile or two on the right and left; while beyond them lay a barren, trackless waste, extending for hundreds of miles to the Arkansas on the one side, and the Missouri on the other. Before and behind us, the level monotony of the plain was unbroken as far as the eye could reach. Sometimes it glared in the sun, an expanse of hot, bare sand; sometimes it was veiled by long coarse grass. Skulls and whitening bones of buffalo were scattered everywhere; the ground was tracked by myriads of them, and often covered with the circular indentations where the bulls had wallowed in the hot weather.

The enormous plain holds parties of Indians, emigrants, Mexicans, like tiny animals moving about in a vast bottle. The figures seem endlessly restless and frustrated by the savage emptiness in which they keep moving in all directions. The shuddering invalid describing all this is able to proceed only with spoonfuls of whiskey to keep him in the saddle.

Parkman's extraordinary seven volumes describing "the struggle for a continent" were written by a man who loved to describe a battle, a siege, the preparations for battle, the march through a forest. The forest was the battleground Parkman always dreamed of. In *Montcalm and Wolfe*, the culminating story of the French loss of Canada, he retells from earlier volumes the story so crucial to American history of General Braddock's defeat at the hands of French troops and Indians in the attempt to capture Fort Duquesne (now Pittsburgh).

century. Here an armed caravan of fur traders crosses what Parkman called the "level monotony of the plain."

Braddock's lieutenant in this battle, the surveyor and experienced mountain man George Washington, was one of the few to survive. He came out of the overwhelming British rout with an enhanced reputation that would set him firmly on the path for future glory against his erstwhile comrades in battle. "At twenty-four," Parkman wrote proudly, "he was the foremost man, and acknowledged as such, along the whole long line of the Western border." Washington knew how to fight Indians in the forest; General Braddock was too vain to learn. Braddock, before leaving for battle, told an actress that "he was going with a handful of men to conquer whole nations; and to do this they must cut their way through unknown woods." Parkman describes June 10, 1755, the ill-fated day when the British marched from Cumberland in Maryland to Fort Duquesne, a route that became the foundation of one national road:

Three hundred axmen led the way, to cut and clear the road; and the long train of packhorses, wagons, and cannon toiled on behind, over the stumps, roots, and stones of the narrow track, the regulars and provincials marching in the forest close on either side. . . . Foot by foot they advanced into the waste of lonely mountains that divided the streams flowing into the Atlantic from those flowing to the Gulf of Mexico,—a realm of forests ancient as the world. The road was but twelve feet wide, and the line of march often extended four miles. It was like a thin, long party-colored snake, red, blue, and brown, trailing slowly through the depth of leaves, creeping around inaccessible heights, crawling over ridges, moving always in dampness and shadow, by rivulets and waterfalls, crags and chasms, gorges and shaggy steeps. In glimpses

43

only, through jagged boughs and flickering leaves, did this wild primeval world reveal itself, with its dark green mountains, flecked with the morning mist, and its distant summits pencilled in dreamy blue.

The "funereal pine-forest" through which this army passed was afterwards known as the Shades of Death. Parkman calls it "this wilderness of death." Braddock's defeat was "a chaos of anguish and terror scarcely parallelled even in Indian war. . . . The field, abandoned to the savages, was a pandemonium of pillage and murder."

Parkman's recurrent images for the forest—the primitive as absolute, the world as it first looked—demonstrate the pull on this invalid Boston Brahmin of the ancient call to battle. Encountering in his history some extraordinary graphic feel for the primordial forest, one falls in with an obsession. His literary power over the seemingly inanimate but growlingly alive forest is of a kind which very few writers of "cool" history can match. Major-General Shirley, embarking at the Dutch village of Schenectady, and ascending the Mohawk,

left behind the last trace of civilized man, rowed sixty miles through a wilderness, and reached the Great Carrying Place, which divided the waters that flow to the Hudson from those that flow to Lake Ontario. . . . Thither the bateaux were dragged on sledges and launched on the dark and tortuous stream, which, fed by a decoction of forest leaves that oozed from the marshy shores, crept in shadow through depths of foliage, with only a belt of illumined sky gleaming between the jagged tree-tops. Tall and lean with straining towards the light, gaunt stems trickling with perpetual damps, stood on either hand the silent hosts of the forest. The skeletons of their dead, barkless, blanched, and shattered, strewed the mudbanks and shallows; others lay submerged, like bones of drowned mammoths, thrusting lank, white limbs above the sullen water; and great trees, entire as yet, were flung by age or storms athwart the current,—a bristling barricade of matted boughs.

Parkman is usually labeled a romantic historian, and he was certainly concerned less with the social facts behind the "struggle for a continent" than with great set passages on the landscape of exploration and battle. But his instinct for the savage sources of history shows a disposition to violence that is kin to the ferocious pages of Melville's *Moby-Dick*.

The forest in Parkman is distinctly not there for his own symbolic purposes. It does serve as a grand concealment if you mean to shoot an enemy foolishly resplendent in scarlet uniforms. Washington's native sense of the forest was to create a lasting picture dear to the American heart not of Indians but of *frontiersmen* behind trees picking off an enemy too vain to use the forest properly. And this forest was Nature; and Nature still in the primeval state was peculiarly America's. Nor was it smooth and easy, as in too-civilized Europe. It was obstruction, wrote Parkman; it "rolled over hill and valley in billows of interminable green, a leafy maze, a mystery of shade, a universal hiding place, where murder might lurk unseen at its victim's side, and nature seemed formed to nurse the mind with wild and dark imaginings."

President Jefferson, on his frequent journeys between Monticello and Washington, was happy to reach the end of the hundred miles without vexatious delay. "Of eight rivers between here and Washington," he wrote to his Attorney General in 1801, "five have neither bridges nor boats."

CHAPTER TWO

ROMANTIC AMERICA

In Concord, Massachusetts, a town so sweetly traditional that it still lacks a movie theater, the short bridge over the sluggish Concord River is dominated by the statue of a sturdy, determined minuteman with rifle at the ready. On the base of the statue is inscribed Ralph Waldo Emerson's *Concord Hymn*:

> By the rude bridge that arched the flood,
>> Their flag to April's breeze unfurled,
> Here once the embattled farmers stood,
>> And fired the shot heard round the world.

On April 19, 1775, British redcoats seeking rebel arms were met here by an enraged citizenry; in the exchange of fire the American Revolution began. At the left of the Battle Monument, looking down upon the bridge, is the "Old Manse." Here Ralph Waldo Emerson's clerical grandfather witnessed the opening of hostilities; here the eighteenth-century relic of Puritanism Ezra Ripley, who married Emerson's widowed grandmother, wrote so many sermons during the decades in which he occupied the Old Manse that bundles of them are still tied up in a hallway desk. Here the ex-minister Ralph Waldo Emerson came to write his extraordinary first book, *Nature*. This was a revolutionary utterance—Nature as an American discovery, Nature as the foundation and refrain of the first influential American books. Emerson's little book was to be almost as great an influence on the American mind as that opening skirmish across Concord River. And here in 1842 Nathaniel Hawthorne and his bride Sophia Peabody came to honeymoon and stayed long enough for Hawthorne to write the stories collected in 1846 as *Mosses from an Old Manse*.

No one was to make more of Concord than native son Henry David Thoreau, who dwelt there most of his forty-four years, and so insistently dwells upon it in the journal from which all his work derives that he incorporated every local landscape into his imagination and made life coterminous with Concord. In the journal, unique even among writers' journals—two million words that fill more than 7,000 printed pages—he wrote (1841), "I think I could write a poem to be called Concord. For argument I should have the River, the Woods, the Ponds, the Hills, the Fields, the Swamps and Meadows, the Streets and Buildings, and the Villagers."

Concord, when it was settled in 1635 just five years after Boston, was the furthest inland point in the wilderness. It was originally the Indian village Musketaquid, a name

The Old Manse, Concord, Massachusetts. Here Emerson's grandfather saw the Revolutionary War begin, Emerson wrote Nature, *and the Hawthornes honeymooned.*

that delighted the villagers because it meant "Sweet Meadow," or was supposed to. "Concord" stood for a never-broken agreement with Indians after the purchase of "six myles of land square." With its tall elms, its eighteenth-century red brick, beautifully proportioned doors and paneled interiors, its fine white houses whose lawns sloped down to the river, Concord, when not engaged in Revolution, was peacefulness itself. Thoreau's first book, *A Week on the Concord and Merrimack Rivers*, was one long reverie. Emerson in his beautiful poem "Two Rivers" contrasted the current of life with the gentle Musketaquid; "they lose their grief who hear his song."

The dreaminess that Thoreau made the very rhythm and theme of life along the Concord River was briefly celebrated by non-transcendentalist Hawthorne. He was Concord's toughest mind, its one novelist as opposed to the amateur mystics and Nature rhapsodists occupying the place. Hawthorne could be acid about them. "Never was a poor little country village infested with such a variety of queer, strangely dressed, oddly behaved mortals, most of whom took upon themselves to be important agents of the world's destiny, yet were simply bores of a very intense water." Although he once enjoyed a trip up the river with Thoreau in Thoreau's boat, he was generally averse to the literary inhabitants.

Nevertheless, Hawthorne's "The Old Manse," his preface to *Mosses from an Old Manse*, suffuses Concord with the radiance of his marriage to Sophia Peabody. With his deep gift for projecting states of mind upon the landscape (and for making landscape a state of mind), Hawthorne in this period, "the flowering of New England," turned his reminiscences of the Old Manse into flowers, earth, spring, summer, the river. These pages were certainly different from the severe and somber fictions, especially *The Scarlet Letter*, which used occasionally bright colors to set off the severity of the Puritan mind. As one of Hawthorne's least sentimental biographers said of the honeymoon period, "The Old Manse was paradise, and Hawthorne and Sophia were the new Adam and Eve."

Hawthorne recalled Sophia and himself lying on a carpet of dried pine leaves.

We walked through the forest, & came forth into an open space, whence a fair broad landscape could be seen, our old Manse holding a respectable place in the plain, the river opening its blue eyes here & there, & waving, mountainous ridges closing in the horizon. There we plucked whortleberries & then sat down. There was no wind & the stillness was profound. There seemed no movement in the world but that of our own pulses.

This idyll was not fashioned entirely by Hawthorne's marital happiness. In "The Old Manse" essay, Hawthorne's recollective rhythms are touched up here and there with the ironic reserve that also contributed to his genius for setting a scene in the past. The past was his natural element; in *The House of the Seven Gables* it dominates a story laid in the present. The ceremonial yet languorous style that serves Hawthorne's collection is markedly different from Emerson's orphic brightness and Thoreau's passionate involvement with every detail of earth and water. Hawthorne's memories of the Manse and the river have the charm of infinite suggestiveness.

Hawthorne had a particular gift for making anything he saw seem ancient and irretrievable—except by his art. So he had only to begin,

Between two tall gate-posts of rough-hewn stone (the gate itself having fallen from its hinges, at some unknown epoch) we beheld the gray front of the old parsonage, terminating the vista of an avenue of black-ash trees

for everything to fall into accents of *un temps perdu*.

The wheel track, leading to the door, as well as the whole breadth of the avenue, was almost overgrown with grass, affording dainty mouthfuls of two or three vagrant cows, and an old white horse, who had his living to pick up along the roadside. The glimmering shadows, that lay half-asleep between the door of the house and the public highway, were a kind of spiritual medium seen through which, the edifice had not quite the aspect of belonging to the material world.

The study in the rear of the house, "the most delightful little nook of a study that ever afforded its snug seclusion to a scholar," looked out on the battlefield and the river. Here Emerson had written *Nature*. A willow tree sweeping against the overhanging eaves had contributed to the writing. *Nature* was a book Emerson had pondered when returning from his first trip to Europe, in 1833. Writing it, he felt that the Atlantic was sounding in his ears again. The great willow tree over the roof "is the trumpet and accompaniment of the storm and gives due importance to every caprice of the gale, and the trees in the avenue announce the same facts with equal din to the front tenants. Hoarse concert: they roar like the rigging of a ship in a tempest."

Hawthorne genially remembering the Old Manse was more cheerful about the now historic study whose walls were once "blackened with the smoke of unnumbered years, and made still blacker by the grim prints of Puritan ministers that hung around." Unlike Emerson in the throes of writing *Nature*—the rhapsody that is half a tone poem celebrating the miracle that every day presents and half the announcement of Nature as the new American deity—Hawthorne was full of the river he could see between the trees.

> It may well be called the Concord—the river of peace and quietness—for it is certainly the most unexcitable and sluggish stream that ever loitered, imperceptibly, towards its eternity, the sea. Positively, I had lived three weeks beside it, before it grew quite clear to my perception which way the current flowed. It never has a vivacious aspect, except when a north-western breeze is vexing its surface, on a sunshiny day. From the incurable indolence of its nature, the stream is happily incapable of becoming the slave of human ingenuity, as is the fate of so many a wild, free mountain-torrent. While all things else are compelled to subserve some useful purpose, it idles its sluggish life away, in lazy liberty, without turning a solitary spindle, or affording even water-power enough to grind the corn that grows upon its banks. . . . It slumbers between broad prairies, kissing the long meadow-grass, and bathes the overhanging boughs of elderbushes and willows, or the roots of elms and ash-trees, and clumps of maples. Flags and rushes grow along its plashy shore; the yellow water-lily spreads its broad, flat leaves on the margin; and the fragrant white pond-lily abounds, generally selecting a position just so far from the river's brink, that it cannot be grasped, save at the hazard of plunging in.

All this mildness, ease and general sweetness became a fixture of the many celebrations of Nature by Concord writers. It was in Concord, thanks to the particular gift of Emerson and Thoreau for seeing Nature clement as themselves, that the harshness of the first American landscapes was transfigured into idyll and pastoral. Nature could be turned into the peaceful Book of Nature, full of symbols. Nature disclosed a wonderful ability to explain itself to Concord authors. There was an apparent beneficence in the air. Even Hawthorne could write, "In the stillest afternoon, if I listened, the thump of a great apple was audible, falling without a breath of wind, from the mere necessity of perfect ripeness."

In transcendentalist Concord Nature became an American art and an American religion. What was a honeymoon mood in the orchard to Hawthorne—"an infinite generosity and exhaustless bounty, on the part of our Mother Nature"—was for Emerson and his genius-disciples, Thoreau and Whitman, a text for living. "Embosomed for a season in Nature," man could be godly without God; he could see through Nature to the infinite structure of the universe and grasp its hidden purpose. This was the true revelation. Nature was the path to supreme knowledge.

> There is a moment in the history of every nation when, proceeding out of this brute youth, the perceptive powers reach with delight their greatest strength and have not

W.H. Stillman's Philosophers' Camp in the Adirondacks *(c. 1857). Boston literary Brahmins were awed by the virgin forest at Ampersand Pond.*

yet become microscopic, so that man at that instant extends across the entire scale, and, with his feet still planted on the immense forces of Night, converses by his eyes and brain with Solar and Stellar creation. That is the moment of perfect health, the culmination of their star of Empire.

Emerson, brought up to be a clergyman like all Emersons before him, left the ministry and turned to nature for his religion. He found the universe "an open secret." Nature was beauty, solace, meaning. Above all, it lent itself to art; the artist, patiently gathering impressions from Nature, could duplicate its form, rhythm, and power. Emerson's own style had a magic effect on his and future generations; he breathed absolute conviction. He created a sense of exaltation between himself and his audience, even from the lecture platform. And this, he claimed in his book *Nature*, actually rested on the common exposure to Nature.

In the presence of nature, a wild delight runs through the man, in spite of real sorrows. Nature says,—he is my creature, and maugre all his impertinent griefs, he shall be glad with me. . . . Crossing a bare common, in snow puddles, at twilight, under a clouded sky, without having in my thoughts any occurrence of special good fortune, I have enjoyed a perfect exhilaration. I am glad to the brink of fear. In the woods too, a man casts off his years, as the snake his slough, and at what period of life, is always a child. In the woods is perpetual youth. Within these plantations of God, a decorum and sanctity reign, a perennial festival is dressed, and the guest sees not how he should tire of them in a thousand years. In the woods, we return to reason and faith. . . . Standing on the bare ground,—my head bathed by the blithe air, and uplifted into infinite space,—all mean egotism vanishes. I become a transparent eye-ball. I am nothing, I see all. The currents of the Universal Being circulate through me; I am part or particle of God.

This astonishing rhapsody can be thought of as the overture to an *American* school of writing founded on the celebration of native landscape. It is more than that. As the famous (and terrible) John Brown was to say when he took up farming in the wild Adirondack mountains of upper New York State, he sought from Nature "those eternal and self-evident truths set forth in our Declaration of Independence." To possess Nature in America *thoroughly* was to confirm in every detail of life and thought America's independence. Emerson threw down the challenge in the first lines of his first book:

Our age is retrospective. It builds the sepulchres of the fathers. It writes biographies, histories, and criticism. The foregoing generations beheld God and nature face to face; we, through their eyes. Why should not we also enjoy an original relation to the universe? Why should not we have a poetry and philosophy of insight and not of tradition, and a religion by revelation to us, and not the history of theirs? Embosomed for a season in nature, whose floods of life stream around and through us, and invite us by the powers they supply, to action proportioned to nature, why should we grope among the dry bones of the past, or put the living generation into masquerade out of its faded wardrobe? . . . There are new lands, new men, new thoughts. Let us demand our own works and laws and worship.

This last sentence distinguishes Emerson from the poetry in Wordsworth and the prose in Coleridge from which he obviously drew. Emerson incorporates America in his romanticism; Wordsworth's greatest poems so transfigure the commonplace that a conversion follows. Emerson writes as the apostle of that new way of seeing which Americans were learning to think of as urgent in "God's Own Country." Unlike the explorers before him, the frontiersmen of his own day, he apprehends Nature not as exertion, but as enchantment and deliverance:

I have seen the spectacle of morning from the hill-top over against my house, from daybreak to sunrise, with emotions which an angel might share. The long slender bars of cloud float like fishes in the sea of crimson light. From the earth, as a shore, I look out into that silent sea. I seem to partake its rapid transformations; the active enchantment reaches my dust, and I dilate and conspire with the morning wind. How does Nature deify us with a few and cheap elements! Give me health and a day, and I will make the pomp of emperors ridiculous. The dawn is my Assyria; the sunset and moonrise my Paphos, and unimaginable realms of faerie; broad noon shall be my England of the senses and the understanding; the night shall be my Germany of mystic philosophy and dreams.

"In the woods is perpetual youth," wrote Emerson, "... decorum and sanctity reign." The gentle landscape of New England retains the qualities that endeared it to him, as to Thoreau and Hawthorne, and one can still see how "the horizon line marched by hills tossing like waves in a storm."

You can trust Nature for anything. Emerson never thinks of it as something that man can destroy by earning his living. It is just one great gift to man. "I have died out of the human world," he once wrote in ecstasy. Just outside his house on the Cambridge pike he had experiences of earth, sky, and water, morning, noon, and night, that were pure pastoral, no danger anywhere!

Last night the moon rose behind four distinct pine tree tops in the distant woods and the night at ten was so bright that I walked abroad. But the sublime light of night is unsatisfying, provoking; it astonishes but explains not. Its charm floats, dances, disappears, comes and goes, but palls in five minutes after you have left the house. Come out of your warm, angular house, resounding with few voices, into the chill, grand, instantaneous night, with such a Presence as a full moon in the clouds, and you are struck with poetic wonder. In the instant you leave far behind all human relations, wife, mother and child, and live only with the savages—water, air, light, carbon, lime, and granite. . . . I become a moist, cold element. "Nature grows over me." Frogs pipe; waters far off tinkle; dry leaves hiss; grass bends and rustles, and I have died out of the human world and come to feel a strange, cold, aqueous, terraqueous, aerial, ethereal sympathy and existence. I sow the sun and moon for seeds.

For all this, Emerson as a popular lecturer was the greatest traveler in America among New England writers, and his Journals in particular provide brilliantly amused snapshots of American places. He started with New England. In 1848, recording his observations in "the coldest November I have ever known," he drew "the finest picture through wintery air of the russet Massachusetts."

The landscape is democratic, not gathered into one city or baronial castle, but equally scattered into these white steeples, round which a town clusters in every place where six roads meet, or where a river branches or falls, or where the pan of soil is a little deeper. The horizon line marched by hills tossing like waves in a storm; firm indigo line. 'Tis a pretty revolution which is effected in the landscape by simply turning your head upside down, or, looking through your legs: an infinite softness and loveliness is added to the picture. It changes the landscape at once from November to June, . . . makes *Campagna* out of it at once. . . . Massachusetts is Italy upside down.

Remembering the superlative use which Emerson's sometimes handyman, Henry David Thoreau, was to make of the following purchase, it is moving to read Emerson's announcement to Thomas Carlyle:

I too have a new plaything, the best I ever had—a woodlot. Last fall I bought a piece of more than forty acres, on the border of a little lake half a mile wide and more, called Walden Pond—a place to which my feet have for years been accustomed to bring me once or twice a week at all seasons. . . . Some of the wood is an old growth, but most of it has been cut off within twenty years and is growing thriftily. In these May days, when maples, poplars, oaks, birches, walnut, and pine are in their spring glory, I go thither every afternoon, and cut with my hatchet an Indian path through the thicket all along the bold shore, and open the finest pictures.

52

The Peaceable Kingdom (Edward Hicks, c. 1848, detail). The Quaker artist painted almost 100 versions of his favorite moral allegory.

My two little girls know the road now, though it is nearly two miles from my house, and find their way to the spring at the foot of a pine grove, and with some awe to the ruins of a village of shanties, all overgrown with mullein, which the Irish who built the railroad left behind them. At a good distance in from the shore the land rises to a rocky head, perhaps sixty feet above the water. Thereon I think to place a hut; perhaps it will have two stories and be a pretty tower, looking out to Monadnoc and other New Hampshire mountains. There I hope to go with book and pen when good hours come.

Emerson never built that hut. He liked walking about Concord, but he was no woodsman, no hermit or saint ambitious to make a whole life out of his encounter with Nature. He could not put his whole life into a book, as Thoreau did, in order to assure himself that he had really lived. He made his living largely by lecturing. Of all American authors he was the greatest educator to his countrymen. They may not have always understood him, but they listened, said James Russell Lowell, "to that thrilling voice of his, so charged with subtle meaning and subtle music. . . . He made us conscious of the supreme and everlasting originality of whatever bit of soul might be in any of us."

Lecturing all over the country, often making his way on foot over the frozen Mississippi, Emerson described a society rapidly leaving him behind. It was typical of the young Emerson to say that in Nature as yet undefiled, "I feel perhaps the pain of an alien world; a world not yet subdued by the thought." In the woods near his house, he admitted in 1840, "I found myself not wholly present there. . . . Nature was still elsewhere. . . . Always the present object gave me this sense of the stillness that follows a pageant that has just gone by."

Nature was a Goddess that Emerson could not keep for himself. He saw all the ways she would elude him. Emerson the traveling lecturer could also describe his own country as if he had gone abroad. His sojourns in the less cultivated parts of New England are always detached, strictly in character. Nantucket he smiled at as a separate "nation"—

Nation of Nantucket makes its own war and peace. Place of winds, bleak, shelterless, and, when it blows, a large part of the island is suspended in the air and comes into your face and eyes as if it were glad to see you.

He is also fastidious, in his mildly underhand manner, about Cape Cod, a region even recently so primitive that writers like Eugene O'Neill and Edmund Wilson could live in the dunes without anyone's noting their presence. In Emerson's time the Cape was famous for the number of ships that regularly came to grief on its shores. He was enchanted to hear the lighthouse keeper on the back side of Cape Cod (facing Massachusetts Bay) report that he found obstinate resistance to the project of building a lighthouse on the ocean side, "as it would injure the wrecking business." At Orleans in the middle of the Cape, Emerson had a good view of the whole Cape and the sea on both sides.

The Cape looks like one of the Newfoundland Banks just emerged, a huge tract of sand half-covered with poverty grass and beach grass, and for trees, abele and locust and plantations of pitch pine . . . the view I speak of looked like emaciated Orkneys . . . made of salt dust, gravel, and fish bones. They say the wind makes the roads, and, as at Nantucket, a large part of the real estate was freely moving back and forth in the air. I heard much of the coming railroad which is about to reach Yarmouth and Hyannis,

Twilight in the Wilderness (*Frederic Church, 1826–1900, detail*).

Cape Cod in Emerson's time was as empty as the West. When Edward Hopper painted Cape Cod Evening *in 1939, he found the same sense of remoteness.*

and they hope will come to Provincetown. I fancied the people were only waiting for the railroad to reach them in order to evacuate the country. For the stark nakedness of the country could not be exaggerated.

Emerson did not invest his soul in every "savage" landscape, as Thoreau certainly invested *his* in Cape Cod, Maine, French Canada, Minnesota. Emerson describing frontier America along the Mississippi is delightful, he is so little swept away by anything he sees. He writes to his wife Lidian about the great river worlds that would soon become Mark Twain's America—

Well, we got away from Cairo, its sailor-shops, tenpin-alleys and faro tables, still on the green & almost transparent Ohio, which now seemed so broad that the yellow line in front for which we were steering, looked hopelessly narrow; but yellow line widened as we drew nigh, and, at last, we reached & crossed the perfectly-marked line of green on one side, & mud-hue on the other, & entered the Mississippi. It is one of the great river landscapes of the world, wide wide eddying waters, low shores. The great river takes in the Ohio which had grown so large, turns it all to its own mud color, & does not become perceptibly larger.

The great sweeps of the Mississippi, the number of its large islands made & unmade in short periods, your distance from either shore, and the unvarying character of the green wilderness on either side from hour to hour, no dents in the forest, no boats almost—we met I believe but one steamboat in the first hundred miles—now & again then we notice a flat wood boat lying under the shore, blow our whistle, ring our bell, & near the land, then out of some log-shed appear black or white men, & hastily put out their boat, a large mud-scow, loaded with corded wood. . . . Then there were planters travelling, one with his family of slaves (6 blacks); peaceable looking farmer-like men who when they stretch themselves in the pauses of conversation disclose the butts of their pistols in their breast-pockets.

It must have amused Emerson to report to Carlyle, that furious resister of all things American,

I went out Northwest to great countries which I had not visited before; rode one day, fault of broken railroads, in a sleigh, sixty-five miles through the snow, by Lake Michigan, (seeing how prairies and oak-openings look in winter), to reach Milwaukee; "the world there was done up in large lots," as a settler told me.

In wilderness Wisconsin Emerson was made much of; his rarity seemed to the first settlers "worth more than venison and quails," their daily diet. Emerson for his part considered this rough country bad for the intellect: "All the life of the land and water had distilled no thought." In St. Louis, where he met the future grandfather of T.S. Eliot, a noble Unitarian minister who had left New England to serve this backward area, Emerson believed "no thinking or even reading man" was to be found "in the 95000 souls" of that city. But then he complained that America as a whole was "formless, had no terrible and no beautiful condensation," was a "great country" with "diminutive minds." "I think Tennyson got his inspiration in gardens, and . . . in this country . . . there are no gardens."

Could this wild country without gardens be mirrored in a book? Henry David Thoreau, emphatically no savage himself, a classical scholar and "bachelor of nature," married to nothing and nobody but the New England countryside, proved that a supremely personal utterance could be located within nature as "the wild." Thoreau staked his life on the belief that man could find his own true nature in the wild. "We need the tonic of wilderness, . . . We can never have enough of Nature," he was to write in the chapter on Spring near the end of *Walden*. "In wildness is the preservation of the world," from his essay on "Walking," has become the motto of the Wilderness Society. Thoreau was too fond of the wilderness in America to imagine a wilderness *society*. And with his tolerant attempt for most of the institutions at hand, this man who went to jail for a night rather than pay a tax that might be used to support the hateful Mexican war saw in wildness *his* preservation and salvation.

The Romantics in this land of Nature held that a book should affect us as Nature itself does. The book of Nature that Thoreau wrote in *Walden* was the book of his life. The theme of *Walden* is that Nature taught Henry Thoreau how to live, and through this book he can now teach others. But *Walden* became the supreme idyll of Romanticism in America because of Thoreau's unique ability (for a writer) to live in Nature. Thoreau himself, for all his many words on the subject, could not entirely convey its mastery over him. The most minute bit of local landscape had a subtle impact on him, infinite in reverberation. Its influence was so pervasive that *Walden* can indeed affect a reader as Nature does.

And in Thoreau's mind Nature is eternal. He made a point of finding anywhere in Concord evidences of an Indian past not known to Indians themselves. What Thoreau saw in Nature as the living world was not "God" but proof that its beauty was order, the cosmos forever giving certainty of an immortality in which man could share. By living *in* Nature—this was still possible—man drew upon the visible signs of eternal life.

One of the many astonishments about Thoreau as a thinker is his awareness of himself as a fragment of such wholeness. When he was dying at forty-four of the lung disease produced by his constant exposure to bad weather plus the graphite he breathed in from making pencils, his friend the Concord sheriff said he had never seen a man dying in such perfect peace. Thoreau was serenely accepting of what he called "succession" in Nature. Emerson in Paris, visiting the Jardin des Plantes, wrote a famous passage in his Journal:

> The Universe is a more amazing puzzle than ever as you glance along this bewildering series of animated forms,—the hazy butterflies, the carved shells, the birds, beasts, fishes, insects, snakes—& the upheaving principle of life everywhere incipient in the very rock aping organized forms. Not a form so grotesque, so savage, nor so beautiful but is an expression of some property inherent in man the observer,—an occult relation between the very scorpions and man. I feel the centipede in me—cayman, carp, eagle & fox. I am moved by strange sympathies, I say continually "I will be a naturalist."

Thoreau became that "naturalist" in his own life, joined himself to Nature and yielded to its inevitabilities. By satisfying his religious instincts in Nature, he attained an extraordinary self-confidence. In *Walden* he compared himself to Chanticleer. "I do not propose to write an ode to dejection but to chant as lustily as Chanticleer in the morning." Although he was emphatically no Westerner in the style of Mark Twain, his satisfaction in Nature proclaimed identity with the onrushing, all-conquering Westward Ho! pioneering America of his day.

It is still truly amazing what unoccupied Nature could do for a fanatically bookish young man in the 1840s who had decided to live by "sauntering." Thoreau would always be a young man—one capable of writing, "Why should I feel lonely? Is not our planet in the Milky Way?" *Walden* has its absurdities: Thoreau offers himself as twice-born, a veritable saint who needs nothing but Nature in the raw outside his door—and lots of paper to write on. The book opens, and thrives upon, the comic energy of a young man (he was in his late twenties when he began the first draft while living in the cabin he built for himself at the Pond). He has made the great discovery that *he* knows how to live, even if his neighbors don't; and is now prepared to instruct his generation that the road to happiness is—to do without. Considering the plenitude of material goods that was to become the daily surface of America, this is proof that Thoreau was as much a humorist as he thought he was (by constantly making puns). Even in the 1840s he showed a gift for living just as he liked that was to become positively rare among "the people of plenty." He showed that it was possible to be honorably poor.

And this in public. Thoreau's famous seclusion at Walden Pond—a mile and a half to Concord Village—was frequently besieged by curiosity seekers. Writing so much about himself in a book entitled *Walden; Or Life in the Woods,* Thoreau archly dramatized his selective isolation. In fact his parents kept a kind of boarding house and he often went home for a good dinner. He had his triumph; he will always be recognized as America's odd man out, the rebel who trumpeted his eccentricity and became a hero to himself as well as to later young people at rebellious stages of their lives.

The persona within and behind *Walden* has many witty things to say about being different. "I should not talk so much about myself if there were anybody else whom I knew as well." "The mass of men lead lives of quiet desperation." "For many years I was self-appointed inspector of snowstorms and rainstorms, and did my duty faithfully, though I never received one cent for it." "I went to the woods because I wished to live deliberately, to front only the essential facts of life, and see if I could not learn what it had to teach, and not, when I came to die, discover that I had not lived." "If a man does not keep pace with his companions, perhaps it is because he hears a different drummer."

Thoreau is refreshing and even inspiring when he brings the full force of his eloquence to being "different." But it is the totally singular way in which he looks at landscape that makes him a classic. He positively blends into the terrain as he searches out the most minute textures and changes in Nature. *Walden* keeps ever fresh a new way of seeing. It creates on every reading a dependable sense of release, of pleasure—and above all, of good will towards the whole of creation.

Thoreau's self-built cabin, drawn by his sister Sophie. He spent 26 months in his "inkstand" on Walden Pond, but walked home to Concord many a night.

D.H. Lawrence, in his sometime enthusiasm for the "old" American books, was most impressed by their "spirit of place." The American situation has famously engendered constant movement. It has always made a virtue of "moving on." Thoreau situated himself, man and artist, by making the most of the genius of place. He hunted up the relics of vanished Indians as if he were the only person still interested in their sacredness. He made an occasional dollar as a surveyor by measuring plots in the neighborhood, then searched out "to exhaustion," as he said, every place he could walk. He played the farmer growing "miles" of beans, the naturalist cataloguing every fresh growth in the woods, St. Francis making friends with birds and beasts, the rhapsodic solitary playing the flute in his boat or beating an oar against the sides to make the hillsides echo. He took to his boat in the night so as to enchant himself with the experience—and possibly to enchant other denizens of what the Quaker painter Edward Hicks called "the peaceable kingdom." The lion and the lamb at last lay down together.

Such roles provided opportunity in *Walden* for Nature as layer on layer of scene, "science," drama. All led to the central theme of the book and Thoreau's special genius: the continuity of man with Nature, man growing out of Nature and, at the last, man returning to it. Though a transient on earth and a mere spectator of the everlasting spectacle and procession in Nature, man joins himself to the everlasting by believing in it.

"The cost of a thing is the amount of what I will call life which is required to be exchanged for it, immediately or in the long run." This is one of Thoreau's many sage pronouncements, his way of putting his life into a single sentence. His genius for the sentence grew out of his way of fixing on Nature for a flash, an epiphany, little monads of being in which his soul rejoiced. He could seize on a particular field, pond, animal as if the ecstasy of the capture were all he needed for life as for art:

> I was seated by the shore of a small pond, about a mile and a half south of the village of Concord and somewhat higher than it, in the midst of an extensive wood between that town and Lincoln, and about two miles south of that our only field known to fame, Concord Battle Ground; but I was so low in the woods that the opposite shore, half a mile off, like the rest, covered with wood, was my most distant horizon. For the first week, whenever I looked out on the pond it impressed me like a tarn high up on the side of a mountain, its bottom far above the surface of other lakes, and, as the sun arose, I saw it throwing off its nightly clothing of mist, and here and there, by degrees, its soft ripples or its smooth reflecting surface was revealed, while the mists, like ghosts, were stealthily withdrawing in every direction into the woods, as at the breaking up of some nocturnal conventicle. . . .
>
> This small lake was of most value as a neighbor in the intervals of a gentle rain-storm in August, when, both air and water being perfectly still, but the sky overcast, mid-afternoon had all the serenity of evening, and the wood-thrush sang around, and was heard from shore to shore. A lake like this is never smoother than at such a time; and the clear portion of the air above it being shallow and darkened by clouds, the water full of light and reflections, becomes a lower heaven itself so much the more important. . . . It is well to have some water in your neighborhood, to give buoyancy to and float the earth. One value even of the smallest well is, that when you look into it you see that earth is not continent but insular. This is as important as that it keeps butter cool. When I looked across the pond from this peak toward the Sudbury meadows, which in time of flood I distinguished elevated perhaps by a mirage in their

seething valley, like a coin in a basin, all the earth beyond the pond appeared like a thin crust insulated and floated even by this small sheet of intervening water, and I was reminded that this on which I dwelt was but *dry land*.

Mark Twain, in a superlative description of sunrise on the Mississippi (*Huckleberry Finn*, chapter XIX), wrote from the point of view of a former steamboat pilot's intense sense of activity: "and by-and-by you could see a streak on the water which you know by the look of the streak that there's a snag there in a swift current which breaks on it and makes that streak look that way . . ." Thoreau sees water as a picture, a scene suffused with peace and quiet—the full beauty of which is opened to him by the peaceful inactivity of contemplation. Nature in Thoreau's eyes *always* makes the picture. When he makes his way home through the woods at night, his route is so firmly established in his own mind that he feels he has been dreaming all the way home. "I have not been able to recall a single step of my walk, and I have thought that perhaps my body would find its way home if its master should forsake it, as the hand finds it way to the mouth without assistance."

In winter, when his idyllic life by the pond required more exertion than usual, Thoreau chopped a hole in the ice to obtain water and lay on the ice to fish through a hole. This he invested with that air of special providence he attached to his smallest doings.

> Standing on the snow-covered plain, as if in a pasture amid the hills, I cut my way first through a foot of snow, and then a foot of ice, and open a window under my feet, where, kneeling to drink, I look down into the quiet parlor of the fishes, pervaded by a softened light as through a window of ground glass, with its bright sanded floor the same as in summer; there a perennial waveless serenity reigns as in the amber twilight sky, corresponding to the cool and even temperament of the inhabitants. Heaven is under our feet as well as over our heads.

Thoreau was an amateur but confident naturalist who liked to keep records. They were the quantitative expression of his immersion in Nature and seemed to him proof positive that he touched Nature on every side. It was necessary to prove that although Walden Pond was unusually deep for its size it was certainly not "bottomless," as the locals liked to say. Thoreau was Emerson's disciple as well as handyman, a leading rhapsodist of the transcendentalist faith. He was forever demonstrating "correspondences" between Nature and human ideals. He could not dwell on any physical surface very long without exhorting the reader to see "higher laws." "Our life is always moral." The wonderful chapter on "The Ponds in Winter" shows the often didactic Thoreau reciting familiar analogy. The depth of Walden Pond, faithfully measured, reveals that "What I have observed of the pond is no less true in ethics."

Yet only Thoreau, having surveyed "the long lost bottom of Walden Pond, . . . before the ice broke up, early in '46, with compass and chain and sounding line," and noting, "It is remarkable how long men will believe in the bottomlessness of a pond without taking the trouble to sound it," would have added, "This is a remarkable depth for so small an area; yet not an inch of it can be spared by the imagination."

Imagination was finally Thoreau's "ethics." Imagination heightened his role as naturalist by fiercely jamming every possible detail, crowding the picture so as to give the fullest possible density to the landscape. Thoreau's favorite role as writer was to give everything he saw the most fervent attention. Exhaustiveness would turn science into art.

While I was surveying, the ice, which was sixteen inches thick, undulated under a slight wind like water. It is well known that a level cannot be used on ice. At one rod from the shore its greatest fluctuation, when observed by means of a level on land directed toward a graduated staff on the ice, was three quarters of an inch, though the ice appeared firmly attached to the shore. It was probably greater in the middle. Who knows but if our instruments were delicate enough we might detect an undulation in the crust of the earth?

Thoreau was clearly looking for things to write about. Fortunately, "ponds in winter" present something external as

a hundred men of Hyperborean extraction swoop down on to our pond one morning, . . . each man was armed with a double-pointed pike-staff, such as is not described in the New-England Farmer or the Cultivator. . . . So they came and went every day with a peculiar shriek from the locomotive, from and to some point of the polar regions, as it seemed to me, like a flock of arctic snow-birds. . . .

To speak literally, a hundred Irishmen, with Yankee overseers, came from Cambridge every day to get out the ice. They divided it into cakes by methods too well known to require description, and these, being sledded to the shore, were rapidly hauled off on to an ice platform, and raised by grappling irons and block and tackle, worked by horses, on to a stack, as surely as so many barrels of flour, and there placed evenly side by side, and row upon row, as if they formed the solid base of an obelisk designed to pierce the clouds. They told me that in a good day they could get out a thousand tons, which was the yield of about one acre. Deep ruts and "cradle-holes" were worn in the ice, as on *terra firma*, by the passage of the sleds over the same track, and the horses invariably ate their oats out of cakes of ice hollowed out like buckets. They stacked up the cakes thus in the open air in a pile thirty-five feet high on one side and six or seven rods square, putting hay between the outside layers to exclude the air; . . . I have noticed that a portion of Walden which in the state of water was green will often, when frozen, appear from the same point of view blue. . . . Ice is an interesting subject for contemplation.

Such fixity of attention became Thoreau's way of life from being his way of writing. His journal in fourteen volumes is the most dogged, meticulous account we have by a major imagination of Nature in America. Its purpose, often treated as natural history, was entirely literary, the transformation of the ordinary into the sense of perfect happiness in Nature. So it contains within itself the story of a writer who made his whole life one with Nature. He hoped that his account would be taken for a life somehow made perfect.

The attentiveness in Thoreau's writing can seem inexorable. The search for an object in which to invest his life quite wore him out and led to early death. To study to exhaustion the object before him became the drive of his life. "Sometimes it is some particular half-dozen rods which I wish to find myself pacing over, as where certain airs blow: then my life will come to me, methinks; like a hunter I walk in wait for it."

Thoreau depended so much on his daily and hourly search of fields around him that he sometimes felt he was wearing Nature out even as it was wearing him out. By 1854 he could admit, "We soon get through with Nature. She excites an expectation which she cannot satisfy. The merest child which has rambled into a copsewood dreams of a wilderness so wild and strange and inexhaustible as Nature can never show him."

As he was dying in 1862, Thoreau prepared for the *Atlantic Monthly* an extraordinary essay, "Walking," that sums up the ultimate meaning of Nature for his country even more than it does for himself. He turned walking into a rehearsal of the westward movement, and Nature into "Nature's Nation." His adoration of Nature, so urgent and even dominating of his daily life, becomes in the merest walk an act sacred to a race in danger of forgetting its primitive roots.

> I wish to speak a word for Nature, for absolute freedom and wildness, as contrasted with a freedom and culture merely civil—to regard man as . . . a part or parcel of Nature, rather than a member of society. I wish to make an extreme statement, if so I may make an emphatic one, for there are enough champions of civilisation: the minister, and the school-committee, and every one of you will take care of that.

In the same breath he likened walking to a "crusade." An accomplished classical scholar, he had the same passion for tracing every bit of Concord ground to its archaic foundation that he had for tracing words to their roots. And with his gift for incorporating more than one national mood into his personal mythology, he wrote in "Walking" a parable for his countrymen at a time when everyone was admiring the advice of the *New York Tribune*'s editor Horace Greeley, "Go west, young man."

> When I go out of the house for a walk, uncertain as yet whither I will bend my steps, and submit myself to my instinct to decide for me, I find, strange and whimsical as it may seem, that I finally and inevitably settle southwest, toward some particular wood or meadow or deserted pasture or hill in that direction. My needle is slow to settle . . . but it always settles between west and south-southwest. The future lies that way to me, and the earth seems more unexhausted and richer on that side. . . . Eastward I go only by force; but westward I go free. . . . I must walk toward Oregon, and not toward Europe.

With this, more than with his rare excursions into frontier lands of the time, Thoreau summed up his hope that "In wildness is the preservation of the world." In "Walking" he boasted "that with regard to Nature I live a sort of border life, on the confines of a world into which I make occasional and transient forays only, and my patriotism and allegiance to the State into whose territories I seem to retreat are those of a moss-Trooper."

Fortunately, Thoreau's longing for the "wild" did not always end in a perfect sentence. In the center of Maine, which is still so raw that it can stun the contemporary visitor, Thoreau frightened himself on the top of Mount Katahdin. Describing the night he spent on the summit, he confessed in *The Maine Woods,*

> I stand in awe of my body, this matter to which I am bound has become so strange to me. I fear not spirits, ghosts, of which I am one . . . but I fear bodies, I tremble to meet them. What is this Titan that has possession of me? Talk of our life in Nature—daily to be shown matter, to come in contact with it—rocks, trees, wind on our cheeks! the *solid* earth, the *actual* world! the *common sense*! Contact! Contact! *Who* are *we*? *where* are we?

The call of the wild, as Jack London was to put it, was not quite what Thoreau heard in his prime passion: to make Nature divine, and thus afford it meaning in every particular. It was possible, as Herman Melville showed, to be a sort of transcendentalist and symbol-hunter in Nature, and yet, if one had been a sailor, harpooner, deserter, jailbird and arch-wanderer in the South Pacific, to describe the wild as an experience of the world and of human nature. As Melville said on listening to Emerson, "To one who has weathered Cape Horn as a common sailor what stuff all this is."

"I have had to do with whales with these visible hands," says Ishmael, Melville's alter ego in *Moby-Dick*; "my splintered heart and maddened hand." He favors the word "isolato" for himself and in the "Knights and Squires" chapter ascribes "high qualities, though dark," to "meanest mariners and renegades and castaways." The ultra-tyrant aboard the *Pequod*, Captain Ahab, bewilders the crew by announcing that the real purpose of the voyage is to destroy the white whale, and explains with infinite condescension that

All visible objects, man, are but as pasteboard masks. But in each event—in the living act, the undoubted deed—there, some unknown but still reasoning thing puts forth the mouldings of its features from behind the unreasoning mask. If man will strike, strike through the mask! How can the prisoner reach outside except by thrusting through the wall? To me, the white whale is that wall, shoved near to me. Sometimes I think there's naught beyond. But 'tis enough. He tasks me; he heaps me; I see in him outrageous strength, with an inscrutable malice sinewing it. That inscrutable thing is chiefly what I hate; and be the white whale agent, or be the white whale principal, I will wreak that hate upon him.

Unlike Emerson and Thoreau, who saw chiefly the beneficence of Nature, and unlike the "household" and "fireside poets" of New England (Byrant, Whittier, Longfellow, Holmes) who were lucky to escape Nature's ravages to their hearths, Melville had great respect for Nature as an almighty power that man could fall in love with (as Ahab loved the whale that took over his life) but that was, as the Book of Job plainly relates, too much for man to harness to his intellect and will. In the more than four years Melville spent roaming the Pacific, he came to know the visible creation as something man might hope to represent but never to dominate. Nature could be glorious in its stupendous force, and the white whale when finally sighted could indeed overpower Ishmael.

A gentle joyousness—a mighty mildness of repose in swiftness, invested the gliding whale. Not the white bull Jupiter swimming away with ravished Europa clinging to his graceful horns; his lovely, leering eyes sideways intent upon the maid; with smooth bewitching fleetness, rippling straight for the nuptial bower in Crete; not Jove, not that great majesty Supreme! did surpass the glorified White Whale as he so divinely swam.

But the "grand god" could not long withhold from sight "the full terrors of his submerged trunk, the wrenched hideousness of his jaw." As soon as Ishmael hears, early in the book, of Ahab's demonic quest, the very whiteness of the whale inspires an amazing hymn to Nature as vacancy and destructiveness. "Though in many of its aspects this visible world seems formed in love, the invisible spheres were formed in fright." When Melville compared his book to "the Horrible texture of a fabric that should be woven of

Ambroise Louis Garneray's Capture of a Sperm Whale *(1850s). "Squall, whale and harpoon had all blended together," wrote Melville in his masterpiece* Moby-Dick.

ships' cables & hawsers,'' he was attacking Romantic America (of which he was certainly a part) where it was most satisfied with Nature and itself. He wanted the true odds against man to be honestly represented. And his main example of this, the awful sea, dominates the book as neither beast nor man can. In the 58th chapter, "Brit," Melville virtually cries out,

> we know the sea to be an everlasting terra incognita, so that Columbus sailed over numberless unknown worlds to discover his superficial western one . . . by vast odds, the most terrific of all mortal disasters have immemorially and indiscriminately befallen tens and hundreds of thousands of those who have gone upon the water. . . . a moment's consideration will teach, that however baby man may brag of his science and skill . . . forever and forever, to the crack of doom, the sea will insult and murder him, and pulverize the stateliest frigate he will make; nevertheless, by the continual repetition of these very impressions, . . . man has lost that sense of the full awfulness of the sea which aboriginally belongs to it.

Professor Longfellow knew all the languages of Europe and cultivated in many translations and imitations any literary atmosphere that could remind the English-speaking races (Queen Victoria was an admirer) of European balladry, legends, folk stories. Many of these became Arcadian landscapes of "men whose lives glided on like rivers that water the woodlands/Darkened by shadows of earth, but reflecting an image of heaven."

Longfellow instilled into his Indian and other "savage" scenes a smoothness and innocence that became dear to the American schoolroom and Victorian parlor. In *The Song of Hiawatha* he drew on the best accounts of Indian life and rolled out in octosyllables

> Should you ask me, whence these stories?
> Whence these legends and traditions,
> With the odors of the forest,
> With the dew and damp of meadows,
> With the curling smoke of wigwams,
> With the rushing of great rivers,
> With their frequent repetitions,
> And their wild reverberations,
> As of thunder in the mountains?

The American government's war with Indian tribes was by no means over when Longfellow made exotic and contented sounds of Indian names:

Longfellow's Hiawatha, illustrated by Frederic Remington. Victorian America's favorite Indian and mythological creature, stoically fishing from his birchbark canoe.

Where the heron, the Shugh-Shuh-gah
Feeds among the reeds and rushes
I repeat them as I heard them
From the lips of Nawadaha,
The musician, the sweet singer

Ye who love the haunts of nature,
. . . Ye who love a nation's legends,
Love the ballads of a people,
That like voices from afar off
Call to us to pause and listen,
Speak in tones so plain and childlike,
Scarcely can the ear distinguish
Whether they are sung or spoken:—
Listen to this Indian Legend,
To this Song of Hiawatha!

Ye whose hearts are fresh and simple,
Who have faith in God and Nature,
Who believe, that in all ages
Every human heart is human,
That in even savage bosoms
There are longings, yearnings, strivings
For the good they comprehend not,
That the feeble hands and helpless,
Groping blindly in the darkness,
Touch God's right hand in that darkness
And are lifted up and strengthened;—
Listen to this simple story,
To this Song of Hiawatha!

John Greenleaf Whittier was a Quaker of New England farm stock who knew a hard punishing life at first hand. The details in his most popular poem, *Snow-Bound*, bring back scenes of labor and isolation that would not reappear in American poetry until Robert Frost. Whittier was so thoroughly a moralist, so eager to show himself a pilgrim of Nature in the sweet provincial style, that his poems swing between actual experience and innocent generalities. What a good good world Americans still possessed in Nature as "teacher!"

The ancient teachers never dumb
Of Nature's unhoused lyceum,
In noons and tides and weather wise,
He read the clouds as prophecies, . . .
Holding the cunning-warded keys
To all the woodcraft mysteries;
Himself to Nature's heart so near
That all her voices in his ear
Of beast or bird had meanings clear.

Whittier is less familiar when he gives us the living details of a now forgotten Yankee land:

> From ripening corn the pigeons flew,
> The partridge drummed in the wood, the mink
> Went fishing down the river-brink.
>   . . .
> We heard the loosened clapboards tost,
> The board-nails snapping in the frost;
> And on us, through the unplastered wall,
>   Felt the light sifted snow-flakes fall . . .
> Down the long hillside treading slow
> We saw the half-buried oxen go,
> Shaking the snow from heads uptost,
> Their straining nostrils white with frost,
>   . . .
> Green hills of life that slope to death,
> And haunts of home, whose vistaed trees
> Shade off to mournful cypresses
>   With the white amaranths underneath.

Emerson appreciated Nature as a source of knowledge. Thoreau venerated it for companionship almost divine. Walt Whitman saw its process and reality as organic, part of himself. "Walt Whitman, a kosmos, of Manhattan the son"—"I am large, I contain multitudes"—returned the compliment of birth and rearing by portraying Nature as incessant creation. Walt Whitman himself, "hankering, gross," knowing "no sweeter smell than that of his own armpits," saw himself as the voice and similitude of that creation.

Amazing insinuations from this man, shameless invitations to the reader: "Stop this day and night with me and you shall possess the origin of all poems." What made Whitman's discovery of poetry so urgent and long-lasting was recognition of himself as a force of nature equal to "Nature." He had a resounding sense of everything outside him as a force that necessarily included him. This was what the wide open sense of Nature in America, "man in the open air," made possible for him. By the force of his attachment, he brings to his "songs" and "chants" a sense of partnership and wholeness.

Only Whitman of the many poets in still pastoral America could have written "Earth, my likeness." And this in the remarkable series of homoerotic love poems he called *Calamus*. Invoking his love as an inextricable part of Nature, he characteristically explained the term by locating it:

a common word here; it is the very large and aromatic grass, or root, spears three feet high—often called "sweet flag"—grows all over the Northern and Middle States. . . .
The recherche or ethereal sense, as used in my book, arises probably from it, Calamus presenting the biggest and hardiest kind of spears of grass, and from its fresh, aromatic, pungent bouquet.

The Much-Resounding Sea (*Thomas Moran, 1884, detail*).

Whitman is above all else a poet of celebrations. In a mid-century America before the Civil War, still thinking of itself as the first entirely virtuous nation in history, who but Whitman could have opened up with "I celebrate myself" and have gone on in tones alternately cosmic and saucy, grandiloquent and street-smart? He portrays himself as being as necessary to the earth—to Nature, America, and freedom—as these are to him. At the same time he is consciously arch and heretical in his efforts to redeem himself from the conventional dutiful American of his time—from the editor Walter Whitman, Jr., that he overthrew to be able to write "I find no sweeter fat than sticks to my own bones."

> What is commonest, cheapest, nearest, easiest, is Me,
> Me going in for my chances, spending for vast returns,
> Adorning myself to bestow myself on the first that will take me,
> Not asking the sky to come down to my good will,
> Scattering it freely forever.

Whitman seems entirely at home with Nature when, with equal confidence, he ends *Song of Myself* with

> I bequeath myself to the dirt to grow from the grass I love,
> If you want me again look for me under your boot-soles

This air of universal acceptance and happy discovery in all things allowed him to exclaim, "Hurrah for positive science! long live exact demonstration!", to illustrate "positive science" by crying, "Fetch stonecrop mixt with cedar and branches of lilac," and to reach his summit of revelation in section 31 of *Song of Myself* with

> I believe a leaf of grass is no less than the journey-work of the stars,
> And the pismire is equally perfect, and a grain of sand, and the egg of the
>   wren,
> And the tree-toad is a chef-d'oeuvre for the highest,
> And the running blackberry would adorn the parlors of heaven, . . .
> And a mouse is miracle enough to stagger sextillions of infidels.

> I find I incorporate gneiss, coal, long-threaded moss, fruits, grains,
>   esculent roots,
> And am stucco'd with quadrupeds and birds all over, . . .

Even the occasionally clumsy, jarring phrase comes in on the tide of so much self-discovery and acceptance:

> In me the caresser of life wherever moving, backward as well as forward
>   slueing,
> To niches aside and junior bending, not a person or object missing,
> Absorbing all to myself and for this song.

What Whitman is forever "moving" toward is the manifestation in Nature of his erotic independence. This produces his special pulsation and rhythm, his threading together

Walden Pond, a mile and a half from Concord Village, where Thoreau secluded himself and wrote about the continuity of man with Nature.

things whose very names proclaim his exhilarated inclusion of the curious, the marginal, the unexpected resourcefulness in Nature—

> The smoke of my own breath,
> Echoes, ripples, buzzed whispers, love-root, silk-thread, crotch and vine,
> My respiration and inspiration, the beating of my heart, the passing of blood
>   and air through my lungs,
> The sniff of green leaves and dry leaves, and of the shore and darkcoloured
>   sea-rocks, and of hay in the barn,
> The sound of the belched words of my voice loosed to the eddies of the wind,
>   . . .

A particular sign of Whitman's ability to be aroused by Nature into all sorts of "abrupt, curious questionings" is his feeling for names. The need to find names for so many unnamed places in a new world was to lead to many deliciously farcical inventions. Whitman's essay "Slang in America" cites Bazoo, Shirttail Bend, Whiskey Flat, Puppytown, Wild Yankee Ranch, Squaw Flat, Loafer's Ravine, Squitch Gulch, Toenail Lake. (George Orwell thought that Americans were curiously deficient in giving names to the land.) Whitman praised slang—"profoundly consider'd, the lawless germinal element, below all words and sentences, and behind all poetry, and proves a certain perennial rankness and protestantism in speech."

Moving toward an American language, which he was the first before Mark Twain to make a continuing essential rhythm of his work, Whitman identified this "lawless germinal element" with his deepest urges as a poet. He described his poems as "sprouting" from nature like grass—the commonest, prolific surface of the daily world. A favorite word was "inception." His occasionally slovenly, indirect, strangely halting way of writing was his way of duplicating the life process. There was a certain ecstasy in the provisional, the effortful. His country was a great experiment, and so was Walt Whitman in his poetry.

> I sometimes think the *Leaves* is only a language experiment that is an attempt to give the spirit, the body, the man, new words, new potentialities of speech—an American, a cosmopolitan . . . range of self-expression.

Whitman's confidently robust persona as "the American poet" was founded on great themes. They were his secret source of strength. He saw them as an inexhaustible series of concentric circles growing out of his country's unique partnership with Nature. Franz Kafka, a shrewd critic, saw that Whitman "combined the contemplation of nature and civilization, which are apparently entirely contradictory, into a single intoxicating vision of life." Whitman turned the physicality of America, America as inventory, into the first transcontinental panorama. *Leaves of Grass* is behind all those twentieth-century novels, notably John Dos Passos's trilogy *U.S.A.*, that sought to find an equivalent in technique and extent to what Whitman celebrated in his insistent lists of American names and occupations. In 1871, obstinate in his hopes for America despite the corruption and cynicism of the Gilded Age, Whitman wrote in his great manifesto *Democratic Vistas* that the country, like his own poetry, was one with Nature. And "the greatest lessons of Nature through the universe are perhaps the lessons of variety and freedom."

Thomas Carlyle sneered that Whitman thought he was a big poet because he came from a big country. But the bigness of America seemed to Whitman, as it did to Jefferson, not a boast but a providential chance for the redemption of millions long starved for land. In a footnote to *Democratic Vistas* Whitman quoted the latest Vice-President's bragging statistics about the extent of the United States after the Civil War and the acquisition of Alaska. The territorial area was fifteen times larger than that of Great Britain and France combined, with a shoreline, including Alaska, equal to the entire circumference of the earth. Whitman had been a patriotic stump speaker before he became the poet of singular gifts, and some of the early fervor never left him. But more than any other major talent of the time, Whitman had been afraid that the breakup of the country in the Civil War meant the end of democracy. It was union he celebrated, not mere size, when in *Democratic Vistas* he crowed: "The triumphant future . . . on larger scales and in more varieties than ever, is certain. In those respects, the republic must soon (if she does not already) outstrip all examples hitherto afforded, and dominate the world." Whitman's exuberance in such matters shows an ability that later writers must envy; he really incorporated "Nature's Nation" into himself. He seems to have thought of America as a kind of universal theater. One of his favorite words was "pageant." There was a startling pageant of occupations, races, talents in "Salut au Monde," "A Song for Occupations," "A Song of the Rolling Earth."

Whitman alone in his time and place was able to turn so intimate and shocking a subject as a child's discovery of sex, "Out of the Cradle Endlessly Rocking," into a glorious ritual of recognition that became his most beautiful single poem. A boy leaves his bed to walk the beach "When the lilac-scent was in the air and Fifth-month grass was growing." "Two feather'd guests from Alabama, two together," entrance the boy; then the "she-bird" disappears. The song of the "he-bird," alone in the tree, unites with the night, "the hoarse surging of the sea" and the boy's awareness that "you singer solitary, singing by yourself," is "projecting me."

> Never more shall I escape, never more the reverberations,
> Never more the cries of unsatisfied love be absent from me,
> Never again leave me to be the peaceful child I was before what there in
>   the night,
> By the sea under the yellow and sagging moon,
> The messenger there arous'd, the fire, the sweet hell within,
> The unknown want, the destiny of me.

But in this recognition is the birth of a poet. Whereupon all around him, "the sea,"

> Delaying not, hurrying not
> Whisper'd me through the night, and very plainly before daybreak,
> Lisp'd to me the low and delicious word death, . . .

Death is the great conjunction with the life process. Earth is father, the sea off Paumanok (the Indian word for Long Island) is mother. The boy has grasped in his separateness the poet he is to be:

Which I do not forget,
But fuse the song of my dusky demon and brother,
That he sang to me in the moonlight on Paumanok's gray beach,
With the thousand responsive songs at random,
My own songs awaked from that hour,
And with them the key, the word up from the waves,
The word of the sweetest song and all songs,
That strong and delicious word which, creeping to my feet,
(Or like some old crone rocking the cradle, swathed in sweet garments,
  bending aside,)
The sea whisper'd me.

Whitman from West Hills, Huntington, Long Island, liked to describe himself "starting from fish-shaped Paumanok." In his childhood Long Island was a paradise of great beaches and peaceful Indian tribes. In the memoirs of earliest youth he attached to his diaries of the Civil War, *Specimen Days*, Whitman lovingly recalled "Paumanok" as

a beautiful, varied and picturesque series of inlets, "necks" and sea-like expansions, for a hundred miles to Orient Point. On the ocean side the great south bay dotted with countless hummocks, mostly small, some quite large, occasionally long bars of sand out two hundred rods to a mile-and-a-half from the shore. While now and then, as at Rockaway and far east along the Hamptons, the beach makes right on the island, the sea dashing up without intervention . . .

The shores of this bay, winter and summer, and my doings there in early life, are woven all through L. of G. . . .

The eastern end of Long Island, the Peconic bay region, I know quite well, too . . . down to Montauk—spent many an hour on Turtle Hill by the old light-house, on the extreme point, looking out over the ceaseless roll of the Atlantic. I used to like to go down there and fraternize with the blue-fishers, or the annual squads of sea-bass takers. Sometimes, along Montauk peninsula . . . met the strange, unkempt, half-barbarous herdsmen, at that time living there entirely aloof from society or civilization, in charge, on those rich pasturages, of vast droves of horses, kine or sheep, own'd by farmers of the eastern towns . . .

Many a good day or half-day did I have, wandering through those solitary cross-roads, inhaling the peculiar and wild aroma. Here, and all along the island and its shores, I spent intervals of many years, all season, sometimes riding, sometimes boating, but generally afoot (I was always then a good walker), absorbing fields, shores, marine incidents, characters, the bay-men, farmers, pilots . . . always liked the bare sea-beach, south side, and have some of my happiest hours on it to this day.

As I write, the whole experience comes back to me after the lapse of forty and more years—the soothing rustle of the waves, and the saline smell—boyhood's times, the clam-digging, bare foot, and with trowsers roll'd up—hauling down the creek—the perfume of the sedge meadows—the hay-boat, and the chowder and fishing excursions;—or, of later years, little voyages down and out New York bay, in the pilot boats. Those same later years, also, while living in Brooklyn (1835–'50) I went regularly every week in the mild seasons down to Coney Island, at that time a long, bare unfrequented shore, which I had all to myself, and where I loved, after bathing,

Looking over the Sand Dunes—East Hampton *(Thomas Moran, 1880). The sea off Paumonok (Long Island) awoke the poet in the young Whitman. "My own songs awaked from that hour,/ And with them the key, the word up from the waves,/the word of the sweetest song and all songs . . ."*

Brooklyn, Long Island *(John Barnet, 1855). The year Whitman printed* Leaves of Grass *off Fulton Street. Brooklyn was a separate city until 1898.*

to race up and down the hard sand, and declaim Homer or Shakespeare to the surf and sea-gulls by the hour.

Whitman could be wonderfully charming and easy in this pastoral mode. He began the first version of "Song of Myself"

> I loafe and invite my soul,
> I lean and loafe at my ease observing a spear of summer grass.

His gift for participating deeply in the mass life of cities—the New York of his youth and Washington during the Civil War—must be discussed in the context of cities as "power centers." But his equal gift for country scenes had a reflowering after the Civil War. Retiring to Camden, New Jersey, on the Delaware, with the paralysis that he attributed to his services as volunteer in the hospitals of war-time Washington, Whitman tried to regain health in the woods. Only Whitman, though certainly no combatant, had been close enough to describe the landscape of war in the fashion that united his reverence for the American land and his passion for the soldier as archetype. We know from his greatest poems that death had supreme significance for him. When he writes in *Specimen Days* of "the million dead summ'd up," his belief in sacrifice, in death as fulfillment of Nature, wins over his horror. The very names of Civil War battles had become sacred to Whitman's generation. There are few testaments to the power over the American imagination of such names as Whitman's rumination over the dead—

> The dead in this war—there they lie, strewing the fields and woods and valleys of the South—Virginia, the Peninsula, Malvern Hill and Fair Oaks—the banks of the Chicahominy—the terraces of Fredericksburgh—Antietam bridge—the grisly ravines of Manassas—the blood promenade of the Wilderness—the variety of the strayed dead . . . the dead, the dead, the dead, *our* dead—or South or North, ours all (all, all, all, finally dear to me)—or East and West—Atlantic coast or Mississippi Valley—somewhere they crawl'd to die, alone, in bushes, low gullies, or on the sides of hills . . . the infinite dead—(the land entire saturated, perfumed with their impalpable ashes exhilaration in Nature's chemistry distill'd, and shall be so in every future grain of wheat or ear of corn, and every flower that grows, and every breath we draw).

In joining his reduced self to the mass "sacrifices" of the Civil War, Whitman was trying to "merge" with his country. By particular attention to the war's devastated landscape he meant to show how much he drew his mystical sense of nationhood from the land. Whitman on a night battle at Chancellorsville:

> It was largely in the woods, and quite a general engagement. The night was very pleasant, at times the moon shining out full and clear, all nature so calm in itself, the early summer grass so rich, and foliage of the trees—yet there was the battle raging, and many good fellows lying helpless, . . . the red life-blood oozing out from heads or trunks or limbs upon that green and dew-cool grass. Patches of the woods take fire, and several of the wounded, unable to move, are consumed—quite large spaces are swept over, burning the dead also. . . . The flashes of fire from the cannon, the quick flaring flames and smoke, and the immense roar—the musketry so general, the light

Reburying the dead; a Civil War photograph. "The dead, the dead, the dead, our dead—or South or North, ours all . . ." Whitman in Specimen Days, *his diary of the war.*

nearly bright enough for each side to see the other—the crashing, tramping of men—the yelling—close quarters . . .

By contrast with these notes on the ferocious engagement of masses, the "old" Whitman (forty-six when the war ended), writing about himself in Camden's woods, is back to the solitude he tried to break out of with "Song of Myself." Charming as these notes are on his effort to restore himself to health through Nature, communing with himself and observing Nature as an all-friendly presence, the picture Whitman presents of his life in the woods, doggedly trying to brush his flesh back to vigor, does not have the excitement of "Song of Myself." It is a return to a Quaker's idyll of "the peaceable kingdom." We are back to Romantic America's fondness for Nature as the perfect friend, Nature easily caught like the golden fish in a fairy tale. He finds himself as pleasing as he does Nature. And his genial self-love, as always, invites us to love Nature. There are little set pieces in *Specimen Days* whose very titles are landscapes—Cedar Apples, Summer Sights and Indolences, Sundown Perfume, Quail Notes, The Hermit Thrush, A Sun-Bath, Nakedness. The sketches Whitman called "notes" are turned by every quick brush stroke into pictures—

As I journey'd today in a light wagon ten or twelve miles through the country, nothing pleased me more, in their homely beauty and novelty (I had either never seen the little things to such advantage, or had never noticed them before) than that peculiar fruit, with its profuse clear-yellow dangles of inch-long silk or yarn, in boundless profusion spotting the dark-green cedar bushes—contrasting well with their bronze tufts—the flossy shreds covering the knobs all over, like a shock of wild hair on elfin pates . . .

Only Mark Twain after Whitman was able to write about Nature with entire naturalness, this spontaneous air of writing as naturally as the mind moves—"like a brook coursing . . ." Whitman writes about Nature as if he were breathing it all in. But toward the end of his life, though benevolent to the last (the "sweet hell within" apparently no longer a trial), he marks the end of Nature seen *entirely* as pastoral glow, America as "picture."

The West that so many Americans were now riding into was to show Nature as something very different from the lovely banks of the sluggish Concord River.

CHAPTER THREE

WESTWARD I GO FREE

In April 1861, a twenty-six-year-old pilot on the Mississippi River, Samuel Langhorne Clemens, found himself without occupation. The Civil War had broken out and river traffic was disrupted. Looking back on his youthful glory as a pilot (it lasted less than two years), Mark Twain was to remember in *Life on the Mississippi* that

> a pilot, in those days, was the only unfettered and entirely independent human being that lived on the earth. . . . The moment that the boat was under way in the river, she was under the sole and unquestioned control of the pilot. He could do with her exactly as he pleased, run her when and whither he chose, and tie her up to the bank whenever his judgment said that that course was best. His movements were entirely free; he consulted no one, he received commands from nobody, he promptly resented even the merest suggestions. Indeed, the law of the United States forbade him to listen to commands or suggestions, rightly considering that the pilot necessarily knew better how to handle the boat than anybody could tell him. So here was the novelty of a king without a keeper, an absolute monarch who was absolute in sober truth and not by a fiction of words.

For perhaps two weeks the young Missourian who had grown up alongside the Mississippi in Hannibal had been part of a small Confederate guerilla band. In later life he was to ridicule this brief and maladroit experience as a "rebel." Then, with the war raging, he seized upon the chance to go out West with his brother Orion, who had been appointed Secretary of the Nevada Territory. The author in Sam Clemens (soon to become "Mark Twain") was made for this experience.

To go all the way out to Nevada in 1861 was the greatest possible experience for someone at once Southern and Western. Mark Twain on the Mississippi already felt himself part of the heady, pushing frontier experience. The basic experience of Americans was to keep moving. As Willa Cather was to write of growing up on the Nebraska prairie in the 1880s, there was still so much motion in the land itself that "the whole country seemed, somehow, to be running." And Mark Twain was definitely and jubilantly not a schooled and restrained "Eastern type." Eventually he became a celebrated frontier humorist, married into a prosperous Buffalo family and settled in Hartford, Connecticut, among extremely respectable literary folk. But his best books, from *Roughing It* to *Life on the Mississippi*, *The Adventures of Tom Sawyer* and, above all, *The Adventures of Huckleberry Finn*, were rooted in the great, still open country, "God's Own Country,"

Crossing the Plains (*Charles Christian Nahl, 1856*). *The story of the West—a story that brought together the pioneering spirit, courage, peril and hardship—became a long-lasting image for American writers at every level.*

that started when you crossed the Mississippi. Another Southerner in the Midwest, Abraham Lincoln, called the Mississippi "the Father of Waters."

When Sam Clemens became Mark Twain, he also became—of all the primary American writers—the incarnation of the Western experience. This was based on the frontier as a place to settle and, just as resolutely, a place to leave. Constantly to move on became the special mark of Mark Twain's writing. An instinct for movement drove his quicksilver prose. His friend William Dean Howells (from Columbus, Ohio, but long settled in Boston) remained enough of a Westerner to appreciate Mark Twain as the perfect Western type, "more dramatically the creature of circumstances than the old Anglo-American type."

What Howells seized in Mark Twain's "circumstances" was the opposition that great man lived between the "primitive" and the modern. The story of the West was rooted in the unsettlement of people from "another country"—Europe or the East. They flocked into an empty country, bearing the old standards with them. As *Huckleberry Finn* more than any other American classic was to demonstrate, the frontier worked on established standards like acid. For people always on the move, a frontier to be "conquered"

82

represented their hardihood as a race. By the end of the nineteenth century, when the historian Frederick Jackson Turner, in his celebrated address at the Chicago World's Fair, proclaimed the "end of the frontier"—there were no longer any parts of the United States still unsettled—the pastoral in American history seemed over. America was no longer synonymous with "Nature."

In 1861, however, Mark Twain exuberantly going out West in a stagecoach felt himself to be the luckiest man alive. *Roughing It* (1872) communicates with the greatest vividness a wholly new *physical* experience—extreme, arduous, intoxicating and bewildering by turns— that the West represented. Nevada today, except for such lurid interruptions of the desert as Reno and Las Vegas, is still largely as arid and empty as when Mark Twain saw it. The United States Energy Commission still finds it highly suitable for (underground) atom bomb tests. Most Nevada rivers go nowhere, end in desolate alkali "sinks." Great arid stretches clothed with sagebrush and creosote bushes (a resinous desert shrub) typify a landscape that defeated usually determined Spanish explorers. They called it the "cruel land."

Mark Twain had a genius for capitalizing on any experience. He reported the journey by regular stagecoach from St. Joseph, Missouri, to Carson City in Nevada as if nothing so jolly had ever taken place before. "St. Joe" on the Missouri River was the classic jumping-off place. "The States" were all behind our twenty-six-year-old hero. The still savage West was obviously waiting to be described by someone just like Mark Twain—brash, delighting in every chance to be impudent, and always with his eye on comedy. Here was Brother Orion, a good Anglo-Saxon Protestant, leaving civilization to be with

> the great plains and deserts, and among the mountains of the Far West, and would see buffaloes and Indians, and prairie dogs, and antelopes, and have all kinds of adventures, and maybe get hanged or scalped, and have ever such a fine time, and write home and tell us all about it, and be a hero . . .

The new Secretary of Nevada Territory took along "about four pounds of United States statutes and six pounds of Unabridged Dictionary." The "poor innocents" did not know that such things could be bought in San Francisco one day and received in Carson City the next. The Secretary's brother armed himself with a "pitiful little Smith & Wesson's seven-shooter," which carried a ball like a homeopathic pill, "and it took the whole seven to make a dose for an adult." A third passenger carried a revolver so unwieldy and unreliable that the stagecoach driver laughed, "If she didn't get what she went after, she would fetch something else." It was a cheerful weapon. "Sometimes all its six barrels would go off at once, and then there was no safe place in all the region round about, but behind it."

The early chapters of *Roughing It* are incomparable descriptions of "morning in America," the Wild West stretched out before young Mark Twain bowling along in a stage:

> It was a superb summer morning, and all the landscape was brilliant with sunshine. There was a freshness and breeziness, too, and an exhilarating sense of emancipation from all sorts of cares and responsibilities, that almost made us feel that the years we had spent in the close, hot city, toiling and slaving away, had been wasted and thrown away. We were spinning along through Kansas, and in the course of an hour and a half

we were fairly abroad on the great Plains. Just here the land was rolling—a grand sweep of regular elevations and depressions as far as the eye could reach—like the stately heave and swell of the ocean's bosom after a storm. And everywhere were cornfields, accenting with squares of deeper green this limitless expanse of grassy land. But presently this sea upon dry ground was to lose its "rolling" character and stretch away for seven hundred miles as level as a floor!

Everything on this journey West is new, and impressions fresh as the beginning of the world rain about the young man taking them all in. The coach is a great swinging and swaying conveyance that makes Mark Twain feel as if it were a cradle enclosing him. Six handsome horses go so fast they have to be changed every ten miles. Except for the three passengers and the six pounds of unabridged dictionary constantly falling against them, the coach is packed with mail bags. A wall of mail rises up to the roof. A great pile of it is strapped on top of the stage. Twenty-seven hundred pounds of mail, but the driver explains that the Injuns will get most of it, "which is powerful troublesome, 'though they get plenty of truck to read."

The "three days mail" they are carrying for Carson City and "Frisco" is so hard on the stagecoach they have to stop for repairs. The newspaper bags are "put out for the Injuns for to keep 'em quiet," and the interior of the coach so lined with the remaining mail bags that the passengers comfortably lie over them, with Mark Twain reading the statutes and the dictionary, "and wondering how the characters would turn out."

It was now just dawn; and as we stretched our cramped legs full length on the mail sacks, and gazed out through the windows across the wide wastes of greensward clad in cool, powdery mist, to where there was an expectant look in the eastern horizon, our perfect enjoyment took the form of a tranquil and contented ecstasy. The stage whirled along at a spanking gait, the breeze flapping curtains and suspended coats in a most exhilarating way; the cradle swayed and swung luxuriously, the pattering of the horses' hoofs, the cracking of the driver's whip, and his "hi-yi g'lang!" was music; the spinning ground and the waltzing trees appeared to give us a mute hurrah as we went by, and then slack up and look after us with interest, or envy, or something; and as we lay and smoked the pipe of peace and compared all this luxury with the years of tiresome city life that had gone before it, we felt that there was only one complete and satisfying happiness in the world, and we had found it.

"So we flew along all day." But "flying" and exhilarated by the sense of boundless adventure, Mark Twain carefully noted the "weird music" of the stage conductor's bugle "winding over the grassy solitudes," the astonishing decrepitude of the station buildings at which they rested, the sudden emergence of a town "after what appeared to us such a long acquaintance with deep, still, almost lifeless and houseless solitudes." Then the quicksands of the "shallow, yellow, muddy South Platte, with its low banks and its scattering flat sand-bars and pigmy islands—a melancholy stream straggling through the centre of the enormous flat plain, and only saved from being impossible to find with the naked eye by its sentinel rank of scattering trees standing on either bank. The Platte was 'up,' they said—which made me wish I could see it when it was down."

Here is America West in the middle of the nineteenth century, in the far middle of a vast continent, in what the novelist William Gass was to call "the heart of the heart of the

The Old Stagecoach of the Plains (*Frederic Remington, 1901*).

country." Mark Twain is fiercely unsentimental about the desert Indians, whom he calls the coyote's "first cousins." He captures the deadly weariness of a Mormon emigrant train of thirty-three wagons driving their herd of loose cows before them. Men, women and children have been walking toward Utah, their promised land, for eight weeks.

Finally, passing Sweetwater Creek, Independence Rock, Devil's Gate and the Devil's Gap, the Clemens stagecoach is in the heart of the Rockies and at last passing through the renowned South Pass. There, perched on the extreme summit of the great range, they are on such an airy elevation above "the creeping populations of the earth, that now and then when the obstructing crags stood out of the way it seemed that we could look around and abroad and contemplate the whole great globe, with its dissolving view of mountains, seas and continents stretching away through the mystery of the summer haze."

OVERLEAF: *Devil's Gate, Wyoming, c. 1871. "It seemed we could look around and abroad and contemplate the whole great globe." Mark Twain.*

This is the exultant note that so many American writers and painters were to get into their Western landscapes. As Mark Twain said, "In cool mornings, before the sun was fairly up, it was worth a lifetime of city toiling and moiling, to perch in the foretop with the driver and see the six mustangs scamper under the sharp snapping of a whip that never touched them; to scan the blue distances of a world that knew no lords but us." The twentieth-century novelist Paul Horgan was to say that he had spent more than half his life among the high plains and mountains of the West, where all marvels were natural ones on a scale so grand as to make man's survival there an historical triumph. Mark Twain's contemporary, the German-born painter Albert Bierstadt, quickly satisfied the American love of bigness in paintings of the Rockies that made them look positively sacred as they ascended into some Valhalla, misty white and pink. Mountains so inhumanly grand were obviously not known to his colleagues in the Hudson River School, but Bierstadt was proud that they were part of "his" continent.

A whole school of frontier types was to manufacture "local color" and "Western humor" out of this still novel landscape. Two dominating political figures in the early life of the United States, Andrew Jackson and Abraham Lincoln, were formed by the Southern frontier as it merged into the West. A superb English-born historian of America, George Dangerfield, wrote that

> The centrifugal impulse of the frontier can be illustrated by the movement of the Lincoln family. The Lincolns rode and walked from Kentucky into southern Indiana in 1816, moving from the path of slavery, which threatened them with the irremediable status of "poor white." Ten years later Thomas Lincoln, no richer, heard the call of the Illinois prairies, and he and his family crossed the Wabash and the Sangamon. Their struggles and tragedies in Indiana were those of all but the most fortunate migrants. At Little Pigeon Creek, for a whole year, they lived in a "half-faced camp," a three-sided cabin, with two trees for corner posts, and an open face looking South, where a log fire burned day and night. "The sides and roof were covered with poles, branches, brush, dried grass, mud; chinks were stuffed where the wind or rain was trying to come through." After a year, they moved into a log cabin, with a dirt floor, no windows, and a hole for a door, and the young Lincoln slept in a minute loft upon a heap of leaves.

Roughing It is vivid and even consciously "picturesque" in its homage to the West. But it is subtle, acrid and enduringly funny because of the human spectacle Mark Twain kept his eye on. He came to Virginia City in Nevada as a prospector himself at a time when the gold and silver in the ground, some of it right under the city pavements, made Nevada the Mecca of thousands upon thousands of American characters desperate to claw this earth and become rich.

Mark Twain turned into frolic the gold and silver rush—a frolic corresponding to his own youth. What he did not care to underline in his exuberant pages on becoming a "millionaire for ten days" was the violence of Nevada. This was not unrelated to a landscape that still looks as if God gave it up as a bad job. The historian Henry Adams was to say that he had never seen a "finished landscape" in America. In Nevada the Creation had broken off; there was some disposition to violence in the very emptiness. This gave countenance and support to the many desperadoes who were finding in the West something equal to their hunger "to make a pile." This would transform them from the social and economic insignificance driving them West.

Raftsmen Playing Cards (*G.C. Bingham, 1847*). "*You feel mighty free and easy and comfortable on a raft.*" (Huckleberry Finn)

Overland Trail *(Albert Bierstadt, 1830–1902, detail); the Oregon Trail, the most famous central route to the Pacific.*

It was the ruggedness and the primeval look—the country "as God made it"—that underlay the saga of "God's Own Country" waiting to be possessed by God's Own People. Enormous distances within the West and the successive hardships to be survived persuaded generations of explorers, plainsmen, ranchers and cowboys that they were more truly American than sedentary folk back East. Westerners saw themselves as the reason for the historic uprooting that had led to America in the first place. Even in Brooklyn, New York, Walt Whitman could unroll an endless diorama of pioneers as the new race of men staking out and settling more free land than had ever been available before:

> Welcome are all earth's lands, each for its kind
>
> > ("Song of the Broad-Axe")
>
> Have the elder races halted?
> Do they droop and end their lesson, wearied over there beyond the seas?
> We take up the task eternal, and the burden and the lesson,
> > Pioneers! O Pioneers!
>
> > ("Pioneers! O Pioneers!")

Mark Twain was right on the spot, at the peak of the frontier spirit, when in the Rockies he was privileged to see a spring which spent its water through two outlets and sent it in opposite directions. He was at the Continental Divide, on one of the Colorado peaks which separate the waters flowing west from those flowing north or east. In the heady style of the period, this gave Mark Twain in *Roughing It* a chance to set up still another panorama of the continental wealth and spread and majesty of the United States. The irresistible sense of momentum behind the Western push became a fixture of Mark Twain's style. On! On! This world is such a miracle!

> . . . one of those streams which we were looking at was just starting on a journey westward to the Gulf of California and the Pacific Ocean, through hundreds and even thousands of miles of desert solitudes . . . the other was just leaving its home among the snow-peaks on a similar journey eastward—and we knew that long after we should have forgotten the simple rivulet it would still be plodding its patient way down the mountain sides, and canyon-beds, and between the banks of the Yellowstone; and by and by would join the broad Missouri and flow through unknown plains and deserts and unvisited wildernesses; and add a long and troubled pilgrimage among snags and wrecks and sand-bars; and enter the Mississippi, touch the wharves of St. Louis and still drift on, traversing shoals and rocky channels, then endless chains of bottomless and ample bends, walled with unbroken forests, then mysterious byways and secret passages among woody islands, then the unchained bends again, bordered with wide levels of shining sugar-cane in place of the sombre forests; then by New Orleans and still other chains of bends—and finally, after two long months of daily and nightly harassment, excitement, enjoyment, adventure, and awful peril of parched throats, pumps and evaporation, pass the Gulf and enter into its rest upon the bosom of the tropic sea, never to look upon its snow-peaks again or regret them.

The zeal with which Mark Twain entered into such successive phases, his sense of itinerary, was like his mastery of Western dialect and dialogue. He readily absorbed a new landscape into himself and made it his own. He stamped his restless, ironic, extraordinarily charged-up temperament on the most fleeting impressions. Sheer personality has rarely been shown to such effect in literature. One is always aware of Mark Twain talking, Mark Twain making points in some slyly assertive way that reflects the bursting vitality of a young man having the time of his life in a new country. The old-time West, the fabled West, the still undiscovered country, is sending out all its freshness through him. But soon he stumbles on ghastly reminders of disasters:

> we . . . sped away, always through splendid scenery but occasionally through long ranks of white skeletons of mules and oxen—monuments of the huge emigration of other days—and here and there were up-ended boards or small piles of stones which the driver said marked the resting-place of more precious remains. It was the loneliest land for a grave! On damp, murky nights, these scattered skeletons gave forth a soft, hideous glow, like the very faint spots of moonlight starring the vague desert. It was because of the phosphorous in the bones.

Whitman in "Earth My Likeness" had said to the earth, "I now suspect there is something fierce in you eligible to burst forth." Mark Twain never swooned over the identity between man and the earth. But he was understandably proud of the powers of observation that new experiences on the frontier gave him.

Turning away from his days as a prospector in Virginia City, as a journalist in San Francisco and Hawaii, as reporter on a cruise ship to Europe and the Holy Land, he married wealth and became a prodigiously successful author on the subscription system. He said of his first book, *The Innocents Abroad*, "it sells right along just like the Bible." He moved into a wealthy enclave of Hartford, settled by genteel folk very different from Sam Clemens and his Western beginnings. But in the moneyed, polite, conventional East, Mark Twain's mind returned to his boyhood days on the Mississippi, his experiences as a steamboat pilot, and to the world of youth that he equated with the freshness of the frontier. Out of these he made his most famous characters in *The Adventures of Tom Sawyer* and *The Adventures of Huckleberry Finn*.

The Mississippi was to become Mark Twain's leading character. T.S. Eliot from St. Louis, born on the banks of what Mark Twain hymned as "the great Mississippi," did not read *Huckleberry Finn* until late in life—in London. The book released images of his childhood along the river that led him in *Four Quartets* ("The Dry Salvages") to write,

> I do not know much about gods; but I think that the river
> Is a strong brown god—sullen, untamed and intractable,
> Patient to some degree, at first recognized as a frontier . . .
> The river is within us, the sea is all about us.

The river was certainly within Mark Twain. One of the most exuberant passages in American writing is the opening of Chapter IV of *Life on the Mississippi*, "The Boys' Ambition," describing the arrival of a steamboat in Hannibal, Missouri, Mark Twain's boyhood home on the west bank of the river.

> Once a day a cheap, gaudy packet arrived upward from St. Louis, and another downward from Keokuk. Before these events, the day was glorious with expectancy;

after them, the day was a dead and empty thing. After all these years I can picture that old time to myself now, just as it was then: the white town drowsing in the sunshine of a summer's morning; the streets empty, or pretty nearly so; one or two clerks sitting in front of the Water Street stores, with their splint-bottomed chairs tilted back against the wall, chins on breasts, hats slouched over their faces, asleep; . . . nobody to listen to the peaceful lapping of the wavelets . . . the great Mississippi, the majestic, the magnificent Mississippi, rolling its mile-wide tide along, shining in the sun; the dense forest away on the other side. . . . Presently a film of dark smoke appears . . .; instantly a negro drayman, famous for his quick eye and prodigious voice, lifts up the cry, "S-t-e-a-m-boat a-comin'!" and the scene changes! The town drunkard stirs, the clerks wake up, a furious clatter of drays follows, every house and store pours out a human contribution, and all in a twinkling the dead town is alive and moving.

Life on the Mississippi is for the most part a memoir of learning to be a pilot in the gaudy days of steamboat piloting before "the wah," when just to be a "steamboat man" was to join the most glorious enterprise in the world. The boats were the wide, topheavy all-dominating "queens" of the river. A pilot had to learn "the face of the water" in its innumerable shifts and turns as it went its way down the center of a continent. He certainly earned his authority. "My boy," Mr. Bixby instructs the young cub, "you've got to know the *shape* of the river perfectly; . . . there isn't any getting around it."

A clear starlight night throws such heavy shadows that, if you didn't know the shape of a shore perfectly, you would claw away from every branch of timber, because you would take the black shadow of it for a solid cape; and you see you would be getting

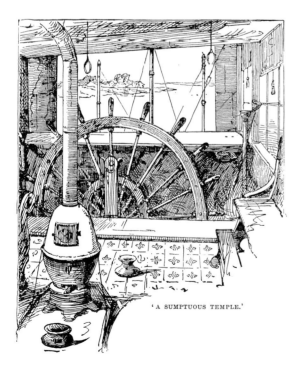

'A SUMPTUOUS TEMPLE.'

A pilot's cabin; illustration from Mark Twain's Life on the Mississippi, *1863. "A pilot, in those days, was the only unfettered and entirely independent human being . . ."*

George Caleb Bingham was the most popular genre painter of the mid-century, specializing in a Twain-like observation of river life. Fishing on the Mississippi (1851).

scared to death every fifteen minutes by the watch . . . you only learn *the* shape of the river; and you learn it with such absolute certainty that you can always steer by the shape that's *in your head*, and never mind the one that's before your eyes.

Learning the shape of the river had much to do with the sinewy, tactile, always responsive style Mark Twain learned to apply to everything in his long itinerant life.

The face of the water, in time, became a wonderful book—a book that was a dead language to the uneducated passenger, but which told its mind to me without reserve, delivering its most cherished secrets so clearly as if it uttered them with a voice. And . . . it had a new story to tell every day. Throughout the long twelve hundred miles there was never a page that was void of interest, never one that you leave unread without some loss. . . . There never was so wonderful a book written by man.

As a writer of books he believed in being spontaneous and unpredictable, like his beloved river: ". . . narrative should flow *as* flows the brook down through the hills and the leafy woodlands, its course changed by every boulder it comes across . . . a book that never goes straight for a minute, but *goes* . . . always going, . . . loyal to the law of *narrative*, which *has no law*." Mark Twain's style is always *rhythmically* right and adroit, and makes its way as a natural phenomenon even when, in the books he tossed off, the style is more

94

St. Louis from the River Below (George Catlin, c. 1832). For Mark Twain, the Mississippi was a world in itself, with secrets barely glimpsed from the luxurious paddle-steamers.

engaging than the content. As a perpetual drifter through life, a "tramp" even when he was visiting Europe in grand style, he believed in obeying the drift of his mind wherever it took him. Writing was in fact like drifting down the river on a raft.

The raft and the river are central to Mark Twain's masterpiece *Huckleberry Finn*. Amidst all the dangers of a frontier society hostile to a runaway boy and a runaway slave trying to make their way down the Mississippi to the Ohio and "freedom," there is the imperishable image of an early America. "The new childhood of the world," the poet Vachel Lindsay called it in his *Three Poems about Mark Twain*. Huck the narrator has a wonderful eye for human caprice and trickery; he is (unwillingly, as he likes to think) the guardian of "Nigger Jim." There is a barely literate boy speaking, not yet fourteen years old, the prey of his father, the town drunk, who wants him under lock and key. But more than any other character in American fiction, he personifies freedom, pluck, and perhaps more than these, the sense of discovery. The world is still entirely new.

In Chapter XIX of *Huckleberry Finn*, Huck tells how he and Jim "put in the day, lazying around, listening to the stillness," and to throw off pursuers traveled by night.

Soon as it was night, out we shoved; when we got her out to about the middle, we let her alone, and let her float wherever the current wanted her to; then we lit the pipes, and dangled our legs in the water and talked about all kinds of things—we was always naked, day and night, whenever the mosquitoes would let us . . . and besides I didn't go much on clothes, nohow.

Sometimes we'd have the whole river all to ourselves for the longest time. Yonder was the banks and the islands, across the water; and maybe a spark—which was a candle in a cabin window—and sometimes on the water you could see a spark or two—on a raft or a scow, you know; and maybe you could hear a fiddle or a song coming over from one of them crafts. It's lovely to live on a raft. We had the sky, up there, all speckled with stars, and we used to lay on our backs and look up at them, and discuss about whether they was made, or only just happened—Jim he allowed they was made, but I allowed they happened; I judged it would have took too long to *make* so many.

Huck's realistic view—there is just too much universe for it to be credited to a single maker—is of a piece with the prodigality of the book, the wonderful flow and involvement of life along the river. Huck the total orphan, the fugitive from his murderous father, slips into one human entanglement after another and just as naturally wins over (almost) everything in his path. All the while he is sheltering Jim the runaway slave and *instructing* him. Huck will not betray Jim to the authorities, though it is his duty as a good citizen under the Fugitive Slave Law to do so. "All right then," he says in a famous passage of the book, tearing up the letter he has written informing on Jim—"I'll *go* to hell." Long before this, Jim has recognized Huck's essential character—"Dah you goes, de ole true Huck; de on'y white genlman dat ever kep' his promise to old Jim."

Huck is in fact *the* Western hero. He is the primary example of Odysseus in the American epic; he is all craft and good sense, and slippery as the devil. His skepticism, his immediate sense of a difficult situation, make him in many ways the most satisfactory hero in American fiction.

Then I thought a minute, and says to myself, hold on,—s'pose you'd 'a done right and give Jim up, would you felt better than what you do *now*? No, says I, I'd feel bad—I'd feel just the same way I do now. Well, then, says I, what's the use you learning to do right, when it's troublesome to do right and ain't no trouble to do wrong, and the wages is just the same? I was stuck. I couldn't answer that. So I reckoned I wouldn't bother no more about it, but after this always do whichever come handiest at the time.

To handle each circumstance just as it came, exactly as if one were fending off hostile Indians or tackling dangerous enemies, became the pride and justification of the "Westerner." He was stoic, taciturn, a "man's man" supremely handling any physical difficulty, but aloof from such unnecessary refinements as the love of woman. He was a predominantly "natural" creature whose good sense and adaptability are drawn from his circumstances. The supreme type was James Fenimore Cooper's Leatherstocking, who in the course of five novels is variously called Bumppo, Hawkeye, Pathfinder, "the trapper," but is always the perfect woodsman, uneasy when he gets anywhere near a human settlement, and above all things cherishes "natur'." In *The Prairie* (1827), which closes the story of Leatherstocking, there is a lament that sums up the conflict of this "natural man" with the civilization he is always trying to leave behind him:

I passed the spring, summer and autumn of life among the trees. The winter of my days had come, and found me where I loved to be,—in the quiet—ay, and in the honesty of the woods: Teton, then I slept happily, where my eyes could look up

Clearing a homestead. Leatherstocking, James Fenimore Cooper's hero, mourns this steady encroachment of agriculture and civilization on the natural world.

Scene from James Fenimore Cooper's The Last of the Mohicans *(Thomas Cole, 1827). Cooper invested America's empty spaces with notable grandeur. Parkman found his descriptions "instinct with the very spirit of the wilderness."*

through the branches of the pines and the beeches, to the very dwelling of the Good Spirit of my people. If I had need to open my heart to him, while his fires were burning above my head, the door was open and before my eyes. But the axes of the choppers awoke me. For a long time my ears heard nothing but the uproar of clearings. I bore it like a warrior and a man; there was a reason that I should bear it; but when that reason was ended, I bethought me to get beyond the accursed sounds. It was trying to the courage and to the habits, but I had heard of these vast and naked fields, and I came hither to escape the wasteful temper of my people. Tell me, Dahcotah, have I not done well?

The West as a province of the imagination required a hero who would bring "law and order" and at the same time "prove his mettle." He had to show himself as rugged and capable in all physical encounters and difficulties as was the country forever testing him. This hero had to be created by gentlemen from the East for whom the testing of their manhood and the planting of "law and order" were expressions of the same quest. Just as

America was an idea first in the minds of Europeans, so the West became in the "effete" East the (mostly masculine) idea of the promised land. The West became an extension and prolongation of the New World, peculiarly companionable to the "virility" of the "Anglo-Saxon race," now represented by Americans responding to the West as their manifest destiny.

The creator of Leatherstocking was a deeply conservative gentleman from Upstate New York who owned thousands of acres around "Cooperstown" off Otsego Lake. He was a Whig, hostile to the popular sentiments behind Jacksonian democracy. But Cooper had grown up in a manorial house at the edge of the frontier wilderness, and he had been a midshipman in the Navy. In his respect for the military life and his nostalgia for an America socially aristocratic though politically democratic, he found his imagination fulfilled in noble Indians uncorrupted by civilization and in Leatherstocking, that child of "natur'" who was a dead shot with a benevolent heart.

Samuel Langhorne Clemens, on the other hand, was the son of a Virginia father who failed in the Midwest, but in distressed circumstances instructed his family to expect wealth from their holdings in "Tennessee land." For all his lack of formal education and the ease with which he adapted himself to "circumstances," Sam was more a gentleman than not. Huckleberry Finn, the ideal Westerner, was created in Hartford in the 1880s by an extremely comfortable fellow who relished every detail of his prosperity. He saw the irony of it and in some biting paragraphs about an excessively genteel family allowed Huck to admire the Victorian bric-a-brac and false sentiment on which "the quality" thrived. But Mark Twain was totally without mercy for the "mudsills," the lowdown squatters he put into Chapter XXI of his greatest novel.

All the streets and lanes was just mud, they warn't nothing else *but* mud—mud as black as tar, and nigh about a foot deep in some places; and two or three inches deep in *all* the places. The hogs loafed and grunted around, everywheres. You'd see a muddy sow and a litter of pigs come lazying long the street and whollop herself right down in the way, where folks had to walk around her, and she'd stretch out, and shut her eyes, and wave her ears, whilst the pigs was milking her and look as happy as if she was on salary. And pretty soon you'd hear a loafer sing out, "Hi! *so* boy! sick him, Tige!" and away the sow would go, squealing most horrible, with a dog or two swinging to each ear, and three or four dozen more a'coming; and then you would see all the loafers get up and watch the thing out of sight, and laugh at the fun and look grateful for the noise. Then they'd settle back again till there was a dog-fight. There couldn't anything wake them up all over, and make them happy all over, like a dog-fight—unless it might be putting turpentine on a stray dog and setting fire to him, or tying a tin pail to his tail and see him run himself to death.

In the expansive decades after the Civil War, when the West was eagerly settled by migrants from all over Europe, and the railroads and industry were coming everywhere, the United States was beginning to relish an imperial destiny. No American leader was to express this more vehemently than Theodore Roosevelt—the only American President born in New York City. Roosevelt was wealthy, Harvard-educated, bookish, a passionate student of natural history from childhood. He belonged to that now vanished

President Theodore Roosevelt on a hunting trip in Colorado, 1905. "I feel as fit as a bull moose!"

The Central Pacific Railroad in the Sierra Nevada *(Joseph Belker, 1869)*, *part of post-Civil War expansion. This was the year when the Central Pacific Railroad, starting from California, joined up with the Union Pacific from Nebraska—the first transcontinental line.*

"aristocratic" New York enclave into which Herman Melville and Edith Wharton were born. He was severely asthmatic as a boy, so nearsighted that "the only things I could study were those I ran against or stumbled over." Life in the open air was a desperate necessity. At first he was shamed by his lack of hardihood. By extreme exertions he turned himself into an athlete and hunter, became a ranchman in the Barrens of South Dakota. He owed his rise in politics to the fact that he was a gentleman not afraid to compete against the lowly "saloon types" from Tammany Hall. "I feel as fit as a Bull Moose!" he boasted.

Would "T.R." have become such an extreme jingo, militarist and preacher of the "strenuous life" if he had not made a career of overcoming his physical handicaps? He described himself as a "caged wolf." An observer in the New York State Assembly said of the young politician on the rise, "Such a super abundance of animal life was hardly ever condensed in a human being." In his *Autobiography* Roosevelt growled that "Love of peace is common among weak, short-sighted, timid, and lazy persons. . . . Justice among nations of mankind, and the uplifting of humanity, can be brought about only by those strong and daring men who with wisdom love peace, but who love righteousness more than peace." Before the 1898 war against Spain, which Roosevelt helped to engineer when he was Assistant Secretary of the Navy, he confessed himself "a good deal disheartened at the queer lack of imperial instinct" the American people displayed. He put constant emphasis on "manliness." His historical account, *The Winning of the West* (1896), now reads like the self-celebration of a master race. "In obedience to the instincts working half blindly within their breasts, spurred ever onwards by the fierce desires of their eager hearts, they made in the wilderness homes for their children, and by so doing wrought out the destinies of a continental nation."

Roosevelt declared the first French inhabitants of the Ohio Valley "in very many cases not of pure blood." He was not shy in his contempt for Indians, "who never had any real title to the soil . . . this great continent could not have been kept as a game preserve for squalid savages." The Indians were the weaker race in the contest for the West. Roosevelt derided them as rootless nomads whose behavior required that they be subjected to that "ultimate arbitrator—the sword." As for the "soft hearted philanthropists defending Indian 'rights,'" Roosevelt termed them "amiable but maudlin fanatics," ignorant of the real facts as supplied by lofty Indian haters like himself and Phil Sheridan, the most famous Northern cavalry leader in the Civil War.

The Indian wars became fierce after the Civil War. Sheridan enlisted crack killers of buffalo so as to cut off the Indians' food supply. They would either starve into invisibility or become wards of the United States. This was traditional stuff for military men. An Indian named Black Elk remembered that when he was in his seventeenth summer Sheridan's presidential aspirations were

spoiled by a group of hungry Indians who had left the reservation to move in search of the dwindling northern buffalo, and looked uncomprehendingly on the white man's slaughter of these animals.

I can remember when the bison were so many that they could not be counted, but more and more Wasichus came to kill them until there were only heaps of bones scattered where they used to be. The Wasichus did not kill them to eat; they killed them for the metal that makes them crazy and they took only hides to sell. Sometimes they did not even take the hides, only the tongues; and I have heard that fire-boats came down the Missouri River loaded with dried bison tongues. You can see that the men who did this were crazy. Sometimes they did not even take the tongues; they just killed and killed because they liked to do that. When we hunted bison, we killed only what we needed.

George Armstrong Custer, who was to die with all his men at the Little Big Horn River in Montana in 1876, wrote in *My Life on the Plains*, "Stripped of the beautiful romance with which we have been so long willing to envelop him, the Indian forfeits his claim to the appellation of the 'noble red man.' We see him as he is, a 'savage' in every sense of the word; not worse, perhaps, than his white brother would be similarly born and bred, but one whose cruel and ferocious nature far exceeds any wild beast of the desert."

The total massacre of Custer's Seventh Cavalry by Sioux under the leadership of Sitting Bull, Crazy Horse, and Gall became the traumatic defeat of American forces in the Indian wars that broke out in resistance to the government's attempt to confine the Sioux on reservations. Unlike the Canadians, who avoided trouble with their Indians by respecting agreements with them, the Americans kept pushing the Indians into confinement—especially when the Black Hills in South Dakota and Wyoming turned out to be rich in mineral deposits. The frightful mutilation of Custer's troups after death has been explained by Evan S. Connell in his valuable book on Custer, *Son of the Morning Star*, as a response to

> the grief and bewilderment these Indians felt. They could not understand why soldiers pursued them when all they ever wanted was to be left alone so that they might live as they had lived for centuries: hunting, fishing, trailing the munificent buffalo. They failed to see why they should live in one place all year, why they should become farmers when they had been hunters. They did not see how the land could be divided, allotted, owned. They thought the earth was created for everybody, that it could not be appropriated by individuals or groups, and to destroy vegetation by plowing was to contradict the obvious plan of a supreme deity.

For the battle at Little Big Horn, the Sioux had a war cry: "It's a good day to die." Because the white men had been wiped out, the government took its revenge in 1890 at Wounded Knee, South Dakota. Indian men, women and children, dogs, horses and tents—a whole village—were blown off the frozen earth in the merciless rake of the Hotchkiss guns attached to poor dead Custer's Seventh Cavalry. "We tried to run," remembered Louise Weasel Bear, "but they shot us like we were buffalo." Wounded Knee was the last great effort to ward off the relentless push of the "Wasichus"; inevitably Indians became a cult when they could no longer menace the pursuit of wealth.

At that same time "Nature" was becoming a wilderness park. Theodore Roosevelt the militarist and Indian hater never forgot the asthmatic child for whom the unspoiled natural world had literally meant life itself. He was a principal force behind the conservation movement that took root during his presidency, 1901–09. In 1903 he created the first unit of the now sprawling refuge system at Pelican Island, a scrubby patch in Florida's sparkling Indian River. Roosevelt designated it as an inviolate sanctuary for nesting birds. His biographer David McCullough notes that Roosevelt increased the area of the national forests by some forty million acres, established five national parks, sixteen national monuments (including the Grand Canyon), four national game refuges, fifty-one

When the Grand Canyon itself had to submit to conquest by the automobile—the year is 1902—it seemed that the wilderness had finally lost its battle against man.

The Grand Canyon of the Yellowstone (1872). Soon after Thomas Moran's painting was made it became obvious that such scenes would need deliberate protection by a national parks movement.

national bird sanctuaries. He made conservation a popular cause. Telling a friend, "I don't know the way the people *do* feel . . . I only know how they *ought* to feel," he exulted that the Presidency was "a bully pulpit," and lectured, scolded, cajoled, charmed the American people into adopting him as a kind of national pet—the Teddy Bear. Roosevelt, the patrician from New York City, became for his people the all-sufficient, endlessly resourceful Westerner he successfully imitated despite his bad eyes and passion for books.

It was another Harvard graduate from the East, Owen Wister, who promoted the cowboy into the ideal American in *The Virginian* (1902); it was a graduate of the Yale School of Fine Arts, Frederic Remington, who became the most accomplished and tireless producer in painting, illustration and sculpture of this "Western type."

The Virginian: A Horseman of the Plains was dedicated to Wister's friend Theodore Roosevelt. The book describes the prevailing nostalgia for the cowboy passing into the sunset of history. With the coming of the movies this was to satisfy mass audiences in a thousand Hollywood Westerns. "The horseman will never come again. He rides in his historic yesterday. . . . A hero without wings, he and his brief epoch make a complete picture, for in themselves they were complete."

"When you call me that, smile!" said early in the book over a poker game in the saloon at Medicine Bow, Wyoming, became the American cowboy's most famous advertisement for himself. Wister, in English clothes and stumbling over his double-barreled English rifle, tells the story with the usual tenderfoot's self-deprecation. The Virginian's bashful courtship of the demure school teacher from New Hampshire was to become stock stuff. The over-civilized Wister first sees his hero sitting on the high gate of a corral, coolly watching several frustrated attempts to rope a recalcitrant horse. Finally bored with other people's inadequacies, he climbs down from the corral "with the undulations of a tiger, smooth and easy, as if his muscles flowed beneath his skin."

He is "a slim young giant, more beautiful than pictures. His broad, soft hat was pushed back; a loose-knotted, dull scarlet handkerchief sagged from his throat; and one casual thumb was hooked in the cartridge-belt that slanted across his hips." Wister's adoration of the "type" is not shy. In 1902 no eager reader of *The Virginian* in city or small town would have snickered at "Daring, laughter, endurance—these were what I saw upon the countenances of cowboys. . . . For something about them, and the idea of them, smote my American heart, and I have never forgotten it, nor ever shall, as long as I live." "In their flesh our natural passions ran tumultuous; but often in their spirit sat hidden a true nobility and often beneath its unexpected shining their figures took a heroic stature."

These were not clichés. They were the heroic phrases Wister's good friend T.R. boomed from the White House. In the first years of the twentieth century, industrial monopoly and violent labor struggles were rocking the nation. Cowboy and cowboy country represented the passing of a great race. "And in a moment we were in the clean plains, with the prairie dogs and the pale herds of antelope. The great, still air bathed us, pure as water and strong as wine; the sunlight flooded the world, and shining upon the breast of the Virginian's flannel shirt lay a long gold thread of hair!" (He is irresistible to the ladies but distinctly not forward.)

By the end of the book the Virginian not only gets the girl and founds a mighty family; he founds a mighty fortune as well. An old New Hampshire lady, questioning him about his life back in Wyoming, laments that "New Hampshire was full of fine young men in those days. But nowadays most of them have gone away to seek their futures in the West. Do they find them, I wonder."

"Yes, Ma'am. All the good ones do."

"But you cannot all be—what is the name?—Cattle Kings."

"That's having its day, ma'am, right now. And we are getting ready for the change—some of us are."

"And what may be the change, and when is it to come?"

"When the natural pasture is eaten off."

As the pasture was getting eaten off, the farmers of the Middle West, not so quick as the cowboys to disappear into movies, more deeply rooted in the land, came to seem the very essence of "true grit," the heartland of a restless race. Whitman in *Specimen Days* would be impressed all his life with "that vast Something, stretching out on its own unbounded scale, unconfined, which there is in these prairies, combining the real and ideal, and beautiful as dreams." A century later John Madson in *Where the Sky Began* called it "The Land of Excesses," "of blazing light and great weathers where a man stood exposed. . . . A prairie never rests for long, nor does it permit anything else to rest. Those first Europeans had no basis for even imagining the wild fields through which a horseman might ride westward for a month or more." But because it seemed to anchor the continent, the rural Middle West became a repository of traditional attitudes, metered out through "the root system in subtle and powerful ways."

That is the Middle West speaking, the backbone and pivot of what was becoming the industrial center of the country as well as its agricultural richness. It was "the valley of democracy," "the heart of the heart of the country," *the* virtuous God-fearing place—New England's day was over. It breathed in a sense of possibility with its unlimited space that was to mark many writers from the Midwest—Theodore Dreiser, Willa Cather, Carl Sandburg, Sinclair Lewis, Sherwood Anderson, Vachel Lindsay, Scott Fitzgerald, Ernest Hemingway, Wright Morris, Saul Bellow, Josephine Herbst, William Gass. "That's my Middle West," Scott Fitzgerald chanted possessively near the end of *The Great Gatsby* in the moving passage that sums up the Midwesterner's feeling of superiority over the tight, crowded, too often corrupt East—

> That's my Middle West—not the wheat or the prairies or the lost Swede towns, but the thrilling returning trains of my youth, and the street lamps and sleigh bells in the frosty dark and the shadows of holly wreaths thrown by lighted windows on the snow. I am part of that, a little solemn with the feel of those long winters, a little complacent from growing up in the Carraway house in a city where dwellings are still called through decades by a family's name. I see now that this has been a story of the West, after all—Tom and Gatsby, Daisy and Jordan and I, were all Westerners, and perhaps we possessed some deficiency in common which made us subtly unadaptable to Eastern life.
>
> Even when the East excited me most, even when I was most keenly aware of its superiority to the bored, sprawling, swollen towns beyond the Ohio . . .—even then it had always for me a quality of distortion.

For such writers the idea of unlimited space and the sense of place were identical. The note was struck perfectly in Willa Cather's *My Ántonia* (1918). Willa Cather, born in Virginia but taken to the far-off Nebraska Divide as a child, never forgot what it was like to come on the prairies for the first time. Her spokesman in the novel for these early experiences, Jim Burden, remembers that first jolting wagon ride along the prairies at night—

> There was nothing but land; not a country at all, but the material out of which countries are made. . . . I had the feeling that the world was left behind, that we had got over the edge of it, and were outside man's jurisdiction. I had never before looked up at the sky when there was not a familiar mountain ridge against it. But this was the complete dome of heaven, all there was of it.

So much space, instead of dwarfing people, released strength and fervor by pitting them against it. The Midwest became legendary for the upright, firm, exceedingly moral but sometimes flinty rural characters it produced. Midwesterners liked to boast that the region made people live up to it. The Nebraska Divide was still virgin soil when Willa Cather roamed it on foot and on her pony in the early 1880s. Immigrant Bohemian families like the Shimerdas in *My Ántonia* lived in earth dugouts. The Burden grandparents in the book had one of the few *wooden* houses on the prairie. A sorghum patch and cornfield were the only broken land in sight. "Everywhere, as far as the eye could reach, there was nothing but rough, shaggy, red grass, most of it as tall as I. . . . As I looked about me I felt that the grass was the country, as the water is the sea. The red of the grass made all the great prairie the colour of wine-stains, or of certain seaweeds when they are first washed up. And there was so much motion in it; the whole country seemed, somehow, to be still running."

Cather's girlhood response to the "great prairie" in the first chapters of *My Ántonia* records classic joy and astonishment over so much space. "The new country lay open before me; there were no fences in those days, and I could choose my own way over the grass uplands, trusting the pony to get me home again. Sometimes I followed the sunflower-bordered roads." (The Mormons on their way to Utah had scattered sunflower seeds.) As the Mississippi becomes a stock character in Mark Twain, so the Nebraska landscape in Willa Cather's work is the ground for everything else. More than other writers even from the Midwest, Cather worked consciously with landscape, was unusually adroit and particular in applying color to her descriptions of character and setting.

Perhaps the all-enveloping sky in the Midwestern farm country, the relative absence of color, pressed Cather to *look* more sharply than others. (Josephine Herbst from Sioux City, Iowa, remembered in the Paris of the 1920s "the arched blue sky, the unwavering sea of wheat unbroken by the spar of a single tree.")

> Trees were so rare in that country, and they had to make such a hard fight to grow, that we used to feel anxious about them, and visit them as if they were persons. It must have been the scarcity of detail in that tawny landscape that made detail so precious. . . .
>
> All those fall afternoons were the same, but I never got used to them. As far as we could see, the miles of copper-red grass were drenched in sunlight that was stronger and fiercer than at any other time of the day. The blond cornfields were red gold, the haystacks turned rosy and threw long shadows. The whole prairie was like the bush that burned with fire and was not consumed.

Prairie Burial (*William Ranney, 1813–57, detail*).

An aching regret over a vanished landscape is even now the splendid thing in Willa Cather's writing and underlies her mastery. *Youth and the Bright Medusa* she called one of her novels; the epigraph to *My Ántonia* is her favorite tag from Virgil: *Optima dies . . . prima fugit.* *Why* she associated her early landscape with so much loss and bitterness is less to the point than the reserves of emotion she brought to her portrait of early Nebraska. Later she lavished abundant feeling on such cherished landscapes as Provence and the deserts of New Mexico. Only physical place retained the sacredness of early attachment. Perhaps Cather's notable gift of passion was a lonely attachment to place itself; place marked the discovery of her powers as an artist.

No other writer on the Midwest saw the physical setting with so much love. She clearly hungered for the past that lay behind and below so much empty country. In *My Ántonia* she remembered:

> Beyond the pond, on the slope that climbed to the cornfield, there was, faintly marked in the grass, a great circle where the Indians used to ride. . . . Whenever one looked at this slope against the setting sun, the circle showed like a pattern in the grass; and this morning, when the first light spray of snow lay over it, it came out with wonderful distinctness, like strokes of Chinese white on canvas. The old figure stirred me as it had never done before.

She was always ready to decry the disappearance of "the best days" she associated with her first years on the open prairie. The father of her heroine, Ántonia Shimerda, had committed suicide under the strain of those inhospitable first years.

> Long afterward, when the open-grazing days were over, and the red grass had been ploughed under and under until it had almost disappeared from the prairie; when all the fields were under fence, and the roads no longer ran about like wild things, but followed the surveyed section-lines, Mr. Shimerda's grave was still there, with a sagging wire fence around it, and an unpainted wooden cross. . . . The grave, with its tall red grass that was never mowed, was like a little island; and at twilight, under a new moon or the clear evening star, the dusty roads used to look like a soft grey river flowing past it. I never came upon the place without emotion, and in all that country it was the spot most dear to me. I loved the dim superstition, the propitiatory intent, that had put the grave there; and still more I loved the spirit that could not carry out the sentence—the error from the surveyed lines, the clemency of the soft earth roads along which the home-coming wagons rattled after sunset.

Elegy became a habit associated with the loss of "her" country. She then applied her trust and love to the residue of Mediterranean cultures in the American Southwest—to the old, still cherished cultural landscapes of Catholicism. Her best novel, *The Professor's House* (1925), an exceptionally authentic characterization of an intellectual, presented the declining years of an American historian whose masterwork was the definitive history of the Spanish explorers in North America. His great work done, rich enough now to have a fine new house, Godfrey St. Peter finds himself weary of his family and academic duties; he obstinately returns every day to the uncomfortable study where he wrote his book in the old house and where he can live in the past. At the center of all his longing and dreaming is the cliff city in New Mexico he once explored with his prize student, Tom

109

"Turn Him Loose, Bill" *(Frederic Remington, 1869–1909, detail).*

Immigrants entering South Loop Valley, Custer County, Nebraska, 1886. "There was nothing but land; . . . the material out of which countries are made." Willa Cather.

Outland, a brilliant scientist killed in the war, whose invention has resulted in wealth for others but whose account of discovering the ancient cliff city (its Indians long lost to history) has remained the one joyful thing in the professor's last days.

Tom Outland, on the Black Canyon trail to the mesa, reminds us in every strongly felt detail that for Willa Cather landscape *was* character, to be cherished at the last more than human character.

> Every inch of that trail was dear to me, every delicate curve about the old piñon roots, every chance track along the face of the cliffs, and the deep windings back into shrubbery and safety. . . . I wanted to see and touch everything.
>
> When I pulled out on top of the mesa, the rays of sunlight fell slantingly on the little twisted piñons—the light was all in between them, as red as a daylight fire, they fairly swam in it. Once again I had that glorious feeling that I've never had anywhere else, the feeling of being *on the mesa*, in a world above the world. And the air, my God, what air!—Soft, tingling, gold, hot with an edge of chill on it, full of the smell of piñons—it was like breathing the sun, breathing the colour of the sky.

By contrast, Tom's friend Rodney sells off keepsakes from the cliff-city. Everything comes to money in the end, says Rodney. Willa Cather never ceased feeling outrage at what had replaced the open country. In *A Lost Lady* (1923) there is total condemnation of a wily commercial type named Ivy Peters:

Now all this vast territory they had won was to be at the mercy of men like Ivy Peters, who had never dared anything, never risked anything. They would drink up the mirage, dispel the morning freshness, root out the great brooding spirit of freedom, the generous, easy life of the great landholders. The space, the colour, the princely carelessness of the pioneer they would destroy and cut up into profitable bits, as the match factory splinters the primeval forest. All the way from Missouri to the mountains this generation of shrewd young men, trained to petty economies by hard times, would do exactly what Ivy Peters had done.

Cather's lament finally expressed itself as homage to the primitive, difficult landscape of New Mexico and the hardships its first bishop, an austere indomitable Frenchman, endured in *Death Comes for the Archbishop* (1927). The harshly unchanged landscape is seen in a radiant light; it shows the difficulties overcome for the Faith. Cather makes the Archbishop the perfect Western hero; even in vestments he is never at a loss. What moves the story is the ardor of overcoming this cruel land, at first glance not merely inhospitable but hostile to human effort. The cult of the Western hero owed much to his gift for improvisation. He created a new culture by overcoming every difficulty; he had the survivor's particular stamp. Father Latour in *Death Comes for the Archbishop* brings Indians and Mexicans back to the true faith. The secret of his appeal lies in his ability to surmount the Southwest territory acquired by America in the war against Mexico, a country described as "a peculiar horror; I do not mean thirst, nor Indian massacres, which are frequent. The very floor of the world is cracked open into countless canyons and arroyos, fissures in the earth which are sometimes ten feet deep, sometimes a thousand."

On one of his many journeys on horseback, Father Latour loses his way and reflects that

The difficulty was that the country in which he found himself was so featureless—or rather, that it was crowded with features, all exactly alike. As far as he could see, on every side, the landscape was heaped up into monotonous red sand-hills, not much larger than haycocks, and very much the shape of haycocks. One could not have believed that in the number of square miles a man is able to sweep with the eye there could be so many uniform red hills. He had been riding among them since early morning, and the look of the country had no more changed than if he had stood still.

Thinking of the Spanish Fathers who had first made their way into this country to convert the Indians, Latour realizes that

A European could scarcely imagine such hardships. The old countries were worn to the shape of human life, made into an investiture, a sort of second body, for man. There the wild herbs and the wild fruits and the forest fungi were edible. The streams were sweet water, the trees afforded shape and shelter. But in the alkali deserts the water was poisonous, and the vegetation offered nothing to a starving man. Everything was dry, prickly, sharp; Spanish bayonet, juniper, greasewood, cactus; the lizard, the rattlesnake,—and man made cruel by a cruel life.

But those early missionaries "threw themselves naked upon the hard heart of a country that was calculated to try the endurance of giants." This is what turns the flinty landscape beautiful for readers of *Death Comes for the Archbishop*. Even the archetypal Western hero, Kit Carson, became a terror during the Civil War. He forced the Navajos from their grazing plains and pine forests to make their last stand in the Canyon de Chelly. He then pursued them into the hidden world between those towering walls of red sandstone, spoiled their stores, destroyed their deep-sheltered cornfields, cut down the terraced peach orchards dear to them.

Those towering walls of red sandstone in the Canyon de Chelly continue to haunt the reader. In a literature that often seems glad to sacrifice human fellowship in order to reclaim *something* from brute Nature, Willa Cather's trust in the remains of some ancient landscape is sometimes unbearably poignant.

*   *   *

At the Chicago World's Fair of 1893 an historian from Wisconsin, Frederick Jackson Turner, made history by announcing that there were no longer any unsettled areas in the United States. The frontier was in effect "closed." This, said Turner, "marks the closing of a great historic movement. Up to our own day American history has been in a large degree the history of the colonization of the Great West. The existence of an area of free land, its continuous recession and the advance of American settlement westward, explain American development."

By the end of the century the industrial power concentrated around the Great Lakes was leading Turner's generation in the West to wonder if their region could retain the pioneers' early ideals. The history of America after the Civil War, said a peppery American sage, John Jay Chapman, was the story of a railroad passing through a town, then dominating it. The great transcontinental trains roaring across the plains not only replaced the pioneers in their covered wagons; they also made it easy for Westerners now living in the East to mark the changes in the West.

The poet Vachel Lindsay from Springfield, Illinois (Lincoln's town), tramped the United States as a troubadour poet "trading rhymes for bread." He chanted and boomed famous oratorical pieces—"The Congo" and "General William Booth Enters Heaven"— and turned every public reading into a revival meeting. Lindsay's populist gospel was vehement but his rhythms were surprising, witty, mock-casual. The West was virtuous, the "moneyed" East not to be trusted. Farmers (especially when they were up against it) were the salt of the earth. Bankers existed to exploit them. The saints were Abraham Lincoln, Mark Twain, the radical governor of Illinois John Peter Altgeld, the young William Jennings Bryan who ran for President of the United States in 1896 shouting, "You shall not crucify mankind upon a cross of gold."

The revival spirit behind Lindsay's public readings would restore poet and people back to the true democracy of equals, friends and brothers all, that had existed before the rule of money invaded the American Garden of Eden. What gave color and zest to Lindsay's political simplicities was his love of wildness, the old animal energy, that could still be felt along the prairies.

In "Bryan, Bryan, Bryan, Bryan," a celebration of the Western forces the Bryan Presidential campaign mobilized against the conservative Republican Party, Lindsay recalled himself at sixteen standing with his best girl, cheering Bryan in Springfield as the embodiment of the Western spirit. Lindsay projected this spirit as wild and funny animals, some real, some farcical, the very sound of whose names summons up the primitive West—

Robidoux Pass, White Mountains of New Mexico (*Richard H. Kern, 1848*), *the primitive and cruel landscape of Willa Cather's* Death Comes for the Archbishop.

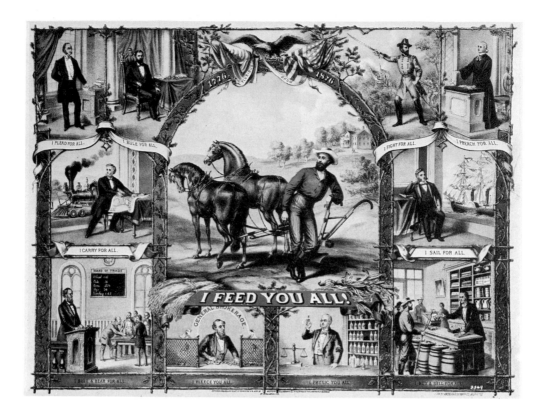

Oh, the longhorns from Texas,
The jay hawks from Kansas,
The plop-eyed bungaroo and giant giassicus,
The varmint, chipmunk, bugaboo,
The horned-toad, prairie-dog and ballyhoo,
From all the newborn states arow,
Bidding the eagles of the west fly on,
Bidding the eagles of the west fly on.

The long, raucously funny poem mounts to ecstasy as Lindsay turns his youth and
Bryan into a single cause. Looking back to early days in the West became an obsession
with native sons and daughters scattered over the great cities of the twentieth century.
The "old" West became the fable of fables, a fixed point in the imagination of those who
had left. Lindsay summoned up all his love and bitterness when he described McKinley's
victory over Bryan.

Defeat of the wheat,
Victory of letterfiles
And plutocrats in miles
With dollar signs upon their coats,
Diamond watchchains on their vests
And spats on their feet.

Victory of custodians,
Plymouth Rock,
And all that inbred landlord stock . . .
Defeat of the aspen groves of Colorado valleys,
The blue bells of the Rockies,
And blue bonnets of old Texas,
By the Pittsburgh alleys.
Defeat of alfalfa and the Mariposa lily. . . .
Defeat of my boyhood, defeat of my dream.

As cities proliferated and land in the West (much of it owned and sequestered by the Federal government) became less available to the public, land turned into an icon for many Americans increasingly disturbed by monopoly in every field. The frontier was indeed closing. Mark Twain's joyous celebration of the unlimited West as a carefree holiday of youth—imagine digging for mineral treasure under the pavements of Virginia City!—was already marking for himself the end of some perfect freedom.

Henry George was an impoverished, self-educated printer from Philadelphia who went out to California before the Civil War to better himself. The financial rapacity surrounding him, and above all the increasing monopolization of California's seemingly unlimited land, went hand in hand with poverty even in "the golden land." Before the American conquest of California in the 1840s, a few Mexican *rancheros* had owned huge stretches of arable land on which they grew crops and grazed cattle. With the Gold Rush

115

and statehood came speculators—new corporations like the Southern Pacific Railroad, which by underhand means acquired massive properties in the rich valleys that lie between the coast and the Sierra Nevada. In the 1870s land speculators Henry Miller and Charles Lux amassed more than a million acres in California and the Pacific Northwest, effectively blocking ownership by small farmers.

Henry George's fierce indictment of the land monopoly in *Progress and Poverty* (1879) drew its force from the widespread disgust such holdings aroused in California. It was the community that made land in California valuable. But the rent on land and the unearned increase in wealth profited just a few. George concluded that a tax on land itself would meet all the costs of government, leave a surplus, and relieve capital as well as labor. "They must stand on equal terms with reference to the bounty of nature. Either this, or Liberty withdraws her light."

Progress and Poverty, which became one of the most famous crusades of the period, was accepted by European intellectuals and by millions of embittered Americans as the only possible solution to increasing class violence in America, "the land of the frontier." George had the pioneer's old-fashioned faith in the land as the symbol as well as embodiment of wealth. "There can be no ownership of anything, no rightful title which does not rest upon the natural right of man to himself." Echoing Jefferson's condemnation of hereditary wealth in land, George insisted that no man was entitled to anything that was not the fruit of his own labor. The "great primary wrong" was committed by the landowner in appropriating to himself the means by which his fellow men must live.

> For what are we but tenants for a day? Have we made the earth that we should determine the rights of those who after us shall tenant in their turn? The Almighty, who created the earth for man and man for the earth, has entailed it upon all the generations of the children of men by a decree which no human action can bar and no prescription determine.

George's reverence for the land as a primary source of wealth, the inherent property of the community, led to the fervent conviction (and fond illusion) that no one really needs more land that he can use. He was almost elected mayor of New York in 1886; his proposed "single tax" on economic rent became a leading prescription for Utopia at a time of enormous social resentment everywhere against monopoly. George's veneration of land showed how hard Jefferson's ideals were dying in America. But his easy assumption that California and the Far West could reassume an earthly paradise was at variance not only with the fierce drive of industrial society but with the intractability of Nature and human nature.

*   *   *

Stephen Crane, the "genius boy" of American literature at the end of the nineteenth century (he died at twenty-eight), was a reporter from New Jersey with eyes distinctly his own. He was not sure that frail, treacherous, self-deceiving human beings were meant to live in so unfriendly a landscape as Nebraska presented in winter.

One of his most startling stories, "The Blue Hotel," describes a fearful and disturbing stranger, "The Swede," who comes upon a hotel on the prairie strangely painted blue: "...a light blue, a shade that is on the legs of a kind of heron, causing the bird to declare its position against any background. The Palace Hotel, then, was always screaming and howling in a way that made the dazzling winter landscape of Nebraska seem only a gray swampish hush. It stood alone on the prairie, . . . and it was not to be thought that any traveler could pass the Palace Hotel without looking at it."

"The Swede" shows an unfathomable fright that unsettles everyone hovering in the hotel, battered by the blizzard outside. He finally forces the proprietor's son to fight him.

No snow was falling, but great whirls and clouds of flakes, swept up from the ground by the frantic winds, were streaming southward with the speed of bullets. The covered land was blue with the sheen of an unearthly satin, and there was no other hue save where, at the low black railway station—which seemed incredibly distant— one light gleamed, like a tiny jewel.

The Swede leaves the hotel, virtually driven out by those Crane calls "the group." The man's fear of everyone around him fits in with the imprisoning weather, and now rebounds on people who in their own anxiety expel him into the storm.

The Swede, tightly gripping his valise, tacked across the face of the storm as if he carried sails. . . . He might have been in a deserted village. We picture the world as thick with conquering and elate humanity, but here, with the bugles of the tempest pealing, it was hard to imagine a peopled earth. One viewed the existence of man then as a marvel, and conceded a glamour of wonder to these lice which were caused to cling to a whirling, fire-smote, ice-locked, disease-stricken, space-lost bulb. The conceit of man was explained by this storm to be the very engine of life. One was a coxcomb not to die in it. However, the Swede found a saloon.

In this saloon the Swede, picking another fight with a stranger, is stabbed to death. He "fell with a cry of supreme astonishment." Stephen Crane's acid denial of any Providence in human affairs has here picked on the West, as he usually picked on the East, for a display of skepticism.

The vital thing about Crane as artist is his unnerving sense of environment. "Environment is a tremendous thing in the world and shapes life regardless," Crane discovered when he was covering New York's Bowery as a reporter. "I always want to be unmistakeable," he once wrote. "That to my mind is good writing." By "unmistakeable" he meant *physical*. "Art is a child of pain." His fascination with environment, showing up man's inability to resist it, led this child of a New Jersey parsonage to the West as it led him to the immigrant slums of New York, war in Cuba, war in the Balkans. In "The Bride Comes to Yellow Sky" he was genial and funny, retelling in his way the stock Western story about the unending duel between the town's "bad man" and the sheriff. Crane wrote stories and sketches about the West when it was still mythical country, and he "covered" it with his usual negligent air and mocking independence. It was just there to be covered. "There is nothing to respect in art save one's own opinion of it."

Crane was a bitingly original artist with a gift for registering every tone in his mind as he covered the Western world. He was always a stranger to the eruptions of the *fin de siècle*. Jack London from Oakland, California, was the ultimate Westerner in harsh personal experience. He became a veritable prisoner of his early hardships; these he recounted over and again in his many books. Living at first from hand to mouth as oyster pirate, hobo, then more recklessly as sailor and prospector in the Far North, he became

Jack London (1876–1916), son of the West and the San Francisco waterfront; author, Socialist and admirer of the Nietzschean "Superman."

one of the most widely read "adventure" novelists in the world. He understandably felt that his greatest work was the life he lived. This did not keep him from reporting with the same excitement the early days along San Francisco Bay, the most beautiful harbor in the United States, his life on the road, at sea, in jail, in the London slums, prospecting in the Klondike. With sudden fame and wealth as a writer, he was able to cruise the world on his yacht, *The Snark*, and to report the social turmoil that had led him to espouse socialism in the name of justice and the Superman in the name of Western hardihood. The Superman was what it took to be Jack London under the most primitive conditions.

London experienced the West fiercely and painfully. Some of his writing is as primitive as he was. Compared with always clever Mark Twain or subtle and deeply feeling Willa Cather, he seems less an artist than a register of the weather, hunger, violence, desolating isolation and constant peril. "Attack," "fierce," "wolf," recur in his titles, in the names and savage contests of his characters, the many dogs in his work. Tearing a creature's skin "to the bone" is a constant event in Jack London's world that never seems to stop man or animal from going on. The all too vivid titles of his books read like a chain of aggressions Western style—*The Son of the Wolf, The Call of the Wild, The People of the Abyss, The Sea Wolf, White Fang, The Iron Heel, Burning Daylight, The White Silence, The Man with the Gash, The Law of Life, The Strength of the Strong, War, The Abysmal Brute, When God Laughs*.

London liked to describe himself as a personality formed entirely by circumstances special to the West. In a typically personal book on his alcoholism, *John Barleycorn*, he described himself stumbling into San Francisco Bay at one in the morning. He enjoyed as ultimate sensation fighting for his life while drunk.

> Some maundering fancy of going out with the tide suddenly obsessed me. . . . Thoughts of suicide had never entered my head. And now that they entered, I thought it fine, a splendid culmination, a perfect rounding off of my short but exciting career. . . . I decided that this was all, that I had seen all, lived all, been all . . . that now was time to cease . . . John Barleycorn, laying me by the heels of my imagination and in a drug-dream dragging me to death. . . .

The water was delicious. It was a man's way to die. . . . So I struck up my death-chant and was singing it lustily, when the gurgle and splash of the current-riffles in my ears reminded me of my more immediate situation. . . .

Daylight, after I had been four hours in the water, found me in a parlous condition in the tide-rips off Mare Island light, where the swift ebbs from Vallejo Straits and Carquinez Straits were fighting with each other, and where, at that particular moment, they were fighting the flood tide setting up against them from San Pablo Bay.

Anywhere in London's work you see and feel and sometimes even taste the struggle for survival. This gave him an astonishing grasp of the Western experience in all its violent detail. In "The Mountain Meadow Massacre," a prisoner in California, condemned to death and because of his aggressiveness strapped into a straitjacket, somehow frees his "spirit" and "recalls" in totality an attack by Mormons in Utah on emigrants from Arkansas whom they mistakenly identify as enemies of their church. The Mormons will not sell food or water to these desperate people. The Western plains have created a frightening sense of place in the migrants even before they have reached the desert beyond Salt Lake City.

First of all, in this awareness, was dust. It was in my nostrils, dry and acrid. It was on my lips. It coated my face, my hands . . . ceaseless movement. . . . All that was about me lurched and oscillated. There was jolt and jar, and I heard what I knew as a matter of course to be the grind of wheels on axles and the grate and clash of iron tyres against rock and sand. . . .

The landscape was an aching, eye-hurting desolation. Low hills stretched endlessly away on every hand . . . only on their slopes were occasional growths of heat-parched brush. Our way followed the sand-bottoms beneath the hills. And the sand-bottoms were bare, save for spots of scrub, with here and there short tufts of dry and withered grass. Water there was none, nor sign of water, except for washed gullies that told of ancient and torrential rains.

They are turned away at the last Mormon outpost. "Beyond lay the vast desert, with, on the other side of it, the dream land, ay, the myth land, of California." California was certainly London's "myth land." But he was so locked into the arduousness of his youth that he made his best books out of the brutality of the seal hunters in *The Sea Wolf* and the struggle to the death between dogs still close to the wolf stage.

It was the Klondike during the mad gold rush of 1897–99 that gave London his greatest opening to the primitive. Starving, freezing prospectors pursued by wolves gave the thrill of the outermost frontier to readers at the beginning of the twentieth century. Western civilization was at the crest of its imperial ambition. But the spell London put on a whole generation (Lenin on his deathbed was read a Jack London story by his wife) suggests that his appeal was founded on that weariness with peace and bourgeois civilization that welcomed the outbreak of war in 1914.

London's crusade for "socialism" was less urgent than his belief in the "blond beast," the "strength of the strong." The struggle for survival on the frontier—from San Francisco Bay to the Canadian mining camps well within the Arctic Circle—became his favorite theme and explains his enduring popularity. He was dominated by the idea of life as a test; the struggle against death was a proof of manhood. (It was a test he deliberately gave

The flat, inhospitable plains of Wyoming and Utah are vividly described by Jack London: "an aching, eye-hurting desolation. Low hills stretched endlessly away . . ."

up at forty.) An astonishing story, "Love of Life," describes a prospector who has made a successful gold strike. Having sprained his leg, he is left behind by his partner and is now bitterly limping through the Canadian Barrens. He is starving, out of ammunition, and so weak that he crawls on all fours. A wolf, also starving and down to skin and bones, follows him at a safe distance. "Then began as grim a tragedy of existence as ever was played—a sick man that crawled, a sick wolf that limped, two creatures dragging their dying carcasses across the desolation and hunting each other's lives. . . . The patience of the wolf was terrible. The man's patience was less terrible. For half a day he lay motionless, fighting off unconsciousness and waiting for the thing that was to feed upon him and upon which he wished to feed."

Wolf and man finally come to grips. The wolf seizes the man. But the man eats the wolf. The Western story.

He did not hear the breath, and he slipped slowly from some dream to the feel of the tongue along his hand. He waited. The fangs pressed softly; the pressure increased; the wolf was exerting its last strength in an effort to sink teeth in the food for which it had waited so long. . . .

The hands had not sufficient strength to choke the wolf, but the face of the man was pressed closer to the throat of the wolf and the mouth of the man was full of hair. At the end of half an hour the man was aware of a warm trickle in his throat. It was not pleasant. It was like molten lead being forced into his stomach, and it was forced by his will alone. Later the man rolled over on his back and slept.

CHAPTER FOUR

LOCAL COLOR

Not every American in the nineteenth century went West, that supreme adventure. In the pretty little New England town of Amherst, Massachusetts, the traditional New England settlement in the "Pioneer Valley" of central Massachusetts that was frontier until the eighteenth century, Miss Emily Dickinson in "The Homestead" on Main Street was famous in town for not going anywhere at all. "I do not cross my Father's ground to any House or Town." This was her only fame until her poetry surfaced after her death in 1886 and made Amherst rather more vivid than it had been before.

The Dickinsons were the leading family in Amherst, which made Emily Dickinson's invisibility all the more interesting to a population of just over 2,500. Her grandfather had gone through all his money helping to establish Amherst College, an institution founded "to check the progress of errors which are propagated from Cambridge [Harvard]." "Father," who in her poetry could easily be mistaken for God, was Squire Edward Dickinson. He was as severe as he looked, a Puritan not ashamed to be an anachronism. When the celebrated Swedish soprano Jenny Lind actually performed one unforgotten evening in nearby Northampton, Emily described Father, not the singer—"Father sat all the evening looking *mad*, and yet so much amused you would have *died* a-laughing. . . . It wasn't sarcasm exactly, nor it wasn't disdain, it was infinitely funnier than either of those virtues, as if old Abraham had come to see the show, and thought it was all very well, but a little excess of *monkey!*"

At seventeen Emily Dickinson entered Mount Holyoke Female Seminary in South Hadley, ten miles away; illness kept her from completing even her first year. She visited Boston twice to consult an eye doctor. "We," she said of Amherst, "were rich in disdain for Bostonians and Boston." Even before her thirties, she kept to The Homestead. It is still imposing—a large square red-brick mansion off the center of town behind a hemlock hedge with three gates. She even stopped visiting the house of her brother Austin and his wife Susan. It was three hundred feet away. The two houses were half-hidden by evergreens.

Except for fifteen years in which the family occupied another house, on Pleasant Street, Emily Dickinson lived for more than forty years exclusively in one house and on its grounds. She worked at a small desk in her circular bedroom on the second floor, kept poems loosely sewn together into little packets in the bottom drawer of a dresser. It may have been the circular bedroom that first made the word "circumference" so dominant in her vocabulary. There was a cupola to which she ascended by a trap-door ladder. There was a conservatory also special to her, an assiduous botanist. She called the hallway past

The Dickinson "Homestead" on Main Street, Amherst, Massachusetts. Emily Dickinson hid herself here for more than forty years ("I do not cross my Father's ground to any House or Town") but closely recorded Nature's moods.

the front door the "Northeast Passage" because it had six exits. She used them to escape visitors.

For many years, especially when her weak and timorous mother had sustained an illness, Emily Dickinson was the family cook. She took great pride in her bread, which once won second prize at the annual cattle show. She had much to do at home, especially after her mother died. In 1861–62, when old friends were being shipped back to Amherst in coffins, she was driven to write several hundred poems a year. As another recluse, Marcel Proust, said about his work, "I have released the genie from the bottle, and it will end by devouring me." Far from seeking to escape the world because of a disappointment in love, she showed in everything she wrote an insistence on loving, on friendship. She anxiously sought "communion" (another favorite word) with the world around her, and more than most poets in America, she actually achieved it.

Like everyone in a small town, Emily Dickinson knew what was going on. Amherst was a tribal village; except for a few Irish servants, everyone was descended from English Puritans. Until well in the middle of the nineteenth century, all five churches in town were Congregationalist. Only "Calvinist clocks" tolled the hours. Austin Dickinson's affair of thirteen years with the wife of the College astronomer, Mabel Loomis Todd, may have astonished the outside world when it was finally revealed in 1974, but it was hardly kept from the village green. Emily and her sister Lavinia aided the affair. For all her own abstinences, Emily Dickinson scorned the idle gossipiness among the "quality." Long before Austin Dickinson and Mabel Todd stirred up the town ladies, Emily acidly noted

> What Soft—Cherubic Creatures—
> These Gentlewomen are—
> One would as soon assault a Plush—
> Or violate a Star—
>
> Such Dimity convictions—
> A Horror so refined
> Of freckled Human Nature—
> Of Deity—ashamed—

Main Street in Amherst is actually a side street. Well into the twentieth century the Dickinsons were surrounded by red barns and extensive fields. The mighty Connecticut River, majestically streaming down the middle of Massachusetts, makes a famous "oxbow" curve in the vicinity of Amherst. It was much painted at the time. The river bottoms made good fertile land. Despite the New England winter, tobacco would some day be grown in the valley. Little Amherst was backed up by farm country on every side. One of Emily Dickinson's major activities was registering the effect of the "blue" mountains surrounding her valley, the Pelham hills on the horizon, the changing shades and *weight* of weather in every season, the light, the birds, insects and snakes in her garden. Nature was the most physical part of her life. Not being a romantic or transcendentalist, she did not find Nature a consoling simile for Deity. Nature was a daily event. It often struck at her with a force that only she would have split into different realms of feeling.

> There's a certain Slant of Light,
> Winter Afternoons—
> That oppresses, like the Heft
> Of Cathedral Tunes—
>
> Heavenly Hurt, it gives us—
> We can find no scar,
> But internal difference,
> Where the Meanings, are—
>
> None may teach it—Any—
> 'Tis the Seal Despair—
> An imperial affliction
> Sent us of the Air—
>
> When it comes, the Landscape listens—
> Shadows—hold their breath—
> When it goes, 'tis like the Distance
> On the look of Death—

Her world inside was the writing table, the sleigh bell, the Franklin fireplace, the dresser, the windows, the view of the front walk and the driveway, the Seth Thomas clock, the ruby glass decanter, the hat box, the pictures of George Eliot, Elizabeth Barrett Browning, Thomas Carlyle. But

> Had I not seen the Sun
> I could have borne the shade
> But light a newer Wilderness
> My Wilderness has made—

Most days and in most seasons, the very air outside her door could make her feel "the little Tippler/Leaning against the—Sun—"

> Inebriate of Air—am I—
> And Debauchee of Dew—
> Reeling—thro endless summer days—
> From inns of Molten Blue—

Her awareness of the life in Nature overlooked by the busy "world" presented another world of which she was the only participant. It also made for separateness as an observer. She had nothing to do but *look*. "Looking" became a way of life and habit of attention. Attentiveness at such a pitch, even without an object in view, became her form of prayer.

> I dwell in Possibility—
> A fairer House than Prose—
> More numerous of Windows—
> Superior—for Doors—
>
> Of Chambers as the Cedars—
> Impregnable of Eye—
> And for an Everlasting Roof
> The Gambrels of the Sky—
>
> . . . For Occupation—This—
> The spreading wide my narrow Hands
> To gather Paradise.

Anything outside the house hit her hard. As she confessed in even a negligent poem,

> The Murmur of a Bee
> A Witchcraft yieldeth me—
> If any ask me why—
> 'T'were easier to die—
> Than tell—
> The Red upon the Hill
> Taketh away my will.

She saw things in Nature positively raining blows. At the same time, the microscopic life she saw made her witty.

> A narrow Fellow in the Grass
> Occasionally rides—
> You may have met Him—did you not
> His notice sudden is—
>
> The Grass divides as with a Comb—
> A spotted shaft is seen—
> And then it closes at your feet
> And opens further on—

Only Dickinson would have noted that a snake moving in the grass resembled "a Whip lash/Unbraiding in the Sun." When "stooping to secure it/it wrinkled, and was gone—" Her affection for country things took an easy, jaunty style. "Several of Nature's People I know, and they know me—I feel for them a transport of cordiality." She described the smallest, most familiar things in Nature momentously. Her gift shows itself in an attachment so driving that it can excite and exhaust the reader, as it plainly did her. With her essential gift for switching within the same poem from shade to shade of feeling, for taking the full count of any situation, she ended her great poem on seeing "a narrow Fellow in the Grass"

> But never met this Fellow
> Attended, or alone
> Without a tighter breathing
> And Zero at the Bone—

Still, there were obvious restrictions placed upon Emily Dickinson living all her life in the same house, the same town. She certainly had a gift for reducing the facts of her life to a few words at once confessional and mischievous. To Thomas Wentworth Higginson, a contemporary critic who tried to take her up but admitted to his wife, "I never was with anyone who drained my nerve power so much," she explained, "My life has been too simple and stern to embarrass any." Nevertheless, she took the measure of Amherst, recorded its moods as cleverly as she did her own, wrote her greatest poems about deathbeds—death was the main event in a small town. If her spinsterhood seemed acceptable—a convention of the period acceptable to everyone but Emily Dickinson— she certainly made claims on many men and women. These developed into a meticulous, witty sense of the life people had to live in such a town.

She was alone, but the solitariness was necessary to her and certainly in the Puritan tradition. There is an unmistakable resonance in poems and letters of loneliness and grief. "I'm Nobody! Who are you?" "I am alive I guess." "I can wade grief." "I cautious scanned my little life." Yet she now seems to have been the subtlest, cagiest, most unafraid spokesman for a wholly personal, unspontaneous faith at a time when church-dominated Amherst, its spires as frequent as its red barns, seemed unmindful of orthodoxy's hollowness. As a poet of the religious life, speaking from the "alone to the Alone," Emily Dickinson has no peer in American writing, and has amazed many a

European reader by her ability, like Rilke's, to put a wholly secular consciousness into the language of sacredness. Herman Melville, the only other major American imagination matching her recognition of faith in crisis, did not silently battle a whole town that regarded itself as the repository of all virtue.

Most American tales of the small town were written by men and women who had to escape in order to write at all. Emily Dickinson wrote hundreds of poems in Amherst about living in Amherst. Yet the name appears only twice in her almost two thousand poems. And she never really wrote anything except in the setting of a country town.

She was just past thirty in the first years of the Civil War, and was perhaps giving up hope that her outward life could change.

> Dare you see a Soul *at the White Heat?*
> Then crouch within the door—

At times she must have felt unhinged. One of her greatest poems describes herself at the end of it as "Wrecked, solitary, here." But accepting as her fate the round of life she had always lived, she was able to make art out of the return of the seasons, the fall of light, the spring of birds, "the angle of a landscape," "the leaves like women interchange," "the dandelion's pallid tube."

> There came a Day at Summer's full,
> Entirely for me—
> I thought that such were for the Saints,
> Where Resurrections—be—

Her central theme is Life Passing. Nature can seem a "fraud" in its sudden beauty.

> These are the days when Birds come back—
> A very few—a Bird or two—
> To take a backward look.

But "I would eat evanescence slowly." So she takes inventory of all the changes, all the masquerades, that Nature provides. Accepting it all, not for a moment pretending that this flow can have a stop, she can break the reader's heart by the stupendous act of resistance that so much precision, this everlasting attention, exerts upon and against the intrusion of death in human affairs.

Her supreme poem, "Because I Could Not Stop for Death," is significantly her best summing up of ordinary life in Amherst and its familiar landmarks. Because she could not stop for Death, Death kindly stopped for her. "The Carriage held but just Ourselves—/And Immortality." They slowly drive through the town on the way to the cemetery, passing "the School, where Children strove/At Recess—in the Ring." They pass the "Fields of Gazing Grain" and go on so steadily that they do not pass the Setting Sun, the Sun passes them. On and on and on! What finally stuns the reader: the round of life in the small town becomes one with the journey to death. They arrive at the cemetery.

Since then—'tis Centuries—and yet
Feels shorter than the Day
I first surmised the Horses' Heads
Were toward Eternity—

Emily Dickinson probably never heard of Herman Melville. Melville would not have heard of Emily Dickinson even when he was living in Pittsfield, Massachusetts, and could see Mount Greylock (looking very like a whale) as he worked at *Moby-Dick*. In his bitterness at the book's failure, he was to dedicate his next book, *Pierre*, "To Greylock's Most Excellent Majesty." Dickinson's only comment on Walt Whitman was that people had told her he was "disgraceful." That was the American style in a vast country, much of it still unoccupied, where writers lived in far separated country towns, and unlike twentieth-century writers felt no need of each other's company.

During Emily Dickinson's lifetime, however, Henry James, brought up in Europe and mesmerized all his life by English institutions and a "tone of time" he sorely missed in his

The Dickinson family plot: "Because I could not stop for Death/He kindly stopped for me."

own country, sharpened his skills as a beginning novelist by "writing up" American towns as if he were a tourist. In a sense he was. "The great thing is to be *saturated* with something," he wrote in an early letter, "and I choose the form of my saturation." In applying his avid sensibility and resonant style to those early travel pieces for magazines, James was adding his distinguished voice to the "local color" or "nativist" writers who in the decades following the Civil War were writing up all sorts of picturesque but overlooked places for the large new magazine audience.

James disdained such material. His eye was on the fashionable places where he could study the newly arrived *parvenus* in the era of blazing greed, national corruption and vulgar display that Walt Whitman lamented in *Democratic Vistas* and Mark Twain satirized in the book that gave a name to the gaudy period, *The Gilded Age*.

James took Saratoga, Newport, and Niagara as "news." In doing this he in his turn, though more fastidious than others, became part of the widespread urge to show life as actually lived—especially in groups—that overtook the new "realists" in America in the aftermath of the Civil War. With the reunification of the country, the new sense of national power, an increasingly materialistic outlook, the age of the social novel and of modern documentary journalism had at last arrived.

James was all his life to be a majestically eloquent travel writer because of his ability to soak up the many rich "impressions" that his unsettled life presented him with. He positively vibrated with impressions. A major side of his genius, early and late, was susceptibility to what in "The Art of Fiction" (1884) he called "the look of things, the look that conveys their meaning, to catch the colour, the relief, the expression, the surface, the substance of the human spectacle." Much later in his career he noted that "Before each scene, I wish really to get *into* the picture, to cross, as it were, the threshold of the frame."

James's father, an eccentrically free spirit, had in dissatisfaction with American education subjected his children to education in Paris, Lyons, Geneva, Boulogne, as well as New York, Boston, and Newport. Europe, where Henry settled for good in 1876, cast such a spell that he cried out in a letter about roaming the streets of Rome—"At last I live!" By contrast, he was to say of Boston, "I don't even dislike it." Living in Europe he associated it with the supremacy of his favorite European writers, like Balzac, George Eliot, Turgenev. These were the exemplars of the social novel he was determined to practice upon his own country.

Positively obsessed by the novel as a form, James complained that society in his native land was too "thin" (when it was not too "harsh"). The still primitive countryside was obviously more interesting to Nature poets like Emerson than the interaction of human beings. This provided the basis for the constant contrast of Europe and America in what came to be James's "international" theme. At the very beginning of an early novel, *The Europeans* (1878), we are asked to see Boston through the eyes of a Baroness Munster, newly arrived in a hotel.

> And indeed, in what met her eyes there was little to be pleased with. The window-panes were battered by the sleet; the head-stones in the grave-yard beneath seemed to be holding themselves askance to keep it out of their faces. A tall iron railing protected them from the street, and on the other side of the railing an assemblage of Bostonians were trampling about in the liquid snow. Many of them were looking up and down; they appeared to be waiting for something.

They are waiting for the bus. Apparently nothing so vulgar was ever seen in Europe. "On the other side of the grave-yard was a row of small brick houses, showing a series of homely, domestic-looking backs; at the end opposite the hotel a tall wooden church-spire, painted white, rose high into the vagueness of the snow-flakes. The lady at the window looked at it for some time; for reasons of her own she thought it the ugliest thing she had ever seen."

James had his fun peering into the Baroness's mind as she looked at a Boston winter "out of one of the windows of the best hotel in the ancient city of Boston." His own prejudices were not altogether absent as "She glanced about her—the room had a certain vulgar nudity; the bed and the window were curtainless—and she gave a little passionate sigh." In the most powerful (and last) novel he was to write about the same scene, *The Bostonians* (1886), James was less guarded in his dislike. The view of Back Bay and the Charles River, with the Massachusetts Institute of Technology and Harvard's residence halls along the river, are so pleasing today that it is a shock to find James writing of the same scene just a century ago:

> The general windows of Olive's drawing-room, looking over the water, took in the red sunsets of winter; the long, low bridge that crawled, on its staggering posts, across the Charles . . . the general hard, cold void of the prospect. . . . There was something inexorable in the poverty of the scene, shameful in the meanness of its details, which gave a collective impression of boards and tin and frozen earth, sheds and rotting piles. . . .

New England—even Boston—no doubt did reflect "something inexorable in the poverty of the scene." In the greatest of American autobiographies, Henry Adams said of the "education" forced on a true son of New England,

> The New England light is glare, and the atmosphere harshens color. The boy was a full man before he ever knew what was meant by atmosphere; his idea of pleasure in light was the blaze of a New England sun. . . . The intense blue of the sea, as he saw it a mile or two away, from the Quincy hills; the cumuli in a June afternoon sky; the strong reds and greens and purples of colored prints and children's picture-books, as the American colors then ran; these were ideals. The opposites or antipathies, were the cold grays of November evenings, and the thick, muddy thaws of Boston winter. With such standards, the Bostonian could not but develop a double nature.

James himself saw Boston as winter, his beloved Europe as the very perfection of summer. In old age he was to write that the most beautiful words in the language were "summer afternoon." And it is a relief to find in Leon Edel's biography James's fond reminiscence of "the splendid American summer" as he recalls a meeting in North Conway, Massachusetts, immediately after the Civil War. Brother William was there, along with the future jurist John Chipman Gray and the beloved cousin Minnie Temple who was to die young and leave something of herself in James's future heroines; James recollected the "play of young intelligence and young friendship, the reading of Matthew Arnold and Browning, the discussion of a hundred human and personal things. The splendid American summer drawn out to its last generosity."

129

In her autobiography, *A Backward Glance*, his old friend Edith Wharton recalled James's lament over "the thin empty lovely American beauty." "Thin," "nudity," along with the "glaring light," recur in James's fictions of New England. And New England, along with his native New York, were virtually the only parts of America that James knew before he visited the country in 1904 after a twenty years absence to write his last and most resplendent travel book, *The American Scene*.

In his early book on Hawthorne (1879) James could not disguise his conviction that the poor fellow would have done much better if he had had the resources of an old and traditional society. "There is in all of [his writings] something cold and light and thin, something belonging to the imagination alone, which indicates a man but little disposed to multiply his relations, his points of contact, with society." In a famous summing up of everything Hawthorne lacked, James listed

> No State, in the European sense of the word, and indeed a barely specific name. No sovereign, no court, no personal loyalty, no aristocracy, no church, no clergy, no army, no diplomatic service, no country gentlemen, no palaces, no castles, nor manors, nor old country houses, nor parsonages, nor thatched cottages, nor ivied ruins; no cathedrals, nor abbeys, nor little Norman churches; no great universities nor public schools—no Oxford, nor Eton, nor Harrow; no literature, no novels, no museums, no pictures, no political society, no sporting class—no Epsom nor Ascot!

The United States was the first state in modern history to constitute itself as a state. Only fourteen years before James lamented that America was not England, the United States had put down the most massive rebellion in history; a widespread and violent civil war had taken almost a million lives. But Henry James was interested in society, not "the state." When he wrote his sparkling early travel pieces (1870–71) for *The Nation* on Saratoga, Newport and Niagara, they reverberated with scorn for the *arrivistes* and *parvenus* in a society not "thin" but greasy, vulgar, fat.

Saragota, at the head of the vast Adirondack preserve in upper New York State, was a popular spa and horse-racing center even before the Civil War. It became the special gathering place of the newly rich in the plush years of the Gilded Age. Once it had been the chosen resort of none but "nice people." James now heard it "constantly affirmed, 'the company is dreadfully mixed.'" With its shining race track, its gambling casino in Congress Park, and above all two gigantic hotels (the "Grand Union" and the "United States") adjoining on the main street to make one continuous terrace lined with rocking chairs in which the moneyed guests displayed themselves, Saratoga was calculated to offend James's fine instincts. Saratoga at the height of the racing season was to be a favorite subject for satire. Edith Wharton opened her last, unfinished novel, *The Buccaneers* (1938), on the scene presented by the guests on the "piazza." Edna Ferber was to make Saratoga a byword for some lovable American corruption in *Saratoga Trunk* (1941). But only Henry James, in a brief magazine piece, could have summed up the special situation presented in Saratoga by the newly "arrived."

The philosopher and theologian Henry James Senior liked to boast that in *his* family (he had a private income) no one was "guilty of doing a stroke of business." His son was all the more interested in the hard look of the businessmen as they took their ease at the hotel. At rest they kept "a look of decision, a hint of unimpassioned volition, the air of 'smartness.'" No longer lean and sallow, as in the Old Yankee days,

Boston Common at Twilight (*Childe Hassam, c. 1885, detail). It is winter, as Henry James always saw Boston in his imagination.*

Saratoga Springs, New York. Guests on the piazza of the Grand Union Hotel. Henry James both sneered at and was fascinated by the nouveau riche *businessmen and their wives who came to Saratoga to be seen.*

they come from the uttermost ends of the Union—from San Francisco, from New Orleans, from Alaska. As they sit with their white hats tilted forward, and their chairs tilted back, and their feet tilted up, and their cigars and toothpicks forming various angles with these various lines, I seem to see in their faces a tacit reference to the affairs of a continent. They are obviously persons of experience . . . they have *lived*, in every fibre of the will. . . . It was not in lounging that they gained their hard wrinkles and the level impartial regard which they direct from beneath their hat rims. They are not the mellow fruit of a society which has walked hand-in-hand with tradition and culture; they are hard nuts, which have grown and ripened as they could.

James's antipathy to commercial types was before long to make him identify the country with nothing but business. When he settled in England, he claimed that his ambition was to be taken as a writer equally English and American. Before his death in 1916, he became a British subject. But even in 1870 he was already removed from the "dense, democratic, vulgar Saratoga of the current year," a brilliant, tart, altogether sniffy observer. He was especially responsive in all his many antennae to the spectacle—of women especially—who had nothing to live for but enjoyment.

All his writing life James pursued some special inquiry of his own: the function and purpose of women in the leisure class consigned to them by their successful husbands. He worried that his own experience of New York was "uptown" with the "pastry cooks," not "downtown" with the business class. In a commercial society, someone who stayed at home writing could be thought of as unmanly. James was to specialize in American heroines separated from society by their "fineness." Isabel Archer in *The Portrait of a Lady* (1881) is the most vivid example. But women as a group—the wives whose ostentatious display of their husbands' wealth was something new in the American picture—brought out all of James's disdain, though as a writer he was fascinated by the picture they made.

> If the men are remarkable, the ladies are wonderful. Saratoga is famous, I believe, as the place of all places in America where women adorn themselves most . . . where the greatest amount of dressing may be seen by the greatest number of people. Your first impression is therefore of the—what shall I call it?—of the abundance of petticoats. . . . You behold a . . . quite momentous spectacle; the democratization of elegance. If I am to believe what I hear—in fact, I may say what I overhear—many of these sumptuous persons have enjoyed neither the advantages of a careful education nor the privileges of an introduction to society. She walks more or less a queen, however, each uninitiated nobody. . . . You look at the coarse brick walls, the rusty iron posts of the piazza, at the shuffling negro waiters, the great tawdry steamboat-cabin of a drawing-room—you see the tilted ill-dressed loungers on the steps—and you finally regret that a figure so exquisite should have so vulgar a setting.

James, fascinated all his life by children as a class, noted that "the part played by children in society here is only an additional instance of the wholesale equalization of the various social atoms which is the distinctive feature of collective Saratoga." Nor did he miss the irony of so much social display on the very edge of the Adirondack forest (in the twentieth century it was to become the largest natural preserve in the country): ". . . a mile or two behind . . . the forest is primeval and the landscape is without figures."

Newport, Rhode Island, at the mouth of Narragansett Bay, had before the Civil War been a natural place for "radicals" like Henry James's father when he removed his family from New York. A long thin neck of land ended on a spectacular cliff facing the ocean. The town early harbored all sorts of refugee groups—Quakers and Jews arrived in the 1650s. The exquisite Synagogue (now a national monument) featured candlesticks reportedly made by Paul Revere and an historic letter of welcome from President George Washington. "The Government of the United States gives to bigotry no sanction, to persecution no assistance."

In the Gilded Age, Newport developed into the fashionable resort of the *very* rich. James revisited it for one of his travel pieces in 1870—before the Vanderbilts and other super-rich of the period built colossal summer palaces like "The Breakers." The Newport of James's youth was fast disappearing into the tides of fashion. Still, "this ancient and

THE DRIVE.

Newport, Rhode Island, the Drive on Bellevue Avenue. After Europe, newly fashionable Newport had no appeal for James, though he found it preferable to Saratoga.

honorable town" was not brazen like Saratoga. "Esthetically speaking, you may remain at Newport with a fairly good conscience; at Saratoga you linger under passionate protest. At Newport life is public, if you will; at Saratoga it is absolutely common." But what was left of the "old" Newport betrayed "the severe simplicity of the generation which produced it." With the feeling for style on a grand scale that was to lead him back to Europe, James now saw something helpless in the Newport being steadily left behind by the splendid equipages streaming down its show street, Bellevue Avenue. "The plain gray nudity of these little warped and shingled boxes seems to make it a hopeless task on their part to present any positive appearance at all.... The magic Newport atmosphere ... makes them scintillate in their bareness.... Their steep gray roofs, barnacles with lichens, reminds you of old barges, overturned on the beach to dry."

Summoning up all his rhetorical power in tribute to Newport's natural advantages, James seemed to be saying farewell to the society he would soon leave behind him.

The peculiar charm of this great westward expanse ... is in an especial degree the charm of Newport in general—the combined lowness of tone, as painters call it, in all the elements of *terra firma* and the extraordinary elevation of tone in the air. For miles and miles you see at your feet, in mingled shades of yellow and gray, a desolate waste of moss-clad rock and sand-starved grass. At your left is nothing but the shine and surge of the ocean, and over your head that wonderful sky of Newport, which has such an unexpected resemblance to the sky of Venice....

The region of which I speak is perhaps best seen in the late afternoon, from the high seat of a carriage on the Avenue. You seem to stand just outside the threshold of the west. At its opposite extremity sinks the sun, . . . with a splendour of the deepest blue, more luminous and fiery than the usual redness of the evening, and all streaked and barred with blown and drifted gold. The whole large interval, with its rocks and marshes and ponds, seems bedimmed with a kind of purple glance. The near Atlantic fades and turns cold with that desolate look of the ocean when the day ceases to care for it.

New England and New York were all James knew of America. But nothing was more evident after the Civil War than that the country itself was turning away from New England, turning West or to the great metropolitan centers. New England, like the South, was being left behind. Three-fifths of Connecticut, three-fourths of Vermont, and nearly two-thirds of New Hampshire and Maine declined in population. The historian Arthur M. Schlesinger, Sr., described "Cellar holes choked with lilac and woodbine, tumble-down buildings, scrubby orchards, pastures bristling with new forest growths, perhaps a lone rosebush—these mute, pathetic memorials of once busy farming communities attested the reversal of a familiar historic process, with civilization retreating before the advancing wilderness."

Beach at Newport, Rhode Island *(John Frederick Kensett, c. 1869). The Newport of James's youth, before society took over.*

New England came to seem "picturesque," a relic for those writers emphasizing "local color." How quickly New England declared itself, seemed virtually to explain itself, in books entitled *The Country of the Pointed Firs, A Connecticut Yankee, The Bostonians, Boston, The Last Puritan, Boston Adventure.* Even the names of characters told the reader that the story was laid in old-fashioned New England—*Mercy Philbrick's Choice, The Rise of Silas Lapham, The Late George Apley, Ethan Frome, The Wapshot Chronicle.* Of all American regions, New England had been the first to be characterized; it was soon the most characterized and for a long time seemed the most characterizable. It was the first to explain itself, to write its own history, to become a character and symbol to everyone else.

The physician-poet Oliver Wendell Holmes, Sr., had given the name "Brahmin" to his company of New England sages, once the nation's cultural authorities. He had lovingly made fun of Boston's assumption that it was "the hub of the universe." As the nineteenth century dwindled, Holmes and similar intellectuals ceased to impress a New England more and more made up of Irish and French-Canadians, factory workers, farmers wearily clawing New England's hard stony soil. New England soon figured as *the* historic place, the most conceivably left-over place that a rapidly self-transforming America could provide. It became at once an icon and a joke. Like the defeated, still powerless South, it was another country.

Realistic novelists found a made-to-order subject in New England when, suddenly detachable from the rest of the country and no longer its conscience, it became aware of itself as—"picturesque." New England became a cultural memory, like Cornwall and Brittany. With its uncompromising landscape, it came to seem quaint to its own writers.

This conscious antiquarianism produced a beautiful book of stories about the Maine Coast, Sarah Orne Jewett's *The Country of the Pointed Firs* (1896).

This exquisite work, as lightly drawn as a *plein air* impressionistic painting of the countryside, is based on wonder. The remote village of Dunnet, on the eastern coast of Maine, has eluded the flattening-out of the rest of the country. Interior Maine even now is still more than half primeval; at the end of the nineteenth century, the inhabitants of the coast and the many islands seemed another race; Jewett, herself from Maine, describes herself visiting and consciously studying these fishermen and islanders for the summer. To escape the endless chatter forced on her by lonely people, she has hired the schoolhouse at fifty cents a week to do her writing in. "I sat at the teacher's desk as if I were that great authority, with all the timid empty benches in rows before me. Now and then an idle sheep came and stood for a long time looking in at the door."

Still, she cannot resist her landlady's talk, mostly about the herbs she gathers for a living, with names that roll off the tongue. "That was in Pennyroyal time, and when the rare lobelia was in its prime and the elacampane was coming on." Mrs. Todd never let her husband Nathan (lost at sea) know about an early attachment.

> "'T'was but a dream with us. I knew it when he was gone. I knew it"—and she whispered as if she were at confession—"I knew it afore he started to go to sea. My heart was gone o' my keeping before I ever saw Nathan; but he loved me well, and he made me real happy, and he died before he ever knew what he'd had to know if we'd lived long together. . . . I always liked Nathan, and he never knew. But this penny r'yal always reminded me, as I'd sit and gather it and hear him talkin'—it always would remind me of—the other one."

Maine characters were unquestionably "quaint." Captain Littlepage "looked like an aged grasshopper of some strange human variety."

Mrs. Todd had told me one day that Captain Littlepage had overset his mind with too much reading; she had also made dark reference to his having "spells" of some unexplainable nature. . . . There was something quite charming in his appearance; it was a face thin and delicate with refinement, but worn into appealing lines, as if he had suffered from loneliness and misapprehension . . . he had the refinement of look and air of command which are the heritage of the old ecclesiastical families of New England.

The Captain: "There's no large-minded way of thinking now: the worst have got to be best and rule everything: we're all turned upside down and going back year by year."
The narrator on her way to meet Mrs. Todd's mother—

Maine Cliffs (*Winslow Homer, 1883*). *The country of Sarah Orne Jewett—and, in the twentieth century, of Edwin Arlington Robinson, Edna St. Vincent Millay, Marsden Hartley.*

On a larger island, farther out to sea, my entertaining companion showed me with glee the small houses of two farmers who shared the island between them, and declared that for three generations the people had not spoken to each other even in times of sickness or death or birth. "When the news came that the war was over, one of 'em knew it for a week, and never stopped across his wall to tell the others."

The Captain: "I must say I like variety myself; some folks washes Monday an' irons Tuesday the whole year around, even if the circus is goin' by!"
Visiting a far island is an event:

We were all moving toward the kitchen as if by common instinct. The best room was all too suggestive of serious occasions, and the shades were all pulled down to shut out the summer light and air. It was indeed a tribute to Society to find a room set apart for her behests out there on so apparently neighborless and remote an island. Afternoon visits and evening festivals must be few in such a bleak situation at certain seasons of the year, but Mrs. Blackett was of those who do not live to themselves, and who have long since passed the line that divides mere self-concern from a valued share in whatever Society can give and take. . . .

At the end of *The Country of the Pointed Firs* the narrator goes off to Europe. We leave these Maine "characters" (they call each other so) as in twentieth-century fiction we leave so many New Englanders behind: stick-in-the-muds. But the resilience of these people is as impressive as their rocky islands and barnacled lobster pots. Sarah Orne Jewett was a writer of unusual charm. A tone of light *gentillesse* pervades her stories, making the gulf between author and characters all the more obvious. If they are forever curiosities to us, it is because the author sees them as such, picks them up and then has done when they are through talking: "What a lot o' queer folks there used to be about here, anyway, when we was young, Almiry. Everybody's just like everybody else, now; nobody to laugh about, and nobody to cry about."

*　　*　　*

Robert Frost's characters all lived "North of Boston." He cherished them as "New Englandly," crabbed and thorny, endlessly speculative and difficult. He had good reason to, since *he* is the chief New England character in his poetry. What it describes, as no other twentieth-century American poet has done, is "the trial by existence." Unlike the many modern poets bewitched by their own stream of consciousness, offering up an endless supply of shining images, Frost in his poetry faced the world as thinker, farmer, husband, survivor. Frost alone made marriage a key subject. Despite his reputation as a "country poet" (the stock phrase for refusing him the Nobel Prize), he was anything but idyllic about Nature; he was a New Englander. "The woods are killing us anyway." In New England, said a nineteenth-century Senator in a nostalgic moment, farming was getting "crops out of granite."

Frost's first book, *A Boy's Will* (1913), was published in England when he moved his family and himself abroad because he was unable to get recognition in his own country. Returning to America when war broke out, he brought out a second volume, *North of Boston* (1914), that astonished readers by its aggressively matter-of-fact language, plain country material, and the subtlety with which Frost put language and material at the service of hard argument and the domestic life of isolated, hard-pressed country folk.

No other poet of such brilliance had sounded so "folksy" (except as a joke), had been so eager to communicate with people unaccustomed to poetry. At the same time Frost was in his refusal of American optimism hard as a diamond. He was equally speculative in his thinking, adroit and mischievous in his handling of the poetic line. When Ezra Pound, an early admirer in England, said that verse should be as well written as prose, he might have been thinking of Frost, who was always aiming at a directness of speech *and* emotion beyond his expatriate countrymen.

Frost was certainly no expatriate. He seized upon New England as his truest material at a time when the region was so obviously low in strength and prestige that it took an uncommon mind to recognize in its very isolation the resilience needed to save poetry from feeble impressionism. When the rich and foolishly self-confident Boston poet Amy Lowell imitated New England speech patterns, Frost told her: "Trouble with you, Amy, is that you don't go out of your back door often enough."

Frost said he felt coaxed into making form by common things and common desires. His constant concern was "The Figure a Poem Makes." This was based partly on his rejection of excess spirituality, essentially on his genius for listening to other New Englanders and himself. He believed with William James in looking for the "truth that grows up inside all finite experiences."

> The background is hugeness and confusion shading away from where we stand into black and utter chaos; and against that background any small man-made figure of order and concentration . . . is velvet, as the saying is, and to be considered for how much more it is than nothing.

Poetry was "a momentary stay against confusion," and "The whole thing is performance and prowess and feats of association." He was quite sure that he *wrote* better than anyone else. Although he was to become a best seller, as popular with Congressmen as with readers who thought him "safe," a refreshing antidote to difficult modernists like Eliot, an "All-American" figure for the general public and every college audience in the land, he was in fact not the wisdom figure he tried to be. The beauty of Frost's poetry arose from the determination with which he faced his own harshly willful temperament, the difficulties of his marriage. In Frost there is a constant sense of necessity: its clamor can be heard within the closeness and sharp whittling of his style, which is dialectical, self-confrontational, continuous struggle.

Frost's best poems start from some governing difficulty: there is a speaker; he seeks a solution by turning a specific landscape into a correlative of his situation. He is usually alone, often enough brooding on some estrangement. What he seeks from the place into which he has wandered is not consolation but companionship in another living form: a correlative to his own state in the wonder world of created and growing natural forms. This he finds in the detail with which nature impinges on his eyes—detail and growth that Frost amazingly captured in the actual strain and sound of speech, especially his own. He created an elasticity of line equal to his sense of speech.

In *A Boy's Will* the outward measure is still formal and even idyllic in a late nineteenth-century fashion that Frost was soon to abandon. The essential Frost can already be heard in "Storm Fear":

When the wind works against us in the dark,
And pelts with snow
The lower-chamber window on the east,
And whispers with a sort of stifled bark,
The beast,
"Come out! Come out!" —
It costs no inward struggle not to go,
Ah, no!

And in "Mowing"

There was never a sound beside the wood but one,
And that was my long scythe whispering to the ground.
What was it it whispered? I knew not well myself; . . .
It was no dream of the gift of idle hours. . . .
Anything more than the truth would have seemed too weak
To the earnest love that laid the swale in rows,
Not without feeble-pointed spikes of flowers
(Pale orchises), and scared a bright green snake,
The fact is the sweetest dream that labor knows.

North of Boston is full of miniature dramas in a style that seemed the heart of American speech. Poem after poem became classic—"Mending Wall," "The Death of the Hired Man," "Home Burial," "After Apple-Picking," "Blueberries," "The Fear." By 1914, when the book came out, vital new magazines like Harriet Monroe's *Poetry: A Magazine of Verse* and *The New Republic* were stirring up an audience for this "new poetry." And here, with the famous opening poem in *North of Boston*, "Mending Wall," was "modern" poetry to the life. But who except Robert Frost had thought that poetry could be so local in diction and cadence, so brusque yet country-slow in movement (as needed)? So redolent of New England stone fences, New England sharpness and crabbedness?

Something there is that doesn't love a wall,
That sends the frozen-ground-swell under it,
And spills the upper boulders in the sun;
And makes gaps even two can pass abreast.
The work of hunters is another thing:
I have come after them and made repair
Where they have left not one stone on a stone,
But they would have the rabbit out of hiding,
To please the yelping dogs. The gaps I mean,
No one has seen them made or heard them made,
But at spring mending-time we find them there.

The speaker and his neighbor meet to restore the fence together. With the humor Frost would not allow himself in "darker" poems ("dark" was a recurrent word), he makes a game of putting the boulders back.

New England wall. "Good fences make good neighbors," Robert Frost's most famous line, was more satiric than not.

And some are loaves and some so nearly balls
We have to use a spell to make them nearly balance:
"Stay where you are until our backs are turned!"

The speaker has the heretical thought that a fence may not be necessary. His neighbor is "all pine and I am apple orchard."

My apple trees will never get across
And eat the cones under his pines, I tell him.
He only says, "Good fences make good neighbors."

This last line became famous, but was mistakenly thought to express Frost's own New England conservatism. The poem actually becomes a mental duel over this line. Spring has put "mischief" in the speaker; he wonders if he can put a new notion in the other's head. "*Why* do they make good neighbors? Isn't it"

Where there are cows? But here there are no cows.
Before I built a wall I'd ask to know
What I was walling in or walling out,
And to whom I was like to give offense.

The other, doggedly insisting on the fence, becomes an ominous figure in Frost's mind.

I see him there
Bringing a stone grasped firmly by the top
In each hand, like an old-stone savage armed.
He moves in darkness as it seems to me,
Not of woods only and the shade of trees.
He will not go behind his father's saying,
And he likes having thought of it so well
He says again, "Good fences make good neighbors."

What surprised and delighted Frost's first readers in every turn and flourish of "Yankee" language was such relish in common speech coming from a subtle, often harshly tragic poet not afraid to tackle the heart's "desert places." The new American poetry of the twentieth century generally aimed at capturing the reality of conversation. No one else in Frost's American generation created so many real-life dialogues within narrative poems that shone with lyric beauty. In perhaps the strongest of these, "The Death of the Hired Man," a shiftless, long undependable old farmhand has taken refuge (it turns out to be his last) in the house of a farm couple fiercely divided over him. The husband wants him out; the wife is full of compassion. Frost was perhaps at his best in poems about marriage. The strife in his own household, for which he blamed his fierce temper, must have helped to give him a complete repertoire of moods and speech tones on the subject. He was writing close to the bone. Husband and wife are sitting together on the wooden steps of their farmhouse. The wife pleads the hired man's case.

> "He's worn out. He's asleep beside the stove.
> When I came up from Rowe's I found him here,
> Huddled against the barn-door fast asleep,
> A miserable sight, and frightening too—
> You needn't smile—I didn't recognize him—
> I wasn't looking for him—and he's changed.
> Wait till you see."

The husband is still bitter at the old man's going off in haying season. He manages in his tirade against him to capture the desolation of the other man's existence. In the midst of this exchange between husband and wife

> Part of a moon was falling down the west,
> Dragging the whole sky with it to the hills.
> Its light poured softly in her lap. She saw it
> And spread her apron to it. She put out her hand
> Among the harp-like morning-glory strings,
> Taut with the dew from garden bed to eaves,
> As if she played unheard some tenderness
> That wrought on him beside her in the night.
> "Warren," she said, "he has come home to die:
> You needn't be afraid he'll leave you this time."

> "Home," he mocked gently.

The wife, agreeing

> "Of course he's nothing to us, any more
> Than was the hound that came a stranger to us
> Out of the woods, worn out upon the trail."

utters the famous lines "Home is the place where, when you have to go there,/They have to take you in."

Frost, going on from success to success in a career that had opened unpromisingly, became an extraordinary national symbol before he died in 1963. Wise sayings extracted from his poetry seemed to console the many Americans increasingly discouraged by the evaporation of their belief in unlimited progress. Frost's real usefulness as a sage lay in his resistance to popular shibboleths; he was downright, even harsh, in his view of life while keeping up the public stance that he entirely shared the founding fathers' faith in the destiny of the republic.

*   *   *

The hallmark of Southern writing was open resistance to the illusion of unlimited progress. The South had been "different" even before the Civil War; afterwards, there was an unbroken sense of regional defeat and backwardness. Southern writers were a particularly valuable corrective as the twentieth century gorged itself on technology, secularism, urbanism, overpopulation and war.

Only the South had known defeat and devastation on its own soil after declaring itself a separate country and vowing to fight to the death for the preservation of slavery as its "peculiar institution." If the South had been indeed "peculiar" to the rest of the country because of its aristocratic pretensions, its dogged race-consciousness, its lack of industrial progress, it was to seem another country entirely in the decades after the Civil War.

When William Faulkner became a world figure a decade before his death in 1962, he said to an interviewer in Japan about his illustrious competitor Hemingway: "He did what he really could do marvellously well, first rate, but to me that is not success but failure . . . failure to me is the best. To try something you can't do, because it's too much [to hope for] but still to try it and fail, then try it again. That to me is success."

"Failure" was still a Southern specialty in the "Silent South" when Faulkner was born near the end of the nineteenth century. The victorious North and Middle West had gone on to become the industrial marvel of the world. The South seemed apart from the century of progress, violent in its politics, unable to escape the hatred between the races that was a lasting effect of slavery.

The South was difficult, even more so than the lonely pockets of stiff, antiquarian New England that were becoming a joke to the country. Without its old Puritan religion, New England could hardly make a traditional case for itself, especially when Irish and Italian and Portuguese immigrants rooted the Catholic Church in industrial areas. The South in its years of decline never lost, could never forget for one moment, the ravages and sacrifices of *the* war for Southern independence, 1861–65. Every Southern town had in the town square the statue of a young Confederate soldier who remained forever young and brave as he waited on his pedestal. On the pedestal were the names that every Southern child knew by heart—Gettysburg, Cold Spring Harbor, The Wilderness, Malvern Hill, Chicamauga, Chancellorsville, Chattanooga, Antietam. Faulkner wrote near the end of his career:

> For every Southern boy fourteen years old, not once but whenever he wants it, there is the instant when it's still not two o'clock on that July afternoon in 1863, the brigades are in position behind the rail fence, the guns are laid and ready in the woods, and the furled flags are already loosened to break out and Pickett himself with his long oiled ringlets and his hat in one hand probably and his sword in the other looking up the hill waiting for Longstreet to give the word and it's all in the balance, it hasn't happened yet . . .

No Southern boy (or girl) becoming a writer would ever lose that intervention into the past and the unshakable dream that it could all have turned out differently. He might regret slavery and acknowledge that it had to end by war. Part of his very being as a Southerner was a reverence for land as well as *the* land of the South—an attachment to earth values long since forgotten in the industrial North. The Southerner made a cult of such attachments, liked to think of himself as the only natural man left in the technological whirligig. He consoled himself in defeat that he had fought for the unspoiled rightness of the Creation.

Light in August (1932) begins with a pregnant young woman from Alabama sitting beside a road in Mississippi, her feet in a ditch, her shoes in her hand, watching a wagon that is mounting toward her.

Decaying plantation house in the South, photographed by Walker Evans as if it were a character (it often is) in William Faulkner's novels.

The sharp and brittle crack and clatter of its weathered and ungreased wood and metal is slow and terrific: a series of dry sluggish reports carrying for a half mile across the hot still pinewiney silence of the August afternoon. Though the mules plod in a steady and unflagging hypnosis, the vehicle does not seem to progress. It seems to hang suspended in the middle distance forever and forever, so infinitesimal is its progress, like a shabby bead upon the mild red string of road. So much is this so that in the watching of it the eye loses it as sight and sense drowsily merge and blend, like the road itself, with all the peaceful and monotonous changes between darkness and day, like already measured thread being rewound onto a spool.

She has been on the road a month, riding in a long succession of farm wagons or walking the hot dusty roads with her shoes in her hand, trying to get to Jefferson in Mississippi. There, she firmly expects, she will find her lover working in a planing mill and ready to marry her, and there—that is the big city she has never seen—she will put on her shoes at last.

This opening scene, so dry and loving in its country humor, centering on the picture of Lena and her precious burden being carried in one wagon or another, by one farmer after another, to her hoped-for destination in a husband, has become a classic example of the pastoral moment central to Faulkner's constant reliving of the Southern heritage. From the first, images have been crowding us with the dust and heat of the country road. Lena (her second name is "Grove") is continually amazed by how far a body can go. This deserted young woman is serene, ever sure that everything will end happily and properly for herself and child. Everything will, though not quite as Lena had innocently anticipated. There will be a satisfactory end to her search because she is the quintessential Southern country girl and earth mother. She draws her strength and faith from the earth and centuries of Southern family life, the tradition of farm and small town.

Lena's face is "calm as a stone, but not hard." She is somehow joined to the "sharp and brittle crack and clatter" of the "wagon's weathered and ungreased wood and metal"—to the identical and anonymous wagons bearing her on, the mules plodding in steady and unflagging hypnosis, the drowsy heat of the afternoon. Lena wears a faded blue dress, carries a palm leaf fan, a small cloth bundle that holds thirty-five cents in nickels and dimes. And the shoes! The shoes she carries in her hand as soon as she feels the dust of the road beneath her feet are as eloquent as her silences. Everything Lena does not have to say, everything she carries—not to forget the unborn baby—show that "she is waging a mild battle with that providential caution of the old earth of and with and by which she lives." A second wagon in which Lena rides "moves slowly, steadily, as if here within the sunny loneliness of the enormous land it were outside of, beyond all time and all haste." From Varner's store to Jefferson it is twelve miles. "Will we get there before dinner time?" she asks. The driver spits. "We mought," he says.

Against this rural world (once thought eternal) are set images of fire and murder, of endlessly desperate wandering and of flight, embodied in the figure who soon enters the book and dominates it in his remorseless gray anonymity. "Joe Christmas" does not even have a name of his own, only a mocking label stuck on him at the orphanage where he was deposited by his mad grandfather because the grandfather thought the baby had "black blood." "Joe Christmas" is worse than any other name could be; it indicates that he has no background, no roots, deserves no name of his own. He is just a *tabula rasa*, a blank sheet of paper on which anyone can write out an identity for him and (temporarily) make him believe it.

The contrast of Lena Grove and Joe Christmas, of the country girl and the American wanderer who is a stranger even to himself, frames the book. Lena Grove begins and ends it—with a newborn baby and a man of her own, if not the one she was first looking for. Joe Christmas's agony in life and final crucifixion are enacted within the circle he runs around in a vain effort to catch up with himself. At the end he knows that he cannot run out of it and stands still, at last, in order to be killed by a mad racist. There was "something definitely rootless about him, as though no town or city was his, no street, no walls, no square of earth his home."

Light in August returns to Lena Grove at the end and her procession up the road with her baby and *her* St. Joseph—Faulkner's version of the Holy Family. There is no deeper, more luminous version in American writing of the Southerner's favorite picture of himself—the contrast between the Southern earth and the Northern city. Joe Christmas seems to walk all smooth city pavements with the same isolation and indifference, eating at the coldly smooth wooden counter. Lena is Mother, Earth Goddess, the true South, love and patience and rebirth—all that is permanent and natural as opposed to anti-life. In Faulkner's *Sanctuary* the impotent gangster Popeye spits into a stream. Joe Christmas seeks all his life for the spirit of Lena Grove without knowing that he does—and, missing it, runs full tilt into the ground.

The title *Light in August* was once supposed to be a country saying: light as a mare or cow after delivery. Faulkner, becoming famous and mischievous, had his fun with this, claiming that the title came to him just because he liked the phrase. Himself a true Southern countryman, living most of his life in the small Mississippi town of Oxford (when he was not in Hollywood making the money that enabled him to write his "real stuff"), Faulkner liked to sound wary of the urban world which published and recognized him. "I think I have written a lot of stuff and sent it off to print," he told the critic Malcolm Cowley, "before I actually realized strangers might read it."

Although he was far from popular back home (the Faulkners were deteriorating Southern "aristocrats" who invited derision by sinking steadily in the social scale), failure was a family obsession the novelist engraved on every reader's mind in *The Sound and the Fury*. In his younger days, often drunk, seemingly incapable of keeping a job, Faulkner was dismissed as "Count No Account." Still, the world-famous novelist he became drew all his material from the local soil. His fervor as a writer was a result of personal struggle against the sense of fatality with which, as a Southerner, he grew up. His novels express a sense of life's final unavailingness that nothing can conceal. In Japan in 1956, Faulkner said he considered Yoknapatawpha County "my own little postage stamp of native soil." It was the epitome of all his work.

> I realized there was a great deal of writing I wanted to do, had to do, and I could simply economize, by picking out one country and putting enough people in it to keep me busy. And save myself trouble, time—that was probably the reason. Or it may have been the same reason that is responsible for the long clumsy sentences and paragraphs. I was still trying to reduce my one individual experience of the world into one compact thing which could be picked up and held in the hands at one time.

Faulkner is the best Southern writer and the one who more than any other put the South on the map of world literature. In Paris in 1945, a young American was moved and gratified to hear Albert Camus say "as a Southerner myself, I love in Faulkner the dust and the heat." Lena Grove was from Doane's Mill, a tiny hamlet too small for any post office list; living in the backwoods, she had not seen the hamlet itself until her parents died. Such "backwardness" became the South's mythic strength. The wagon taking Lena Grove away from Doane's Mill and all those country ways would soon be replaced by speedier vehicles taking the South right into the United States and its intercontinental highways. Lena Grove and her people now seem as "slow" and mythic as characters in fairy tales. Lena getting out of the wagon—"She reached the earth, in the heavy, dusty shoes. She looked up at him, serene, peaceful. 'It's been right kind,' she said." At another point in *Light in August* a fire breaks out.

> ". . . and then his wife said 'That house is afire.' And I reckon maybe he stopped the wagon and they sat there in the wagon for a while, looking at the smoke, and I reckon that after a while she said, 'It looks like it is.' And I reckon it was his wife that made him get down and go and see. 'They don't know it's afire,' she said, I reckon. 'You go up there and tell them.'"

Faulkner, beyond any other writer of his century, demonstrated that Americans are not a homogeneous mass but in imagination cling to some past of their own. He wrote of the wilderness left in Mississippi as if he could not bear to part with the time of "deep woods." The first white characters in Faulkner's historical chronicle were Scots like the Faulkners, Highlanders who had fought for the Stuarts, barely escaped with tartan and claymore from the English hunting down survivors of the last Jacobite campaign. Their descendants crossed the Appalachians to the last Southern frontier—the delta country of Mississippi occupied by Chickasaws. These Indians kept Negro slaves (and buried them with their master when the master died).

The Chickasaws eventually went to Oklahoma, originally reserved for Indians driven from the South. (As early as Emerson's time, he had vainly protested to President Van Buren against the forced migration of the Cherokees of Georgia, rounded up and driven westward for a thousand miles on the grounds that they were nomadic hunters and had no right to take up farming.) The "deep woods"—what was left of them—became a hunting preserve. In the most famous of Faulkner's powerful hunting stories, "The Bear" (often compared to *Moby-Dick* because of its evocation of the primeval), Faulkner describes hunters in the Fall, moving into "the tall and endless wall of dense November woods under the dissolving afternoon and the year's death, sombre, impenetrable . . ."

> the surrey moving through the skeleton stalks of cotton and corn in the last of open country, the last trace of man's puny gnawing at the immemorial flank, until, dwarfed by the perspective into an almost ridiculous diminishment, the surrey itself seemed to have ceased to move . . . as a solitary small boat hangs in lonely immobility, merely tossing up and down, in the infinite waste of the ocean . . . the wilderness closed behind his entrance as it had opened momentarily to accept him . . .

Faulkner's driving style sought to reproduce some ancient picture in his mind. The "deep woods" were somehow still impenetrable, gave men no sense of being at home there, even when they had made camp and were on the alert for "Old Ben," the towering bear tyrant of the woods, whom they unsuccessfully sought season after season. Faulkner's story is centered around the sixteen-year-old Ike McCaslin, heir to one of the best families in the county, who is taken to hunt the great bear so that, in a *rite de passage*, he may show his courage and be initiated into the ranks of men. Ike has been "learning the woods" since he was ten. When he was thirteen, the hunting guide Sam Fathers, Indian and black, "had marked his face with the hot blood" of the first buck he had killed. "In the next November he killed a bear."

Old Ben has killed dogs, a fawn, a colt. Sam Fathers has trained an almost wild dog, Lion, to hold the bear; Lion and Old Ben maul each other to death. When he is twenty-one and married, Ike decides to give up the plantation he has inherited so as to free himself from property. The land is cursed because of his grandfather's incestuous relations with slaves. But his mentor and symbolic father, Sam Fathers, has by his Indian blood taught Ike the sacred meaning of Nature as represented not by the land—an object of ownership, soon to be cleared and taken over by loggers and developers—but by Ben the bear beast, the true owner of the woods, who has left the memory of his force despite the vanishing wilderness.

Faulkner's sense of the old South in retreat before the juggernaut of industrial progress gives a particular luminosity to each actor in this drama of the irreversible.

Roasting Ears *(Thomas Benton), an expressionist view of the South.*

. . . a new planing-mill already half completed which would cover two or three acres and what looked like miles and miles of stacked steel rails red with the light bright rust of newness and of piled crossties sharp with creosote, and wire corrals and feeding troughs for two hundred mules at least . . . [Ike] could not look any more, mounted into the long-train caboose with his gun . . . and looked no more save toward the wall of wilderness ahead within which he would be able to hide himself from it once more anyway. . . .

   He had already inherited then, without ever having seen it, the big old bear with one trap-ruined foot that in an area almost a hundred miles square had earned for himself a name, a definite designation like a living man: . . . It ran in his knowledge before he ever saw it. It loomed and towered in his dreams before he even saw the unaxed woods where it left its crooked print, shaggy, tremendous, red-eyed, not malevolent but just big, too big for the dogs which tried to bay it, for the horses which tried to ride it down, for the man and the bullets they fired into it; too big for the very country which was its constricting scope . . . that doomed wilderness whose edges were being constantly and punily gnawed by men with plows and axes who fear it because it was wilderness, men myriad and nameless even to one another on the land where the old bear had earned a name.

Faulkner's accomplishment was hard on Southern writers. "Nobody wants his mule and wagon stalled on the same track the Dixie Limited is roaring down," complained Flannery O'Connor in Milledgeville, Georgia. She was a deeply Catholic writer of Irish descent in the very heart of what H.L. Mencken had called the "Bible Belt." She wrote formidably severe short stories—"A Good Man is Hard to Find," "Everything that Rises Must Converge," equally brilliant novels, *Wise Blood*, *The Violent Bear It Away*—about people remarkably committed to pettiness of heart and the grotesque situations they fall into. She wrote as if she had been locked up in Milledgeville with some extraordinarily painful people and had been forbidden to write about anything else. Fortunately, she was as talented as she was uncompromising.

This emphasis on the smallness and freakishness of human nature was intensely Southern. Faulkner never ceased to praise the "courage" and "folly" of humanity in battling so hopelessly against the odds of what O'Connor at least would have called original sin. The South's long-endured experience of defeat, of being "different" in having, still, to bear the burden of slavery, had created in the twentieth century a distinctly Southern appetite for irony, the hard-bitten, the tragic. The most popular of Southern novels, *Gone with the Wind* (1936), had conveyed this event in its title for all the nostalgic romanticism it brought to the "Lost Cause." Flannery O'Connor was more given to a cold-eyed skepticism about the human lot than other writers. She was ill much of her short life (1925–64) with the hereditary disease of lupus. The Bible Belt in her section, the very heart of the South, was given to an hysterical fundamentalism that aroused all her adversary powers as an Irish Catholic.

Flannery O'Connor's personal situation in the South was in every detail anomalous enough to furnish her with story after story of misfits. Like so many Southern characters, they seemed to have been born in a state of rage. Faulkner repeatedly described such people in a florid, vehemently expressive style, trying to catch the unavailing *effort* he saw as central to the human scene. He often described this in a tone despairing of the attempt to describe "this" and "this."

By contrast, Flannery O'Connor wrote in little drops of acid. What moved her as an artist was some inexhaustibly rigid, ultramontane sense that human beings are absolutely limited. Her point never really varied—people have a crazy disposition to error. Her characters are plainly in a world wrong for them, are totally resentful; they express themselves in ominous silences and inevitably do themselves in through sudden acts of violence. But her positively imprisoned sense of locale gave her a fixity on Southern landscape that no reader can forget: her eye seems to be on you as well. In "A Good Man is Hard to Find"

They stopped at The Tower for barbecued sandwiches. The Tower was a part stucco and part wood filling station and dance hall set in a clearing outside of Timothy. A fat man named Red Sammy Butts ran it and there were signs stuck here and there on the building and for miles up and down the highway saying, TRY RED SAMMY'S FAMOUS BARBECUE. NONE LIKE FAMOUS RED SAMMY'S! RED SAM! THE FAT BOY WITH THE HAPPY LAUGH! A VETERAN! RED SAMMY'S YOUR MAN!

To the murderer "The Misfit," who just cannot keep from murdering almost anybody he gets hold of, the grandmother says, "You could be honest too if you'd only try. Think how wonderful it would be to settle down and live a comfortable life and not have to think about somebody chasing you all the time." "No, lady," the Misfit replies as he buttons up the shirt of a man he has just murdered, "I found out that crime don't matter. You can do one thing or you can do another, kill a man or take a tire off his car, because sooner or later you're going to forget what it was you done and just be punished for it."

The stupidity, unwillingness, meanness are beyond control. But how the human race can kill! In perhaps Flannery O'Connor's cruelest story, "Greenleaf," there is an overpowering description of human helplessness in the face of human nature. Mrs. May's outrageously inefficient tenant farmer, Greenleaf, can never keep the bull penned in. She is finally gored to death through a "carelessness" on Greenleaf's part that is an act of total hostility by a poor white to the class above him, a theme that runs through Southern fiction but never attained such frightening vividness as this—

She looked back and saw that the bull, his head lowered, was racing toward her. She remained perfectly still, not in fright, but in a freezing unbelief. She stared at the violent black streak bounding toward her as if she had no sense of distance, as if she could not decide at once what his intention was, and the bull had buried his head in her lap, like a wild tormented lover, before her expression had changed. One of his horns sank until it pierced her heart and the other curved around her side and held her in an unbreakable grip. She continued to stare straight ahead but the entire scene in front of her had changed—the tree line was a dark wound in a world that was nothing but sky—and she had the look of a person whose sight had been suddenly restored but who finds the look unbearable.

CHAPTER FIVE

POWER CENTERS

New York has for so long been a favorite landing place for writers, the promised city for artists in every field, that no one complains or perhaps even notices how little recognition the city gives the extraordinary talents that have walked its streets. New York University periodically puts up a tablet to mark the birth of Henry James on Washington Place just off Washington Square Park, but it has been known to vanish for years at a time. Herman Melville was born on Pearl Street just off the Battery, whose great view of New York harbor is rapturously described on the first page of *Moby-Dick* as a lure for "thousands upon thousands of mortal men fixed in ocean reveries." But though American rebels and French movie directors have been known to change their last names to Melville in homage to the great man, the only sign of Melville's long existence in New York at 104 East 26th Street, off "Park Avenue South" (it was once plain Fourth Avenue), is a tablet put up by worshipful academics that, like so much in this violently energetic city, is regularly stolen.

Long ago a Warden of All Souls, Oxford, noted, "My impression is that in New York anything might happen at any moment." And in *The Tenants*, which ends with a fight to the death between a Jewish writer and a Black writer, squatters in an abandoned tenement, the novelist Bernard Malamud observed: "In New York who needs an atom bomb? If you walked away from a place they tore it down."

In Brooklyn Heights, on the corner of Fulton and Pineapple Streets, Walt Whitman in 1855 himself set the first edition of *Leaves of Grass* in the print shop of Rome Brothers. For many years a tablet commemorating the event became more and more lopsided, and finally disappeared with everything else on that ancient corner to make room for a smart-looking "project." In Italy one is never allowed to forget that Ibsen once lived in Amalfi, that Liszt and an aristocratic mistress spent a night or two in Bellagio. Chelsea on the far West Side of New York couldn't care less that Edith Wharton was born on West 23rd Street. Union Square knows not that a distinguished historian, Theodore Roosevelt, who liked to describe himself as "straight New York," spent his first years on East 20th.

There is a splendid photograph of Mark Twain in bed in the house on Fifth Avenue and Tenth Street where, cigar in hand, he dictated his autobiography. This was to be published only after his death. "Only dead men tell the truth," he explained. His autobiography was to be the most shockingly true account of a man's real life that was ever written. It was actually too loose, disjointed and altogether familiar to shock anybody. But Mark Twain made quite a figure as he paraded up Fifth Avenue followed by a crowd of gawking admirers. The ex-steamboat pilot and prospector now wore a top

Sunset, West 23rd Street, New York (detail) by John Sloan, c. 1905, brings out the slightly sinister quality of a city where "anything might happen at any moment."

Washington Arch, Spring *(Childe Hassam, 1890); a typical monument of Henry James's New York, in Washington Square, the setting of one of his most powerful stories.*

Washington Square Park, New York, c. 1880. James was born nearby, on Washington Place.

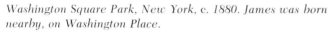

hat over his shining white locks (washed every morning with laundry soap). At home he wore his Oxford gown over the white suit he displayed summer and winter even when he was playing billiards.

At the other end of the social scale young Stephen Crane as a reporter so exasperated the police in the Times Square district that they tried to bar him from the city. The district was known as "The Tenderloin" because of the graft the police collected. Crane, with his usual need to defy any establishment, had defended a prostitute from police molestation. Crane's father was a leading New Jersey Methodist minister; his mother was a founder of the Women's Christian Temperance Union. What was Stephen Crane doing in the slums of lower New York, in the huddled and squalid Five Points area virtually unchanged from the criminality that had horrified Dickens in the middle of the century? He was first in New York as a reporter on the Bowery; there he absorbed the color and full tide of Irish immigrant life that went into his famous early stories—*Maggie: A Girl of the Streets* and *George's Mother*.

New York so dimly recalls the great writers who have passed through it that when a sign was put up commemorating Edgar Allan Poe's once having lived in the West 80s (when it was all country), his middle name was misspelled. New York neither knows nor cares that Willa Cather lived for years in Greenwich Village on Bank street (the house was pulled down to make an extension of the Seventh Avenue subway). William Dean Howells in 1881 managed all by himself to remove the literary center of the country from Boston to New York when he left the *Atlantic Monthly* to edit *Cosmopolitan*. Theodore Dreiser, Eugene O'Neill, Willa Cather, John Reed, John Dos Passos and a dozen others at one time or another occupied the same boarding house on Washington Square. The city is totally indifferent to every vestige of Thomas Wolfe and Marianne Moore in Brooklyn, Hart Crane on Columbia Heights, Allen Tate in Greenwich Village, E.E. Cummings on Patchin Place, W.H. Auden on St. Mark's Place, Wallace Stevens as a reporter and law student in downtown New York, the great Spanish poet Federico García Lorca at Columbia. But what an array! Ralph Ellison from Oklahoma and Saul Bellow from Chicago on Riverside Drive, James Baldwin off Lenox Avenue, Edmund Wilson in the East 80s, Isaac Bashevis Singer on West 86th Street. New York has given shelter to European exiles from Lorenzo da Ponte to Giuseppe Garibaldi, Tom Paine to John Butler Yeats, Maxim Gorky to Leon Trotsky, Piet Mondrian to Marc Chagall. Yehudi Menuhin said in 1943 that "One of the great war aims is to get to New York."

New York has been the capital of American book and magazine publishing since the mid-nineteenth century. It has been a prodigious subject for the literary imagination: perhaps the largest. This would have surprised Henry James, a native son proud to call his collected works "the New York edition": James was sure that his favored form, the novel of society, depended on a rich traditional background like Victorian England. Returning to the city in 1904 to write that extraordinary example of his late genius, the most highly charged of "travel books," *The American Scene* (1907), James, seeing modern New York and its skyscrapers for the first time, recorded in eloquent amazement what a powerhouse—beginning at the bay—the city had become,

The aspect the power. wears then is indescribable; it is the power of the most extravagant of cities, rejoicing, as with the voice of the morning, in its might, its fortune, its unsurpassable conditions, and imparting to every object and element, to the motion and expression of every floating, hurrying, panting thing, to the throb of ferries and tugs, to the plash of waves and the play of winds and the glint of lights and the shrill of whistles and the quality and authority of breeze-borne cries—all, practically, a diffused, wasted clamour of detonations.

New York, since the Civil War "the greatest harbor," was the lodestar for the world's immigrants, the financial center, the metropolis, America's one world city. Even old-stock patrician Americans like Henry Adams, who had always been indifferent to New York, had to admit being dazzled, painfully, by the New York he saw when he returned from Europe.

As he came up the bay again, November 5, 1904, he found the approach more striking than ever—wonderful—and like nothing he had ever much cared to see. The outline of the city became frantic in its effort to explain something that defied meaning. Power seemed to have outgrown its servitude and to have asserted its freedom. The cylinder had exploded, and had thrown great masses of stone and steam against the sky. The city had the air and movement of hysteria, and the citizens were crying, in every accent of anger and alarm, that the new forces must be at any cost brought under control. Prosperity never before imagined, power never yielded by man, speed never reached by anything but a meteor, had made the world irritable, nervous, querulous, unreasonable and afraid.

Port of New York was the wholly appropriate title of a book by the critic Paul Rosenfeld, at the height of the "golden twenties," about such artists as Alfred Stieglitz, John Marin, Georgia O'Keeffe, Marsden Hartley. The harbor, with Liberty raising her lamp to the entering world, was the world's dream. As Emma Lazarus wrote in "The New Colossus," inscribed on the pedestal of the great statue,

> Send these, the homeless, tempest-tossed, to me:
> I lift my lamp beside the golden door.

The New Yorker Herman Melville spent the last twenty-five years of his life as a customs inspector of cargoes along the Hudson River docks. Melville resented his birthplace as a symbol of his merchant father's bankruptcy and early death, and his patrician family's decline. Above all he identified New York with his own worldly failure as an author. He wrote his greatest books and stories in the rustic peace of Pittsfield in the Berkshires, but was compelled to return to New York in the middle of the Civil War in order to obtain regular employment. For all his bitterness at the hazards of the literary life—"If I were to write the Gospels in this century," he wrote to Hawthorne, "I should die in the gutter"—New York as the great port of entry retained its fascination for a writer whose imagination was always bound up with the sea.

In *Redburn*, the fictionalized account of his first voyage, to Liverpool as a cabin boy, Melville rejoiced in the emigrants setting off for America. The ancient myth of a new world seemed very real.

The other world beyond this, which was longed for by the devout before Columbus's time, was found in the New; and the deep-sea lead, that first struck these soundings, brought up the soil of Earth's Paradise. Not a Paradise then, or now; but to be made so, at God's good pleasure, and in the fullness and mellowness of time. The seed is sown, and the harvest must come; and our children's children, on the world's jubilee morning, shall all go with their sickles to the reaping. Then shall the curse of Babel be revoked, a new Pentecost come, and the language they shall speak shall be the language of Britain.

Melville's awesome creation, *Moby-Dick* (1851), begins as a tribute to New York at the Battery.

The Battery, New York. The round structure at the left is the old immigrant receiving station. Melville was born a few minutes away.

There now is your insular city of the Manhattoes, belted round by wharves as Indian isles by coral reefs—commerce surrounds it with her surf. Right and left, the streets take you waterward. Its extreme down-town is the battery, where that noble mole is washed by waves, which a few hours previous were out of sight of land. Look at the crowds of water-gazers there.

Circumambulate the city of a dreamy Sabbath afternoon. Go from Corlears Hook to Coenties Slip, and from thence, by Whitehall, northward. What do you see?—Posted like silent sentinels all around the town, stand thousands upon thousands of mortal men fixed in ocean reveries.

In *Pierre* (1852), following the failure of his great effort in *Moby-Dick*, Melville satirized his own early idealism and Grub Street in New York.

As he was finishing *Moby-Dick* in June 1851 he complained to Nathaniel Hawthorne, "In a week or so, I go to New York, to bury myself in a third-story room, and work and slave on my 'Whale' while it is driving through the press. *That* is the only way I can finish it now,—I am so pulled hither and thither by circumstances." And later the same month he wrote, "The 'Whale' is only half through the press; for, wearied with the long delays of the printers, and disgusted with the heat and dust of the Babylonish brick-kiln of New York, I came back to the country to feel the grass, and end the book reclining on it, if I may."

In *Pierre* he summed up this period in New York more savagely.

The chamber was meager even to meanness. No carpet on the floor, no picture on the wall; nothing but a low, long, and very curious-looking single bedstead, that might possibly serve for an indigent bachelor's pallet. . . . A wide board of the toughest live-oak, about six feet long, laid upon two upright empty flour-barrels, and loaded with a large bottle of ink, an unfastened bundle of quills, a pen-knife, a folder, and a still unbound ream of foolscap paper, significantly stamped, "Ruled, Blue."

Now look around at that most miserable room, and at that most miserable of all the pursuits of a man, and say if here be the place, and this be the trade, that God intended him for. A rickety chair, two hollow barrels, a plank, paper, pens, and infernally black ink, four leprously dingy white walls, no carpet, a cup of water, and a dry biscuit or two. . . . Civilization, Philosophy, Ideal Virtue! behold your victim!

Before leaving the Berkshires for New York, Melville composed a book of extraordinary stories, *The Piazza Tales* (1856). The 'piazza' of the title was at his country house, "Arrowhead," but the story with the greatest personal allusions in it, "Bartleby the Scrivener," was another satire on the literary life and set in New York's "Babylonish brick-kiln." Bartleby, a meek, totally dutiful copyist in the office of a Wall Street lawyer, suddenly and irrevocably refuses to do any more copying, quietly refuses to say anything more than "I prefer not to." His thoroughly conventional-minded employer is exasperated and finally almost disoriented by this painfully strange creature, who refuses to copy, and just as adamantly refuses to quit the premises. Finally the lawyer abandons his own office. But carted off by the police and starving himself to death in jail—"I prefer not to have dinners"—Bartleby haunts and spiritually overcomes his former employer, who has been shaken out of the usual complacency of his existence.

Melville's grudge against New York—against failure, poverty, anonymity—reached its peak in 1863 when he witnessed the worst riot in the city's history. A mob mostly of

Maiden Lane, Wall Street district, 1885. In one of these offices, Melville's Bartleby put down his pen and said that he "preferred not to."

Row of brownstone fronts, West 46th Street, New York. Edith Wharton grew up in just such a street, typical of those which once occupied many square miles of Manhattan.

Irish immigrants, protesting the Draft Act, fired buildings, including a Negro orphanage, lynched Negroes from lampposts, and rendered the police so helpless that regiments had to be pulled from the front to restore order. Melville, who had just moved to 104 East 26th Street, described himself in a poem, "The House-Top," standing on the roof of his house on a steamy July night listening to

<pre>
                                          a mixed surf
          Of muffled sound, the Atheist roar of riot.
          Yonder, where parching Sirius set in drought,
          Balefully glared red Arson—there—and there.
          The Town is taken by its rats—ship-rats
          And rats of the wharves. All civil charms
          And priestly spells which late held hearts in awe—
</pre>

Fear-bound, subjected to a better sway
Than sway of self; these like a dream dissolve,
And man rebounds whole aeons back in nature.

Crime in New York was not a subject Melville was prepared for. Edgar Allan Poe, born in Boston and living much of his life in New York, was fascinated by crime. Like Baudelaire, who was mesmerized by Poe's stories and imagined himself to be Poe's double, Poe was—for his time—positively unAmerican in his attraction to the sordidness of great cities. His was a devilishly original imagination: an inventor of the detective story, he was as dependent on the violence of early New York as a police reporter. "The Mystery of Marie Roget" was based on the last days of a New York shop assistant, who was found dead in the Hudson River after what is now believed to have been a botched abortion. This may have been the first detective story written in an attempt to solve an actual crime. Poe died under mysterious circumstances in Baltimore in 1849. It is no longer certain that he died as the result of being voted around the town on Election Day by a mob while he was drunk. But poor Poe was given to drink, and was often entangled with "low" urban life.

Melville's angry attachment to his birthplace was deep and entirely personal. A lowly inspector of cargoes on the Hudson River docks, he was outraged by the eclipse of the great names in his family. Gansevoort Street near the Hudson was named after his maternal grandfather, a hero of the Revolutionary War. He once went into a barroom on Gansevoort Street to buy a cigar and discovered that no one knew where the name came from. And this was a time when Melville's startling achievement in *Moby-Dick* was beginning to be recognized abroad. British visitors, for whom Melville was a "Titan," came looking for him, only to be told that "Melville is living somewhere in New York." Even at a salary of $4 a day (it was later reduced to $3.60), he did not have assurance of tenure in his job, a political appointment.

Edith Wharton, another New Yorker born into its old merchant aristocracy, was to admit in her autobiography, *A Backward Glance*, that she "never heard Melville's name mentioned." But she knew that he was "a cousin of the Van Rensselaers, and qualified by birth to figure in the best society." Mrs. Wharton would probably not have been amused by Melville's "The Two Temples," a vindictive sketch of Grace Church, the Gothic shrine built on Lower Broadway for New York's better sort. In it Melville described his ejection by the beadle after being chased up and down the church.

In *A Backward Glance* Mrs. Wharton provided a scornful picture of the rows and rows of New York brownstones, first put up by venal landlords in the 1860s, that made Lewis Mumford call his cultural history of this period *The Brown Decades.*

Out of doors, in the mean, monotonous streets, without architecture, without great churches or palaces, or any visible memorials of an historic past . . . cursed with its universal chocolate-covered coating of the most hideous stone ever quarried, this cramped horizontal gridiron of a town without towers, porticoes, fountains or perspectives, hide-bound in its deadly uniformity of mean ugliness. . . .

This was New York during the Gilded Age. But this was also the period that saw the completion of Frederick Law Olmsted's Central Park and John August Roebling's Brooklyn Bridge. Both creations were to be described at the close of Walt Whitman's

Specimen Days, his diary of Washington life during the Civil War. Before the war Whitman, as a "jour printer," reporter and editor in New York, was to show himself more lovingly attached to the city than any other of its native sons. "Oneself I sing, a simple separate person/Yet utter the word Democratic, the word En-Masse." These words were put at the head of *Leaves of Grass* when this epic of a lifetime—Whitman's and America's—was finally all collected. Only Whitman among New York writers a century ago sought the masses of New York as a correlative to his "ongoing soul," caught the note of a city in his key term *ensemble*. Whitman even called *Leaves of Grass* a city; he would have liked Auden's calling Eros the builder of cities. "I can hardly tell you why," Whitman said about his book during the Civil War, "but feel very positively that if anything can justify my revolutionary attempts and utterances, it is such *ensemble*—like a great city to modern civilization & a whole combined cluttering paradoxical unity, a man, a woman."

Whitman's lovable archaic faith was that New York was not just a legal construction but a true community based on faith in the people. In the most expressive poem he ever wrote from New York, "Crossing Brooklyn Ferry," he portrayed himself as one of the crowd. And the crowd crossing on the ferry between Brooklyn and Manhattan was as alive and irresistible as the tidal movements of the East River; together they gave the poet his scope.

Of course Whitman could feel separated from the life around him. "I too felt the curious abrupt questionings stir within me, . . ./I too had been struck from the float forever in solution." His faith in "*you*," his future reader, was like his faith in the crowd surrounding him on the ferry

> Closer yet I approach you,
> What thought you have of me now, I had as much of you—
> I laid in my stores in advance,
> I considered long and seriously of you before you were born.

So he put into "Crossing Brooklyn Ferry" "The glories strung like beads on my smallest sights and hearings, on the walk in the street and the passage over the river." The crowd entering the gates of the ferry, the shipping around Manhattan and the heights of Brooklyn, the winter seagulls floating with motionless wings but in slow-wheeling circles as they gradually edge south. The shadowy group of steamtug, barges, hay-boat, the belated lighter; "the foundry chimneys burning high and glaringly into the night,/Casting their flicker of black contrasted with wild red and yellow light over the tops of houses, and down into the clefts of streets."

At the end of "Crossing Brooklyn Ferry" these objects reveal themselves as "dumb, beautiful ministers,"—the "appearances" that places present, and that have waited ("you always wait") to connect with the human soul. "We fathom you not," he cries at the end—"we love you—there is perfection in you also, . . ./Great or small, you furnish your parts toward the soul." The most ordinary day to day fixtures of the landscape can be absorbed into the deepest urges of our being. Such a connection to be grasped out of the tidal heart of the East River! As Yeats said, belief makes the mind abundant. Whitman's genius, in this as in so many things, was to merge some immanent erotic glow with his positive confidence (already old-fashioned) in "the people, yes."

Besides, he had nowhere to go but up, this stalwart of the Brooklyn streets who learned as much bravado there as he did from Emerson. "I was simmering, simmering,

Brooklyn Bridge in construction (Harper's Weekly, 1877). *The bridge inspired many writers who saw it as part of the "epic of modern consciousness" (Hart Crane's words).*

Looking through Brooklyn Bridge (*C.R.W. Nevinson, 1919–20*). *John Augustus Roebling's crisscrossing of supporting cables inspired Crane to cry, "O harp and altar, of the fury fused."*

Emerson brought me to a boil." Whitman was and is like no one else. It was some mysterious confidence in both "the Me" and the "Not Me" (favorite terms) that enabled him to make conjunction with the most ordinary materials and with the immortality of the earth itself.

Seventy years later Hart Crane from Columbus, Ohio, was living in Whitman's Brooklyn; he set out in the "Proem" to *The Bridge* a more wistful effort at connection with New York's fullness:

> O harp and altar, of the fury fused,
> (How could mere toil align thy choiring strings!)
> Terrific threshold of the prophet's pledge,
> Prayer of pariah, and the lover's cry,—

His aim was epical: in fifteen sections to envelop American history stemming westward from Brooklyn Bridge. The launching pad was the dream-long day from dawn in "Harbor Day" to midnight in "Atlantis." Through the dream, the single day takes in vast stretches of time and space; from a subway ride in the morning to a railroad journey to the Mississippi, then going beyond De Soto's crossing of the river to the primeval world of the Indians, then forward to the West of the pioneers.

Like so many American poets attempting a long poem, Crane conceived an epic about American history as personal myth rather than consecutive narrative. It was not the poets but the novelists—Melville in *Moby-Dick* and Mark Twain in *Huckleberry Finn*—who captured convincingly the strain and hardihood of the national experience. What Crane really caught in his effort to make Brooklyn Bridge a pivot for all American history was the material confidence of the 1920s. Lindbergh, the Empire State and Chrysler Buildings, the Florida boom, the first cross-country highway system impart their frantic energy to Crane's swollen effort. The Empire State Building was climbing a story a day to the height of 102 floors. Stifling in an advertising agency, Crane admitted, "Maybe I'm just a little jealous of Lindy." To Waldo Frank in 1926 he also acknowledged—"Intellectually judged, the whole theme and project seems more and more absurd, these forms, materials, dynamics are simply non-existent in the world. . . . The bridge today has no significance beyond an economical approach to shorter hours, quicker lunches, behaviorism and toothpicks."

A month later, having composed the "Proem":—"I feel an absolute music in the air again, and some tremendous rondure floating somewhere." The "Proem" provides so powerful an entrance to *The Bridge*, that the forced eloquence of the rest, with random shots of American history yoked together by Crane's amazingly chromatic style, is an inevitable letdown. But the "Proem," set in New York itself, is wonderful. By a fortunate accident Crane had come to live at 110 Columbia Heights overlooking the harbor. There Washington Roebling, son of the bridge's originator, John Augustus Roebling, had directed the actual completion of his father's bridge from a wheelchair: he had become paralyzed directing work at the bottom of the East River on the foundations of the Brooklyn tower. The concluding section of *The Bridge*, "Atlantis," opens powerfully:

> Through the bound cable strands, the arching path
> Upward, veering with light, the flight of strings,—
> Taut miles of shuttling moonlight syncopate

The whispered rush, telepathy of wires.
Up the index of night, granite and steel—
Transparent meshes—fleckless the gleaming staves—
Sibylline voices flicker, waveringly stream
As though a god were issue of the strings. . . .

And through that cordage, threading with its call
One arc synoptic of all tides below—

Crane said of this: "I have attempted to induce the same feelings of elation, etc.—like being carried forward and upward simultaneously—both in imagery, rhythm and repetition, that one experiences in walking across my beloved Brooklyn Bridge." What is personal and even intimate in the opening and closing sections of *The Bridge* now seems more lasting than all the rest.

Under thy shadow by the piers I waited;
Only in darkness is thy shadow clear.
The City's fiery parcels all undone,
Already snow submerges an iron year . . .

O Sleepless as the river under thee,
Vaulting the sea, the prairies' dreaming sod,
Unto us lowliest sometime sweep, descend
And of the curveship lend a myth to God.

Crane was of course a stranger in New York, another writer from the Midwest's "heartland" of America escaped to New York as the supreme power center. In literature, New York sometimes seems to exist just for strangers. Vladimir Mayakovsky from Moscow was also fascinated by Brooklyn Bridge in the 1920s.

Hey, Coolidge boy,
make a shout of joy!
when a thing is good
                        then it's good,
Blush from compliments
                        like our flag's calico,
even though you're
                        the most superb united states
                                                of
America.

Equally fascinated with Brooklyn Bridge was Federico García Lorca from Granada, who as a sometime student at Columbia University wrote "Unsleeping City: Brooklyn Bridge Nocturne." Lorca identified the bridge not with some historic epic, as Crane hoped to do, but with the loneliness Crane actually evoked in his best lines. Lorca did not cry, as Crane seems to, "Only connect!" He excoriated New York as a city impossible to sleep in—

Brooklyn Bridge from below. For Roebling, its builder, the bridge was a philosophical statement. He wanted, he said, to "bring in harmony all that surrounds me."

Life is no dream! Beware and beware and beware!
We tumble downstairs to eat of the damp of the earth
Or we climb to the snowy divide with the choir of dead dahlias.
But neither dream nor forgetfulness, is:
brute flesh is. Kisses that tether our mouths
In a mesh of raw veins.
Whomsoever his woe brings to grief, it will grieve without quarter.
Whom death brings to dread will carry that death on his shoulders.

The 1920s marked the triumph of American entrepreneurship conceived as rugged individualism, nowhere more blatantly than in the city famous for Wall Street. The poets preferred to circle around Brooklyn Bridge. Roebling, the builder of the bridge, called himself Hegel's favorite student when he fled to the United States from the Prussian police. He was then a utopian socialist, and actually kept a kind of commune in Saxonburg, Pennsylvania, where he invented the wire rope that made possible the suspension of Brooklyn Bridge. Everyone who recognizes the unique beauty of Roebling's bridge still marvels over the central promenade. The latest bridges in New York have no promenade at all. But Roebling—in Germany an Hegelian, in America a transcendentalist—said, "It is a want of my intellectual nature to bring in harmony all that surrounds me. Every new harmony I discovered is to me another messenger of peace, another pledge of my redemption." In his treatise *The Condition of the United States Reviewed by the Higher Law*, he urged his fellow citizens to consider the country not as a business partnership but as a family—"parental estate."

"This elevated promenade," Roebling wrote in his prospectus, "will allow people of leisure and old and young to stroll over the bridge on fine days. I need not state that in a crowded commercial city such a promenade will be of incalculable value." Roebling the visionary had designed the great stone towers after the Gothic cathedral in his native Muhlhausen. He never could separate Brooklyn Bridge, the greatest technical feat of his day, from the ancient myth of connection and protection that bridges express. The lone individual walking Brooklyn Bridge was now to be included and developed in some mighty work of harmony. The theme was not E.M. Forster's wistful cry "Only connect!" but connection made social. This in the tumultuous often brutal city of New York was to be accomplished by synoptic experience of the "greatest harbor," the already imperial city. New York, the world's great port of call, allowed no one to forget the passage from Old World to New and the power through freedom that became, truly, the American dream.

The drive to own and exploit every fraction of New York's tight space was so marked early in the nineteenth century that the intellectual leaders of the city—the once romantic poet and longtime editor of the *New York Post*, William Cullen Bryant, was fundamental in this—conceived a central park to keep the masses from crowding each other to death. What still astonishes and exhilarates one about the plan offered by Frederick Law Olmsted before he became the park's superintendent is the vision of a public place that would somehow elevate and expand what this practical visionary called the soul. Democracy was still each individual's romantic adventure.

Olmsted detested the terrible regularity of New York streets, the gridiron plan. For his park he wanted a rural unkemptness, picturesque roads. In the vast planting to replace the old swamp wasteland he emphasized wild plants, random tufts, a thick growth of low brambles, ferns, asters, gentians, irregularly spaced trees. And of course the boulders of

Bird's Eye View of Central Park, Looking South (c. 1870). Frederick Law Olmsted's great plan to graft open country on to New York's rigid grid.

Central Park (*Maurice Prendergast, 1901*). *Prendergast liked to depict the "carriage-riding classes," like characters in novels of "high society."*

rock left from the demolition of the rock stratum underlying great parts of New York that made possible the skyscrapers.

"Fine old trees may be left standing," Olmsted wrote, "and to save them, the wheel-way carried a little to the right or left, or slightly raised or lowered. Such conditions . . . far from blemishes . . . add to other charms of picturesqueness, and they are a concession to nature, tending to an effect not of incongruity and incompleteness, but of consistent and happy landscape competition." Olmsted, in collaboration with the professional landscape architect Calvin Vaux and Jacob Wrey Mould, designed every structure, miniature bridge, terrace, arch, stairway, fountain, bench, each piece of masonry work, fence, gate, lamppost and mosaic design, never overlooking the innumerable details of every description that needed to be drawn for fabrication.

Olmsted described the park-to-be as "throughout a single work of art, and as such subject to the primary law of every work of art, that it shall be framed upon a single, noble motive, to which the design of all its parts, in some more or less subtle way, shall be confluent and helpful."

I shall venture to assume to myself the title of artist. . . . The main object and justification is simply to produce a certain influence in the minds of the people. . . . The character of this influence is a poetic one and it is to be produced by means of scenes, through observation of which the mind may be more or less lifted out of moods and habits into which it is, under the ordinary conditions of life, in the city, likely to fall. . . .

Of course Walt Whitman was right to complain that the plan was suited mostly to New York's elite. Fifteen miles of perfect roads and bridle paths would attract mainly the "carriage-riding classes," "the full oceanic tide of New York's wealth and gentility." But Whitman admitted that the park "represented at least a trial marriage of art and enlightened enterprise, nature and the life of the city." Even Harvard's super-refined Charles Eliot Norton said that of all American artists, Olmsted stood "first in the production of great works which answer the need and give expression to the life of our immense and miscellaneous democracy."

Olmsted saw the representative New Yorker as someone walking through "The Ramble," as he called one of his more pastoral creations in the park, breathing New York's air in an access of Wordsworthian sublimity. Little could he anticipate the sexual mayhem now more common in "The Ramble." New York, "the promised city," was to become in twentieth-century literature no less promising and even more glittering than it had been in the nineteenth; but, as Henry James thundered in *The American Scene*, the trouble with New York would now be the crush of democracy itself.

James could be amusing about the pressure on Central Park that was so at variance with Olmsted's vision of it as a "poetic" scene. He compared the park to an innkeeper compelled to take in everybody. He admired—it was a positive thrill to his majestic sensibility—the power that the "terrible town" exhibited. The masses, especially the immigrants jamming his old neighborhoods on the East Side of lower New York, he called the agency of future ravage.

171

Orchard Street, the heart of New York's Jewish immigrant district at the turn of the century; silent on Saturday, roaring with trade on Sunday.

More than Theodore Dreiser in *Sister Carrie*, Edith Wharton in *The House of Mirth*, Stephen Crane in *Maggie*, William Dean Howells in *A Hazard of New Fortunes*, Jacob Riis in *How the Other Half Lives*, it was James in *The American Scene* who caught the physical thrill of New York, the boundless energy and impatience expressed in the harbor, the new skyscrapers and bridges. "The subject was everywhere—that was the beauty, that was the advantage; it was thrilling, really, to find oneself in the presence of a theme to which everything directly contributed, leaving no touch of experience irrelevant." Before leaving the country thirty years earlier, he had thought of *Europe* as the great imperial idea. His old boredom with the "thin empty lovely American beauty" had now to be replaced by strictures against the vulgarity of the prospering lower class.

> . . . the collective sharpness, so to speak, of this vocal note, offering any price, offering everything, wanting only to outbid and prevail, at the great auction of life. . . . It was as if, in their high gallery, the bidders, New Yorkers every one, were before one's eyes; pressing to the front, hanging over the balustrade, holding out clamorous importunate eyes. . . . It was not, certainly, for general style, pride and colour, a Paul Veronese company. . . . But my vision has a kind of analogy; for what were the Venetians, after all, but the children of a Republic and of trade?

It was typical of Henry James to tolerate New York—as Henry Adams tolerated Chicago at the World's Fair in 1893—by comparing such trading cities to Venice. But in truth James the Anglophile, who in England dined out with bishops and peers, was as irritated by modern New York as James the artist was excited by its energy. Of Brooklyn Bridge he magnificently captured the force, but this he also identified with the mass surge that repelled him.

> The universal *applied* passion struck me as shining unprecedently out of composition; in the bigness and bravery and insolence, especially, of everything that rushed and shrieked; in the air as of a great intricate frenzied dance, half merry, half desperate, or at least half defiant, performed on the huge watery floor. This appearance of the bold lacing-together, across the waters, of the scattered members of the monstrous organism . . . does perhaps more than anything else to give the pitch of the vision of energy. One has the sense that the monster grows and grows, flinging abroad its loose limbs even as some unmannered young giant at his "larks," . . . the future complexity of the web, all under the sky and over the sea, becoming thus that of some colossal set of clockworks, some steel-souled machine-room of brandished arms and hammering fists and opening and closing jaws. The immeasurable bridges are but as the horizontal sheaths of pistons working at high pressure, day and night, and subject, one apprehends with perhaps inconsistent gloom, to a certain, to fantastic, to merciless multiplication.

James's genius for capturing the clamor of New York dominates harbor and bridge alike. This is truly, as he said of the ideal critic, "perception at the pitch of passion." But what has he done with his own, his native city? He has turned it into an art object. The life in the streets affronts him, shows democracy on a rampage. The crudity of people—some actually eating in the streets—is unbearable. The "land of consideration" James found in upper-class England seems unintelligible to New York. James went on in his overflowing memoir of earliest youth, *A Small Boy and Others*, to linger fondly on New York sights and sounds before the Civil War. There is always genius at work in the all-devouring subjectivity of James's "late" manner. But the New York James idyllicly remembers was still Walt Whitman's city. Compare Whitman in "Song of Myself"—"The blab of the pave, tires of carts, sluff of boot-soles, talk of the promenaders" (Whitman expressing the city's mass life)—with James. James remembers himself as alone, the artist-to-be, getting everything on Lower Broadway, as he says, to rub his contemplative nose. "For there was the very pattern and measure of all he was to demand: just to be somewhere—almost anywhere would do—and somehow receive an impression or an accession, feel a relation or a vibration."

Did James revisiting New York in 1904–05 overlook anything of consequence? Nothing whatever. This is already *our* New York. None of us in our more harried moments at the rush hour can honestly scorn James's picture of "the consummate monotonous commonness of the pushing male crowd, moving in its dense mass—with the confusion carried to chaos for any intelligence, any perception; a welter of objects and sounds in which relief, detachment, dignity, meaning, perished utterly and lost all rights." The city has indeed become so pressing and unsafe that the crudity James merely sniffed at is now something more ominous. There is a constant fear of the city even among those most stimulated by its possibilities.

James is magnificent but outside. The city, for those who live in it, can hardly remain an esthetic object. James could never have noticed about New York what Thomas Paine did in early Greenwich Village—"The contrast of affluence and wretchedness is like dead and living bodies chained together." The energy and plenitude of New York were more than esthetic objects, as one brilliant intelligence after another, usually from "out of town," came to make New York *the* metropolitan subject, the shining jewel. The procession became sumptuous. Scott Fitzgerald in *The Great Gatsby*, John O'Hara in *Butterfield* 8, Dorothy Parker in "Big Blonde," Eugene O'Neill in *The Iceman Cometh*, John Dos Passos in *The Big Money*, John Cheever in "The Enormous Radio," Thomas Wolfe in *Of Time and the River*, Saul Bellow in *The Victim* and *Seize the Day*, Truman Capote in *Breakfast at Tiffany's*, J.D. Salinger in *The Catcher in the Rye*, Ralph Ellison in *Invisible Man*, James Baldwin in *Go Tell It on the Mountain* and *The Fire Next Time*.

There were the poets: E.E. Cummings, Marianne Moore, W.H. Auden, Elizabeth Bishop, Robert Lowell, Frank O'Hara, John Ashbery, and how many others. There were the magazines, especially *The New Yorker*, which was such a nursery and gallery of talent that people all over the country felt they knew New York, the New York manner, the supreme voice of New York, just from turning its pages. New York's native writers might complain that Scott Fitzgerald from St. Paul thought New York was the Plaza Hotel. But even Norman Mailer from Brooklyn Heights described New York in *An American Dream* with the same rapture. And when after World War II New York displaced Paris as the capital of twentieth-century art, all the rancor of an exhausted and frustrated Europe melted into tributes to its variety by foreign artists happily settled in New York. Visitor after visitor observed that it was not only more difficult to sleep in New York but often unnecessary. Cyril Connolly after the war could not get over Greenwich Village bookstores open at midnight. New York seemed "the supreme metropolis. . . . If Paris is the setting for a romance, New York is the perfect city in which to get over one, to get over anything. Here the lost *douceur de vivre* is forgotten and intoxication of living takes its place."

* * *

LEFT: *The Plaza Hotel in 1922. On the right is General Sherman on his horse and in the center the fountain into which Scott and Zelda Fitzgerald jumped one heady night.*

OPPOSITE: *New York skyscrapers at night in the giddy 1920s. The Sixth Avenue "El," long gone, runs diagonally across the lower right section of the picture.*

New York as a literary capital has had only one predecessor in American history: Boston. It was merrily admitted, by Boston, to be the Athens of America, the "hub of the universe." Since then Boston writing about Boston has had no other subject except its lost tradition. When Elizabeth Hardwick from Kentucky was married to the poet Robert Lowell and living in the very heart of tradition-conscious, ancestor-worshipping Beacon Hill, she acidly wrote: "With Boston and its mysteriously enduring reputation, the 'reverberation is longer than the thunderclap.'"

Boston—wrinkled, spindly legged, depleted of nearly all her spiritual and cutaneous oils, provincial, self-esteeming—has gone on spending and spending her inflated bills of pure reputation decade after decade. . . . History, indeed, with its long, leisurely, gentlemanly labors, the books arriving by post, the cards to be kept and filed, the sections to be copied, the documents to be checked, is the ideal pursuit for the New England mind. . . . For money, society, fashion, extravagance, one went to New York. . . .

Boston is not a small New York, as they say a child is not a small adult but is, rather, a specially organized small creature, with its small-creature's temperature, balance, and distribution of fat. In Boston there is an utter absence of that wild electric beauty of New York, of the marvelous, excited rush of people in taxicabs at twilight, of the great Avenues and Streets, the restaurants, theatres, bars, hotels, delicatessens, shops.

Puritan Boston's Christ Church, "The Old North." Paul Revere's lanterns in the steeple warned patriots that the British were marching on Lexington and Concord.

To the complaint that Boston is not New York, Boston replies—or used to—that at least it knows its own history and has even polished it up. New York from the first was an imperial prize fought over by European rivals. Puritan Boston was founded as a token to God by His elect. Before sailing from England on the *Arbella*, in 1630, Governor John Winthrop of the Massachusetts Bay Company wrote,

> Thus stands the case between God and us. We are entered into a Covenant with Him for this work. We have taken out a commission. . . . Now if the Lord shall please to hear us, and bring us in peace to the place we desire, then hath He ratified this Covenant and sealed our Commission, and will accept a strict performance of the articles contained in it. . . .
>
> We shall find that the God of Israel is among us, when ten of us shall be able to resist a thousand of our enemies; when He shall make us a praise and a glory, that men shall say of succeeding plantations, "The Lord make it like that of New England."

Boston, beyond any other American town, helped to foment and support the American Revolution. The Puritan clergy created at Harvard the first and most famous American university. The descendants of the Puritans became the first and most lasting of American thinkers, from Emerson and Hawthorne to Justice Oliver Wendell Holmes and Edmund Wilson. Up to nearly the end of the nineteenth century, Boston as itself and as the center of New England understandably regarded itself as American literature. William Dean Howells, a literary pilgrim from Columbus, Ohio, was still in awe when he remembered meeting Dr. Oliver Wendell Holmes and James Russell Lowell in 1860:

Nothing else so richly satisfactory . . . as the whole affair could have happened to a like youth at such a point in his career; and when I sat down with Doctor Holmes and Mr. Fields, on Lowell's right, I felt through and through the dramatic perfection of the event. The kindly Autocrat recognized some such quality of it in terms which were not the less precious and gracious for their humorous excess . . . he leaned over towards his host, and said, with a laughing look at me, "Well, James, this is something like the apostolic succession; this is the laying on of hands."

The one great novelist to come out of New England in the nineteenth century, Nathaniel Hawthorne, described tiny Boston in *The Scarlet Letter* (1850) as a theocratic tyranny horribly at war with the freedoms for which the Puritans had come to New England. Hawthorne's novel, which he felt so deeply that he broke down reading it to his wife, took place in the seventeenth century. Boston, where H.L. Mencken was arrested in the 1920s for selling his iconoclastic magazine *The American Mercury* on the Common, seemed to many Americans to have remained in the seventeenth century. The Puritans had been America's most profound thinkers; "The Puritan" became a symbol of humorlessness and repression. Boston had pioneered the China trade and anesthesia, Harvard the professional study in America of Dante, Sanskrit, and what Professor William James called "the stream of consciousness." But it was a Massachusetts governor, a Harvard president and still another Harvard alumnus (both judge and social novelist) who finally put Sacco and Vanzetti in the electric chair. Writers like John Dos Passos, Edna St. Vincent Millay and Katherine Anne Porter, bitterly protesting the execution, felt that Sacco and Vanzetti were paying for the Boston elect's resentment of the Irish and Italian immigrants who seemed to be taking over Boston. One of the many writers arrested outside the Boston State House, John Dos Passos (Harvard, '16) wrote in *The Big Money* that the Sacco-Vanzetti case had radicalized him.

they have clubbed us off the streets   they are stronger   they are rich
they hire and fire the politicians the newspaper editors   the old judges   the
small men with reputations   the collegepresidents   the wardheelers (listen
businessmen collegepresidents judges America will not forget her betrayers) they
hire the men with guns   the uniforms the police cars the patrol-wagons

all right you have won   you will kill the brave men our friends tonight

America our nation has been beaten by strangers who have turned our language inside out who have taken the clean words our fathers spoke and made them slimy and foul

their hired men sit on the judge's bench they sit back with their feet on the tables under the dome of the State House   they are ignorant of our beliefs they have the dollars the guns the armed forces the powerplants

they have built the electricchair and hired the executioner to throw the switch

all right we are two nations

To satirize Boston became as much a tradition as Boston itself. T.S. Eliot's most famous early poem, "The Love Song of J. Alfred Prufrock," made immortal the contrast between the protagonist's timidity and the vapidity of culture. "In the room the women come and go/Talking of Michelangelo." The routine!

> For I have known them all already, known them all—
> Have known the evenings, mornings, afternoons,
> I have measured out my life with coffee spoons;
> I know the voices dying with a dying fall
> Beneath the music from a farther room,
>   So how should I presume?

Eliot's satires on Brahmins, Brahmin relatives, Beacon Hill—"Cousin Harriet," "Aunt Helen," "Cousin Nancy," "The Boston Evening Transcript"—like his sardonically sorrowful portrait of Prufrock, the ultimate Puritan driven to near-madness at the end—was a *Kulturkampf* against Boston-Cambridge that lies behind his joy in getting to England "away from the college bell." "Cambridge seems to me a dull nightmare now." After the war he explained from England, "I settled over here in the face of strong family opposition, on the claim that I found the environment more favorable to the production of literature."

There was a return of the oppressed in Eliot's early poems. *Preludes*, with its melancholy round-the-clock example of a sallow, joyless existence, had the great Eliot line, an effort to transcend this too, too ordinary life—"You had such a vision of the street as the street hardly understands." Equating Boston with repression had become a tradition even before Henry James's *The Bostonians* (1886), in which he reduced the most venerated personages of Back Bay to cranks and strident reformers. The plot centered around the struggle for an attractive but passive young woman, a sort of "medium," waged between the aggressively feminist, man-hating Olive Chancellor and the contemptuously reactionary ex-Confederate Basil Ransom. Henry James's parting shot at Boston was: "I don't even dislike it!"

To take Boston down was a habit. *The Education of Henry Adams*, portraying the most sacred citadels of ancestral power in New England, sourly contrasted rigid, cold-hearted Boston with the delightful countryside in Quincy.

> Resistance to something was the law of New England nature; the boy looked out on the world with the instinct of resistance; for numberless generations his predecessors had viewed the world chiefly as a thing to be reformed, filled with evil forces to be abolished, and they saw no reason to suppose that they had wholly succeeded in the abolition; the duty was unchanged. . . . The chief charm of New England was harshness of contrasts and extremes of sensibility,—a cold that froze the blood, and a heat that boiled it,—so that the pleasure of hating—oneself if no better victim offered,—was not its rarest amusement; . . . Winter and summer, cold and heat, town and country, force and freedom, marked two modes of life and thought, balanced like lobes of the brain.

The indictments never stopped—from Upton Sinclair's Sacco and Vanzetti novel, *Boston*, to Jean Stafford's *Boston Adventure*, John Marquand's *The Late George Apley* and the dry ironies in popular histories of the "elect" inevitably titled *The Proper Bostonians*.

The most brilliant of these books is George Santayana's *The Last Puritan* (1936), a parting shot indeed, delivered twenty-five years after the famous Spanish-born philosopher at Harvard had shaken off its respectability. Santayana's theme is central— the price Boston has always paid for being Boston. At a time when many Americans were irritated with the Yankee as a type, Santayana's satire brought to a boil this movement of feeling. *The Last Puritan* is so crowded with Santayana's asperities that the Aldens and Bumsteads can hardly be said to develop or change. His thesis is that such people never leave themselves room for development; in their own minds, destinies are fixed from birth. So we see them always rigid, always saying what is socially the right thing and humanly the impossible thing, buttering themselves with the petty moral restrictions of their class—strangers to their real natures and to general human nature. Where in the world, Santayana asks on every page, did people get such ridiculously inflated notions of their importance? How did they get so rigid, stiff, unhappy? Above all, why do they preposterously think so well of themselves when it has been so long since they led the nation in any important particular?

If in the seventeenth century Boston thought itself Jerusalem and in the nineteenth Athens, by the middle of the twentieth century it was really the last word in academia, technology, science. Route 128 circling Boston was a technological powerhouse. Boston's hospitals were as world-famous as the awesome scientific establishment overlooking the Charles at the Massachusetts Institute of Technology and at Harvard. Boston also had the worst race relations in the Northeast; for decades the federal courts grimly tried to desegregate Boston's schools, and just as grimly whole areas of the local population resisted "bussing" with a vehemence paralleled only by the mutual hatred of Protestant and Catholic in Northern Ireland.

It finally took a poet more traditionally Boston than contemporary Boston, Robert Lowell, to write the great poem in *For the Union Dead* (1964) that portrayed Boston's angry undoing of its Brahmin reputation. Long before the rise of John Fitzgerald Kennedy (born the same year as Robert Lowell, 1917) showed in the highest scales of American life that power was hardly the prerogative of "proper Bostonians," Robert Lowell proved that one historic family still had an important card to play. Lowell was descended from a Boston family supposedly so exclusive that his very name had become a symbol. In 1910 an Irish toastmaster at a Holy Cross College banquet in Worcester (definitely not part of Boston) raised his glass to intone these immortal lines:

> And this is good old Boston,
> The home of the bean and the cod,
> Where the Lowells talk to the Cabots,
> And the Cabots talk only to God.

In *For the Union Dead* Robert Lowell recalled that the first Black regiment in the Civil War was raised in Boston. Its colonel was the Boston patrician Robert Gould Shaw, who was eventually buried in the same ditch as his Black troops after they had fruitlessly attacked Fort Wagner in South Carolina. The march of Colonel Shaw and his men through Boston is commemorated by Augustus Saint-Gaudens's bas-relief at the entrance to Boston Common facing the State House.

Saint-Gaudens's memorial showing Colonel Robert Shaw leading black troops in the Civil War.
"Two months after marching through Boston/half the regiment was dead ..."Robert Lowell.

One morning last March,
I pressed against the new barbed and galvanized

fence on the Boston Common. Behind their cage,
yellow dinosaur steamshovels were grunting
as they cropped up tons of mush and grass
to gouge their underworld garage.

Parking spaces luxuriate like civic
sandpiles in the heart of Boston.
A girdle of orange, Puritan-pumpkin colored girders
braces the tingling Statehouse,

shaking over the excavations, as it faces Colonel Shaw
and his bell-cheeked Negro infantry
on St. Gaudens' shaking Civil War relief,
propped by a plank splint against the garage's earthquake.

Two months after marching through Boston,
half the regiment was dead;
at the dedication,
William James could almost hear the bronze Negroes breathe.

Their monument sticks like a fishbone
In the city's throat.

*   *   *

Chicago bewails its fate as "the second city," but in the eyes of its writers it is all energy and push, rude strength, more muscular than New York and proud that its traditions are those Chicago has made for itself. A New Yorker seeing Chicago for the first time at the Great Lakes Naval Training Station in 1943, when Chicago was turning out sailors as Detroit turned out tanks, was as excited by the city on the lake, the city of terrible winters and its indigenous American force, as another writer might have been by Paris. A wild energy poured in from Lake Michigan, from the sailors pummeling each other to keep warm, from the stiffly silent Black recruits. It all brought home the street corner savagery of the gangs in James T. Farrell's *Studs Lonigan*, the unleashed power of Black resentment in Richard Wright's *Native Son* and, most picturesquely, Carl Sandburg's poem "Chicago," as relevant then as it had been in 1916, for all the civic changes.

> Hog Butcher for the World,
> Tool Maker, Stacker of Wheat,
> Player with Railroads and the Nation's Freight Handler;
> Stormy, husky, brawling,
> City of the Big Shoulders: . . .
> Come and show me another city with lifted head singing so proud to be alive
>   and coarse and strong and cunning,
> Flinging magnetic curses amid the toil of piling job on job, here is a tall bold
>   slugger set vivid against the little soft cities . . .

Chicago stockyards, in the days when the raw capital of the Midwest was described by Carl Sandburg as "Hog Butcher for the World."

Chicago, 1893: the World Columbian Exposition celebrating the 500th anniversary of Columbus's landing in the New World. "The first astonishment became greater every day," wrote Henry Adams.

For the literature of the American *people* one went to Chicago writers and their early associations. Vachel Lindsay's "The Eagle that is Forgotten," his tribute to the brave Illinois governor whose career ended because he pardoned the imprisoned Haymarket Anarchists, ended in good populist style: "To live in mankind is far more than to live in a name." No one else had caught the raw poignance of Chicago creating itself out of the prairie as Theodore Dreiser did in *Sister Carrie* (1900), a first novel that its own publisher tried to kill but that set American realism on its brave new path of sexual honesty. Chicago, the center and king of the railroad age, was caught unforgettably in Scott Fitzgerald's *The Great Gatsby*. Students coming back West at Christmas time from prep school and college in the East "would gather in the old dim Union Street station at six o'clock of a December evening, with a few Chicago friends, already caught up into their own holiday gayeties, to bid them a hasty good-bye. . . . And last the murky yellow cars of the Chicago, Milwaukee & St. Paul railroad looking cheerful as Christmas itself on the tracks beside the gate." To be fond of Chicago literature was never to tire of the description of the 1893 "Columbian Exposition" in *The Education of Henry Adams*, of the newly rich in Thorstein Veblen's *The Theory of the Leisure Class* (1899) and Henry Blake Fuller's *With the Procession* (1893), of Chicago's Bohemia in stories by Hamlin Garland and Sherwood Anderson, of the immortal wisecracks about the unduly great delivered by

"Mr. Dooley" (Finley Peter Dunne) in his neighborhood saloon. And all this was before the rich naturalistic fiction of lower-class Chicago started in the 1930s by Richard Wright, James T. Farrell, Saul Bellow, Nelson Algren, Meyer Levin. The tone of *this* was described for all time by Nelson Algren. Living in Chicago "is like making love to a woman with a broken nose."

Chicago was not just the capital of the Midwest—it was *new*, and much of its literature described what it was like always to feel "new." Henry Blake Fuller, a delicate, over-sensitive upper-class Chicagoan, wrote in *With the Procession* that Chicago was America "materialized." The town

> labors under one disadvantage; it is the only great city in the world to which all its citizens have come for the one common, avowed object of making money. There you have its genesis, its growth, its end and object. . . . In this Garden City of ours every man cultivates his own little bed and his neighbor his; but who looks after the paths between?

Chicago was the first goal for Midwesterners to conquer. Theodore Dreiser left Terre Haute in Indiana for Chicago when he was sixteen. In his autobiography, *Dawn*, he remembered that to a boy just off the train, raw and muddy Chicago appeared "an Aladdin's view in the Arabian Nights. . . . Had I one gift to offer the world, it would be the delight of sensing the world as I then saw it."

Dreiser began as a reporter in the 1880s on the old Chicago *Globe*. As late as 1925, his best novel, *An American Tragedy*, invested Clyde Griffiths's childhood in Kansas City with details from Dreiser's early life in Chicago. Dreiser walking the streets of Chicago at the end of the century felt in his bones the stupendous fact of being a new man in a new city. He never got over the rawness of unfinished Chicago, the city trailing out into prairie. The earliest houses there occupied his imagination as "sentinels." "Sister Carrie" is eighteen in 1889—Dreiser's age— when she arrives in Chicago. In the innocence and awkwardness of his heroine, who will succeed without knowing why, who succeeds because she is a prize that her lover Hurstwood will die for, Dreiser caught the brazenness that Chicago writers were proud of.

Realism in America would have been nothing without Chicago; Chicago was nothing without realism. Henry James visited it in 1904 to read his lecture "The Lesson of Balzac." Balzac would certainly have found Chicago grist to his mill. James did not. A local reporter described James casting a weary eye on "the bleak parks, the jumbled stray masses of tenements and the engulfing avenues of warehouses and freight sheds." One day James was returning with the novelist and University of Chicago professor Robert Herrick from a luncheon on the far South Side by way of a suburban train, along the wintry shore of the lake. They travelled, says Leon Edel, "the smudged purlieus of the untidy city into the black gloom of the Loop." James sat huddled on the dingy bench of the railway car, draped in the loose folds of his mackintosh, his hands clasped about his baggy umbrella, his face haggard under the shuttling blows of the Chicago panorama. "What monstrous ugliness!" he murmured.

A better term for Chicago than "realism" was the "social question." Chicago was a gathering of all the forces pressing on the old rural America. The city, still jacking itself out of the mud cast by Lake Michigan on the low-lying streets, was jammed to suffocation with immigrants. Even their local Catholic churches were divided by countries of origin. 183

The Haymarket Affair of 1886, when four Anarchists were hanged because their propaganda had supposedly incited an unknown person to throw a bomb into the crowd, had already demonstrated the violence of class feeling. Then came the Panic of 1893, the Pullman Strike of 1894, President Cleveland's calling out the troops against the protests of Governor John Peter Altgeld.

Chicago was American battleground. Thanks to Jane Addams's Hull House and the rise of social investigation at the new University founded by John D. Rockefeller, Chicago also became a prime social specimen for novelists at the university like Robert Herrick, poets like William Vaughan Moody, liberals like Robert Morss Lovett, pioneer theoreticians like Thorstein Veblen, philosophers like George Herbert Mead and John Dewey.

The pioneer modern architect Louis Sullivan, allowed at the World's Fair in 1893 to show his stuff only in the Transportation Building, bitterly protested the domination of the Fair by the Beaux-Arts neo-classicists. Henry Adams laughed that "all trading cities had always shown traders' taste. . . . No art was thinner than Venetian Gothic. All traders' taste smelt of bric-a-brac; Chicago tried at least to give her taste a look of unity."

Sullivan's former draftsman Frank Lloyd Wright finally got his chance to build private homes in Chicago; Chicago's architecture, universities and flamboyant literary reporters were to impart famous energy to the twentieth-century scene. It was still a fact that Chicago writers were aggressively tough and sullen. One reason was the enduring hold of New York and even of Boston on the literary marketplace. Chicago has never been an easy city for book and magazine publishing. Harriet Monroe's *Poetry: A Magazine of Verse* (1912) symbolized the pre-war "Chicago Renaissance." It was actually quite timid; its European editor, Ezra Pound, complained that he had to bombard genteel Miss Monroe into accepting the new modern stuff by his friends H.D. and T.S. Eliot.

Chicago would never be altogether right for an *avant-garde*. Margaret Anderson started *The Little Review* there in 1914, but inevitably moved it to Paris. It died twenty-five years later after publishing stories and poems by all the twentieth-century masters first rejected by established magazines. Chicago relished the popularity of local bards like Carl Sandburg. Sandburg as the personification of brawling America became dear to high-school teachers otherwise afraid of modern poetry and to practically anyone else looking for a way to affirm the great twentieth-century energies centering on Chicago. For an ex-Wobbly and Socialist, Carl, as everyone in Chicago called him, was certainly a town booster. Robert Frost called him a fraud; Edmund Wilson complained that his biography of Lincoln was full of made-up stuff. Yet Sandburg knew better than Wilson what the Civil War was about. His biography of Lincoln is Sandburg's greatest poem. It is a collective myth to the people, yes, who recognized the war as one for their freedom. The book is a masterpiece because it weaves together thousands of American voices that finally establish Lincoln as the awaited hero of a common people.

Sandburg's poetry suffers from the glib emotions common to a swashbuckling Chicago newspaperman in the days when anyone with a byline was a prima donna who could get away with anything. *The Front Page*, the stage comedy by Ben Hecht and Charles MacArthur, preserves the tradition in Chicago newspaperdom of irresistible outrage. Sandburg himself became an artifact as truly American as the cigar-store Indian. What he supplied in addition to his personal minstrel act with guitar was populism, the radical democratic faith so expressive of the angry farmers and villagers of the early twentieth century. There was an almost visceral regional instinct for protest that would be strange indeed to Eliot, Pound, Stevens, and other masters of the international new style.

Chicago was a vast patchwork of immigrant groups, each retaining its national identity. It became a cliché that there were more Poles in Chicago than in Warsaw.

Still, the loyal traditionalism and severe intellectualism of the University of Chicago (even before President Robert Maynard Hutchins established the Great Books program in the 1930s), was an obvious turning away from the localism and wilful primitivism of Chicago bards. James T. Farrell managed to attend the University in defiance of the family faith; Saul Bellow came under its influence and remained to teach there. It is remarkable that portraitists of Chicago low life reflected a style that was fond of theory and sharply argumentative.

At the same time Chicago writers like Farrell seemed professionally tough, abrasive, militant. In all this harshness there was a Chicago self-advertising that impressed a New Yorker. Chicago writers—was this because they were always in New York?—put themselves forward, let their characters be grasped in the quickest way. They were blunt to a point. If New York, as Lyndon Johnson was to say about Miami, was to many Midwesterners "not an American city," why was Chicago, with its solid ethnic wards and ethnic divisions even in the Catholic Church, more "American?"

The answer was that Chicago was always visibly and raucously making itself; it was a concentrate that worked on writers like some abrasive chemical. Richard Wright's extraordinary *Native Son* (1940), about the murder of a white woman by a Black raised in the slums of Chicago, showed what triumphant art could be made out of a naturalistic tradition peculiarly Chicago's own. James T. Farrell's *Young Lonigan* (1932) was considered so scabrous that its publisher put it out as a clinical document in a special wrapper. Actually, Farrell's social-science approach to his own experience was exceptional. Farrell said he had been liberated by the University of Chicago's sociology department to put the city, the street, the gang, in a theoretical frame. At the same time he felt so buttressed by the racial intensity of his upbringing that he dismissed more elegant writers like Saul Bellow as "straw."

By contrast with Farrell, whose doggedness in repeating his early life story in dozens of volumes finally sank him—his mind was simply not interesting enough to feed an interminable personal history—Saul Bellow made his own exceptional intelligence and powers of observation the exciting center of novels from *Dangling Man* (1944) to *The Dean's December* (1982). Bellow's novels constitute another personal epic, divided between Chicago and New York. But what lifted Bellow from the gritty naturalism of Farrell, as it saved him from the tribalism of many other Jewish writers?

Bellow took himself seriously, he took his *mind* seriously, in a way that most novelists of the city streets never could. Admittedly, he was the hero of his books, their only hero, his own hero. But this central observer showed extraordinary powers as he dwelt on the physical world, the hardihood of people, the thickness of their skins, the strength in their hands, the force in their chests.

This was the Chicago note over and again: the world around us is pure grit but fascinating in the show it puts up. One of Bellow's best stories, "Looking for Mr. Green," recalls the time when the future Nobel Laureate was a welfare worker in Chicago. The story hangs on the central observer's inability to find a "Mr. Green" for whom he is holding a welfare check. Chicago in the depression was a particularly desolate place. Yet

> it wasn't desolation that this made you feel, but rather a faltering of organization that set free a huge energy, an escaped, unattached, unregulated power from the giant raw place. . . . People were compelled to match it. In their very bodies. He no less than others, he realized . . . his parents had been servants . . . they had never owed any service like this, which no one visible asked and probably flesh and blood could not even perform. Nor could anyone show that it should be performed; or see what the performance would lead to. That did not mean that he wanted to be released from it, he realized with a grimly pensive face. On the contrary. He had something to do. To be compelled to feel this energy and yet have nothing to do—that was horrible; that was suffering . . .

*   *   *

In 1877 the brilliant, sardonic and most artistically gifted of American historians, Henry Adams, resigned his Harvard professorship of history to take up residence in Washington just across Lafayette Park from the White House. "The fact is, I gravitate to a capital by a primary law of nature." "This is the only place in America where society amuses me, or where life offers variety." "Cambridge is a social desert that would starve a polar bear." Alone among the primary writers of his generation, Adams was interested in studying power as an *American* phenomenon. Even more oddly, he thought he could study it best in Washington.

Washington after the Civil War was trying, but not too hard, to show itself as the head and fount of a great nation. It was a Southern town on the marshes of the Potomac, long

Chicago's South Side near the end of the Depression. Chicago writers such as Farrell and Wright brought American readers disconcertingly close to poverty and violence.

accustomed to slavery, still capable of infecting visitors with malaria. It was so full of unfinished projects and memorials (the Capitol, the Washington Monument) that "the city of magnificent distances," as Prosper L'Enfant's plan of 1791 envisaged it, had been ridiculed by Dickens in the 1840s as "the city of magnificent intentions."

Still, Washington was a magnificent idea, like the founding of the United States itself. This was the first self-created government of a new nation, the first to create a capital exclusively for its seat of government. President Washington himself had selected the site, a compromise between Northern and Southern interests; it was at the President's request that the French-born architect L'Enfant submitted the plan that was not fully carried out until the end of the nineteenth century. L'Enfant himself was an early victim of political rivalries.

Washington in the last decades of the twentieth century looks so gracious and splendid—to be "monumental" was the dream—that it is touching to recall the raw beginnings. Two centuries before, the banks of Rock Creek were a rubbish dump. The city on the Potomac river was not to exceed ten miles square "at some place between the mouths of the Eastern Branch and the Comnogocheague." L'Enfant reported that "After much search for an eligible situation, I could discover no one so advantageously to greet the congressional building as that on the west end of Jenkins's hill, which stands as a pedestal waiting for a monument." L'Enfant even designated a square on a small hilltop overlooking the Potomac beyond the executive mansion as the site for a national university. The university was to be a particular dream of John Quincy Adams, the sixth president, but Congress never approved the plan.

John Quincy Adams was the son of the second president, John Adams. The Adamses had reason to think of American history as a family connection. John and Abigail Adams were the first presidential couple to occupy the White House. It was typical of the first Adamses and the simplicity of the early republic that Abigail was not ashamed to put the laundry up to dry in the East Room of the White House. When her great grandson Henry first saw Washington in 1850, President Zachary Taylor's horse "Old Whitey" was grazing in a paddock in front of the White House. "And inside, the President was receiving callers as simply as if he were in the paddock too."

Washington in 1850 was remembered in *The Education of Henry Adams* as a shock:

> . . . the sudden change that came over the world on entering a slave State. . . . The mere raggedness of outline could not have seemed wholly new . . . in truth, he had never seen a finished landscape; but Maryland was the raggedness of a new kind. The railway, about the size and character of a modern tram, rambled through unfenced fields and woods, or through village streets, among a haphazard variety of pigs, cows and negro babies. . . .
>
> Coming down in the early morning from his bed room in his grandmother's house— still called the Adams building—in F street, and venturing outside into the air reeking with the thick odor of the catalpa trees, he found himself on an earth-road, or village street, with wheel-tracks meandering from the colonnade of the Treasury hard by, to the white marble columns and fronts of the Post Office and Patent Office which faced each other in the distance, like white Greek temples in the abandoned gravel-pits of a deserted Syrian city. Here and there low wooden houses were scattered along the streets, as in other Southern villages, but he was chiefly attracted by an unfinished square marble shaft, half a mile below, and he walked down to inspect it before

Washington; an imaginative rendering of the Capitol in an 1852 lithograph.

breakfast. His aunt drily remarked that at this rate, he would soon get through all the sights; but she could not guess—having lived always in Washington,—how little the sights of Washington had to do with its interest.

The unfinished square marble shaft was to hold the great spire of the Washington Monument, not completed until 1884. Even the "wings" of the Capitol were not in place until 1859. In the 1980s the sights of Washington have much to do with its interest for the "mere spectator." Henry Adams was remarkably prescient in this as in everything else when he chose to live in Washington between 1877 and 1918, just across from the White House. Within the ragged and indolent Washington of 1850 lay the future. And the future represented power, a concentration of national forces that at last represented the unity of history Adams would always be looking for. He called it "the height of knowledge."

The idea that any *city*, even a nation's capital, could embody the apex of understanding would have astonished the eighteenth-century founders of the American Republic. Nothing was so natural to them as fear of the city. "The mobs of great cities," Thomas Jefferson had written, "add just so much to the support of pure government, as sores do to the strength of the human body." "Virtue" was what Jefferson, the cultivated aristocrat on his country estate at Monticello, had sought for America. This cut out the swarms and mobs that disturbed him in London and Paris. Only a leading American sage even in the nineteenth century, Ralph Waldo Emerson, could have written, "Alone is wisdom, Alone is happiness." Emerson's fellow idealists irritated him when they met at a hotel to lay plans for Utopia-to-be, Brook Farm. "To join this body would be to traverse all my long trumpeted theory, and the instinct which spoke from it, that one man is a counterpoise to a city—that a man is stronger than a city, that his solitude is more prevalent and beneficent than the concert of crowds."

Henry Adams acidly described the Washington scene for almost half a century from the splendid house built for him by his gifted classmate Henry Hobson Richardson. From his windows he could see Andrew Jackson on his prancing horse in the park. Presidents real and in effigy (he would also supply the effigy) were his special delight. He did not abhor mobs and swarms; he ignored them. His interest was in power at the top *trying* to control the tides of history; history was ironic. Hence the double vision that went into Adams's *History of the United States during the Administrations of Thomas Jefferson and James Madison* (1889–91), his novel *Democracy* (1880), and the great *Education* (privately published 1907). Although Adams tried to be a "scientific" historian, measuring the social and economic forces that mold society, his literary interest was in the establishment, the leaders, even when they came out as figureheads.

For Adams, Washington was the inside track of those in the know, in command. His best friend was John Hay, once Lincoln's private secretary, who became Secretary of State. Adams's circle was so famous for its exclusiveness that their friend Henry James satirized them in a story, "Pandora"—"Hang it all, the season's almost over. Let's be democratic and invite the President." Adams saw no one but the leaders, but he could not respect them. He described a White House reception in *Democracy*:

Madeline found herself before two seemingly mechanical figures, which might be wood or wax, for any sign they showed of life. These set figures were the President and his wife; they stood stiff and awkward by the door, both their faces stripped of every sign of intelligence, while the right hands of both extended themselves to the column

191

of visitors with the mechanical action of toy dolls. . . . To the President and his wife this was clearly no laughing matter. There they stood, automata, representatives of the society which streamed past them. . . . What a strange and solemn spectacle it was. . . . She felt a sudden conviction that this was to be the end of American society; its realization and its dream at once. She groaned in spirit.

Madeline Lee, a pretty young widow, weary of New York, comes down to Washington to find a new interest in life: the workings of American government. A leading political figure, Senator Silas P. Ratcliffe from Illinois, the "Prairie Giant," falls in love with her, as does an ex-Confederate lawyer, John Carrington, in Washington to restore his family fortunes ruined by the war. Her sister, baffled by Madeline's interest in Washington politics, asks derisively, "Haven't you got to the heart of the great American mystery yet?" She is alarmed that Madeline may accept the excessively ambitious and crafty Ratcliffe, who dominates the clumsy "Western farmer" in the White House. Ratcliffe plans, with Madeline as his consort, to become president. Fortunately, his corrupt record is betrayed to Madeline by his rival Carrington. In bitterness Madeline turns her back on Washington.

Madeline Lee is one of the many heroines who dominate Henry Adams's writings as symbols of purity, intelligence—and vulnerability. Adams was the Saint-Simon, the Proust, the avid chronicler, of Washington society. Women hardly dominated the world of political Washington then or later. But Adams believed (as did Henry James) that because American men were entirely absorbed in business or politics, their women were unsoiled by the greed for power and were more attractive human beings.

Alice Roosevelt Longworth, Theodore Roosevelt's daughter, spanned the Washington scene from T.R. to Ronald Reagan. Late in life she described Washington as "a small, cozy town, global in scope. It suits me." Such superior raillery was unknown to New York, Boston, Chicago. In Los Angeles it would not have been understood at all. Mrs. Longworth understood, as did Henry Adams, that the romance of Washington was the show it put on. In a way totally unlike the development of other American power centers, Washington *looked* consistent, all of a piece along its white Roman fronts. It was what the founders had hoped for, perhaps the only thing that the wildly heterogeneous America of the late twentieth century could look up to—a *center*.

Behind the marble columns and the extraordinary museums that late Washington provided on a scale inconceivable even during the New Deal (the rumor then was that the capital had returned from Wall Street to Washington), the business of Washington was compromise, the deal. Everyone in the halls of Congress was involved with everyone else in Washington—lawyers, columnists, bureaucrats. There was not much fine literature about Washington, but there was certainly a lot of information, much in the form of confidential "leaks" from governmental big shots to newspapermen. Washington was the inside story.

Yet in a fashion entirely appropriate to contemporary Washington—Lyndon Johnson once described himself to a reporter as "the head of the free world"—Washington was certainly a splendid show. The show was everywhere, from Abraham Lincoln brooding in his memorial to the crowds that haunted the Vietnam Memorial at night, under dim lamps, to search out some of the almost 60,000 names inscribed there. Washington more than other cities was statuary and memorials. Out in Rock Creek Cemetery was Augustus Saint-Gaudens's famous hooded figure, a memorial to Henry Adams's wife Marian.

Washington, D.C. The memorial to President Washington on "The Mall." When Henry Adams saw it in 1850 it was still an "unfinished square marble shaft."

Augustus Saint-Gaudens's memorial to Mrs. Henry Adams in Rock Creek Cemetery, Washington, D.C.

People came from all over the world to look at it. For so intensely private a man who not once directly mentioned his wife in his "autobiography," the *Education,* Henry Adams had certainly created one of Washington's great tourist attractions. John Galsworthy called it the most beautiful thing in the United States. Adams himself liked to sit on the magnificent bench he had had Stanford White design, listening with some amusement to the comments of many visitors.

That, too, was Washington, a place so public that it represented an idea more than it did the people walking its streets. A President of the United States had reason to believe that the very sight of him held together the most diverse population imaginable. On December 12, 1985, Ronald Reagan, returning from his summit meeting in Geneva with Soviet leader Gorbachov, went straight from the airfield to the halls of Congress. He went there in a helicopter that was bathed in light as it swooped down upon what Major L'Enfant in his plan for the capital had known as "Jenkins's Hill." The millions of television viewers watching the presidential helicopter bearing its important passenger down to earth might well have associated the sight with something out of classical mythology, Zeus alighting. In any event, it was a scene entirely suitable. Other cities represented money, energy, push. Washington alone had a touch of the transcendent.

CHAPTER SIX

TO CALIFORNIA AND BEYOND: THE ROVING AMERICAN

In the summer of 1834 a Harvard student, whose eyes were suffering after an attack of measles, worked his way back to health by shipping out to California as a common sailor. Richard Henry Dana was a Boston patrician, son of a notable literary figure, grandson of a leading Revolutionary War patriot. He was not overcome, in the hundred and fifty days it took *The Pilgrim* to reach Santa Barbara by way of Cape Horn, by "The change from the tight frock-coat, silk cap, and kid gloves of an undergraduate at Harvard, to the loose duck trousers, checked shirt and tarpaulin hat of a sailor." Incessant labor and the many dangers he faced left little room for introspection. Dana's capacity for objective fact was to make him a famous lawyer. It first showed itself in the unpretentiously direct, precise and vivid account of life at sea and in early California, *Two Years before the Mast* (1840), which was recognized instantly as a classic of its kind. "A voice from the forecastle" had hardly been heard before.

Dana's calm, always considered, record of the excruciating labor and physical hardships that were regularly experienced on a sailing ship is like nothing else in American sailor literature. "In no state prison are the convicts more regularly set to work and more closely watched." We share Dana's outrage at the maddening tyranny of the captain, "the tendency to make the most of inequalities, natural or artificial," the humiliating silence enforced between sailors at work, the mingled exultation and panic of having to climb the foremast during the usual storm while rounding Cape Horn, the desolating monotony of salt beef and salt pork every day for half a year. Dana was always the observer, on land and at sea. We owe to his remarkable book images of Mexican California a decade before Americans took over, images prior to the frontier days.

California after the 1849 gold rush symbolized the destination and prize of American history. Emerson, visiting after the Civil War, called California America's garden. Whitman felt that everything was going in the direction of California. Dana was less excited about the place. Americans, he found, were in Mexican California just to collect hides for the home market. After all the labor and vexations of life at sea—"tarring, greasing, oiling, varnishing, painting, scraping, scrubbing, watching at night, steering, reefing, furling, bracing, making and sorting sail, pulling, hauling, climbing in every direction"—Dana found himself dragging rough heavy skins of slaughtered cattle up the hill lining the beach. Then, after flinging them down, the men had to press hides into the hold so tightly that some 40,000 could be delivered at Boston.

Behind the beach at Santa Barbara was the mission built by Spanish friars. The town lay "on a low plain, but a little above the level of the sea, covered with grass, though entirely without trees, and surrounded on three sides by an amphitheatre of mountains,

195

THE
CALIFORNIA
INDIANS.

LEFT: *California Indians, pictured in their "quaint" customs after they had come under American control.*

CATCHING GRASSHOPPERS

OPPOSITE, ABOVE: *Mission at Santa Barbara, California coast. The Harvard-educated Richard Henry Dana disapproved of Mexican Catholicism, which was too relaxed for his Puritan soul.*

OPPOSITE, BELOW: *San Joaquin County, California, before irrigation. Frank Norris was to plan a trilogy of novels based on the San Joaquin Valley, which became one of the most productive farm areas in history.*

which slant off to a distance of fifteen or twenty miles." The houses were all made of adobe, constructed in bricks of desert-dried clay and straw; the hills had no large trees, "they having all been burnt by a great fire which swept through everything in sight." Great fires are recurrent and devastating in Southern California to this day.

The primitive bareness of Mexican California sometimes intimidated Dana. "Here we were, in a little vessel, with a small crew, on a half-civilized coast, at the ends of the earth, and with a prospect of remaining an indefinite period, two or three years at the least. . . . We were in the remote parts of the earth, on an almost desert coast, in a country where there is neither law nor gospel, and where sailors are at their captain's mercy." At the same time he had a heady sense of adventure whenever he could get away from dragging and carrying hides. *The Pilgrim* moved between Santa Barbara, San Pedro, San Diego. Thirty miles from San Diego was the Pueblo de Los Angeles, the largest settlement in California, and several of the wealthiest missions. Horses abounded—"the cheapest thing in California; very fair ones not being worth more than ten dollars apiece. . . . In taking a day's ride you pay for the use of the saddle, and for the labour and trouble of catching the horses. If you bring the saddle back, they care but little what becomes of the horse."

Life along the coast was hard but there was the rapture of a new country. Dana thought little of the local Indians, found their language brutish, a mere "slabber." Cock fighting was scary but a thrill, as was the horse-racing on Easter Sunday. Dana disapproved of Mexican Catholicism, which abounded in church holidays: "Yankees can't afford the time." But in Spring the harbor at San Pedro was filled with whales, as were all other open ports upon the coast. The whales

Santa Barbara Mission.
from the hill —
(Island of Santa Cruz in the distance 26 miles)

had come in to make their annual visit upon soundings. For the first few days that we were here and at Santa Barbara we watched them with great interest, calling out "There she blows!" every time we saw the spout of one breaking the surface of the water; but they soon became so common that we took little notice of them. They often "broke" very near us, and one thick, foggy night, during a dead calm, while I was standing anchor-watch, one of them rose so near that he struck our cable, and made all surge again.

San Juan in those days was

the only romantic spot on the coast. The country here for several miles is a high table-land, running boldly to the shore, and breaking in a steep cliff, at the foot of which the waters of the Pacific are constantly dashing. For several miles the water washes the very base of the hill, or breaks upon ledges and fragments of rock which run out into the sea. Just where we landed was a small cove, or bight, which gave us, at high tide, a few square feet of sand-beach between the sea and the bottom of the hill. This was the only landing-place. Directly before us rose the perpendicular height of four or five hundred feet. How we were to get hides down, or goods up, upon the table-land on which the mission was situated, was more than we could tell. . . . we strolled about, picking up shells, and following the sea where it tumbled in, roaring and spouting,

Cypress Point at Monterey, California. The peninsula, a retreat for artists and writers, formed the background for Steinbeck's early novels.

The California coast, described by Richard Henry Dana in the 1840s.

Carmel, California; the old whaling station. Robinson Jeffers was to move to Carmel during the First World War and celebrate its isolated, rocky coast.

The embryonic site of San Francisco in 1847, a view from the hills overlooking the bay. The following year gold was discovered in California.

among the crevices of the great rocks. What a sight, thought I, this must be in a south-easter! The rocks were as large as those of Nahant or Newport, but to my eye, more grand and broken. Besides, there was a grandeur in everything around, which gave a solemnity to the scene, a silence and solitariness which affected every part! Not a human being but ourselves for miles, and no sound heard but the pulsations of the great Pacific! and the great steep hill rising like a wall, and cutting us off from all the world but the "world of waters"!

As a good Yankee Dana was scornful of California in Mexican hands, called its *administradores* "strangers sent from Mexico, having no interest in the country, not identified in any way with their charge and for the most part, men of desperate fortunes—broken down politicians and soldiers—whose only object is to retrieve their condition in as short a time as possible." Describing an encounter between Mexicans and Americans, he notes as a matter of course that "forty Kentucky hunters, with their rifles, and a dozen of Yankees and Englishmen, were a match for a whole regiment of hungry, drawling, lazy half-breeds."

Such are the people who inhabit a country embracing four or five hundred miles of sea-coast, with several good harbours, with fine forests in the north; the waters filled

200

Panning Gold (*William McIlvaina, 1813–67, detail*): *a picturesque convention applied to an activity that was usually the reverse of picturesque.*

with fish, and the plains covered with thousands of herds of cattle; blessed with a climate, than which there can be no better in the world; free from all manner of diseases, whether epidemic or endemic; and with a soil in which corn yields from seventy to eighty-fold. In the hands of an enterprising people, what a country this might be! We are ready today. Yet how long would such a people remain so, in such a country? The Americans (as those from the United States are called) and Englishmen, who are fast filling up the principal towns, and getting the trade into their hands, are indeed more industrious and effective than the Mexicans; yet their children are brought up Mexicans in most respects, and if the "California fever" (laziness) spares the first generation, it is likely to attack the second.

Dana need not have worried about "California fever." Returning to California in a steamship just before the Civil War, he was startled by modern, bustling San Francisco. He recalled the

remote and almost unknown coast of California . . . the vast solitude of the bay of San Francisco. All around the stillness of nature . . . on the whole coast of California there was not a lighthouse, a beacon, or a buoy. Birds of prey and passage swooped and dived about us, wild beasts ranged through the oak groves, and as we slowly floated out of the harbor with the tide, herds of deer came to the water's edge, on the northerly side of the entrance, to gaze at the strange spectacle.

San Francisco had become "the sole emporium of a new world, the awakened Pacific." With the discovery of gold in 1848, California had indeed become the promised land. The "Forty-Niners," the prospectors, were called Argonauts. They were drawn to the finds of gold in California stream beds as Jason and his Argonauts were drawn by the glittering fleece. And of course California was the land of the sun. Even before the gold rush the entrance to San Francisco Bay had been named the "Golden Gate" by the explorer John C. Fremont after the "gate" and "horn" identified with Constantinople. The gold fever became positively patriotic when President Polk made an official announcement of the gold strike at the end of 1848 and displayed 230 ounces of California gold.

The "Forty-Niners" came from Oregon, the Sandwich Islands, Mexico, South America, Europe. The greatest influx was from the United States. Sailors deserted and passengers decamped as soon as ships from all over the world arrived in San Francisco. Three main routes were open to the California-bound: down the Atlantic, across the Isthmus of Panama (or Nicaragua) and up the Pacific: by ship around Cape Horn; across the plains, the Rockies, the Sierras by the overland California trail. This followed the earlier Oregon Trail, beginning at the Missouri River, and moved across Kansas and Wyoming to South Pass. The "mother lode" was supposed to be a hundred and twenty miles long, a single vein of quartz from which most of the gold came. The search for rich spots along the river beds led to mining camps called Fiddletown, French Camp, Greenhorn Bar, Humbug Hill, Sixbit Gulch, Whiskey Flat. Enormous fortunes were made by such characters as George Hearst, the father of William Randolph Hearst. In 1850 he walked across the continent from Missouri to prospect in California without much success. Then he struck it rich in Nevada, as did the Irish immigrant John W. Mackay, founder of the international telegraph system. Gold dust was a regular circulating medium in the cities as well as in the mining districts.

MAP OF SAN-FRANCISCO. CALIFORNIA.

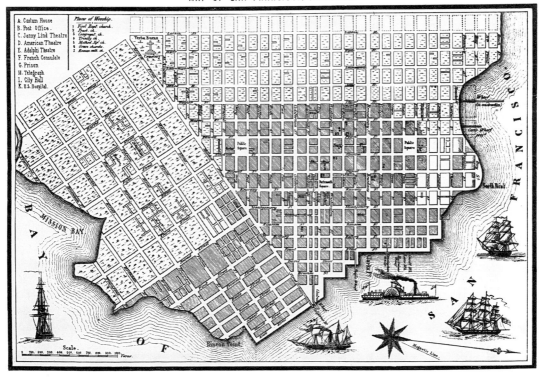

TOP: *San Francisco, California, a general view in 1856;* BOTTOM, *a nineteenth-century map.*

The gold rush was virtually over by the 1860s, but the deserted camps made the literary fortune of Bret Harte in highly picturesque "Western" stories for the *Atlantic Monthly* back in Boston and appealingly sentimental stories, such as "The Luck of Roaring Camp," for his own *Overland Monthly*. Mark Twain captured a literary audience in the East with "The Celebrated Jumping Frog of Calaveras County." In a drawling tone and affectedly "plain" style, the story told of the jumping frog Dan'l Webster, pet of the gambler Jim Smiley, which is defeated in a jumping contest when a stranger slyly packs its gullet with quail shot. The story became so "celebrated" that Mark Twain wrote a "Private History of the 'Jumping Frog Story'" in which he explained that, although the story had been written in English, it had to be translated back into English— "Clawed Back into a Civilized Language Once More by Patient, Unremunerated Toil."

All this was part of the California myth, necessary to the end of the continent. Americans, it was agreed by all hands, rode on space; space was peculiarly their medium. California was the gateway to new conquests; the Pacific would be next. In 1851 appeared the greatest epic of the American obsession with space, *Moby-Dick*. Of all American writers influenced by the "wild world" opened to Americans by every circumstance of exploration and settlement, Melville was the most marked. He had a particular genius for seizing on the most alien, "far-out," landscapes and translating them into his extreme sense of things. Melville as artist vibrantly lived up to a favorite admonition from the great explorer-scientist Von Humboldt: "A book on nature should elicit the same feelings we get from nature herself." No one else in American writing came so close to this as Melville: "extraordinary works of man . . . affect the imagination like the works of Nature." Melville as a young sailor in the Pacific between 1841 and 1844 never saw California, but writing up his adventures in *Typee, Omoo, Mardi, White-Jacket, Moby-Dick* and the great stories "The Encantadas" and "Benito Cereno," he evoked the endless wonder and seeming infiniteness of the world's largest ocean, a third of the globe. There was no one like Melville for making a part of the reader's own life a casual visit to the end of the earth. In "The Encantadas" he recalled his first view of the primal scene in the Galápagos, six hundred miles off the Ecuador coast—

> . . . to them change never comes; neither the change of seasons nor of sorrows. Cut by the Equator, they know not autumn and they know not spring; while already reduced to the lees of fire, ruin itself can work little more upon them. . . . in these isles, rain never falls. Like split Syrian gourds left withering in the sun, they are cracked by an everlasting drought beneath a torrid sky. . . .
>
> In many places the coast is rock-bound, or more properly, clinker-bound; tumbled masses of blackish or greenish stuff like the dross of an iron-furnace, forming dark clefts and caves here and there, into which a ceaseless sea pours a fury of foam; overhanging them with a swirl of gray, haggard mist, amidst which sail screaming flights of unearthly birds heightening the dismal din. However calm the sea without, there is no rest for these swells and those rocks; they lash and are lashed, even when the outer ocean is most at peace with itself. . . .

He then described the Galápagos tortoises:

> I looked down over the ship's high side as if looking down over the curb of a well, and dimly saw the damp boat deep in the sea with some unwonted weight. Ropes were dropt over, and presently three huge antediluvian-looking tortoises after much straining were landed on deck. They seemed hardly of the sea of earth. . . . behold these really wondrous tortoises—none of your schoolboy mud-turtles—but black as widowers' weeds, heavy as chests of plate, with vast shells medallioned and orbed like shields, and dented and blistered like shields, that have breasted a battle, shaggy too, here and there, with dark green moss, and slimy with the spray of the sea. These mystic creatures suddenly translated by night from unutterable solitudes to our peopled deck, affected me in a manner not easy to unfold. They seemed newly crawled forth from beneath the foundations of the world.

The Pacific carried profound intimations for Melville. Captain Ahab in *Moby-Dick* destroys his crew, ship and himself in his maddened struggle with the great whale. But the final confrontation takes place in the "great trench" of the Pacific, supposed to mark the greatest ocean depth on the globe. There is a legend that the moon was pulled into the heavens out of the earth, creating the void filled with the Pacific Ocean. Mythology, the lore of the most ancient of worlds, is never far from America as the newest of worlds. In Chapter 111 of *Moby-Dick* Melville unites all that is most meditative and lyrical in the book into a replication of the ocean's very rhythms.

> When gliding by the Bashee isles we emerged at last upon the great South Sea; were it not for other things, I could have greeted my dear Pacific with uncounted thanks, for

now the long supplication of my youth was answered; that serene ocean rolled eastwards from me a thousand leagues of blue.

There is, one knows not what sweet mystery about this sea, whose gently awful stirrings seem to speak of some hidden soul beneath; like those fabled undulations of the Ephesian sod over the buried Evangelist St. John. And meet it is, that over these sea-pastures, wide-rolling watery prairies and Potters' Fields of all four continents, the waves should rise and fall, and ebb and flow unceasingly; for here, millions of mixed shades and shadows, drowned dreams, somnambulisms, reveries; all that we call lives and souls, lie dreaming, dreaming, still; tossing like slumberers in their beds; the ever-rolling waves but made so by their restlessness.

To any meditative Magian rover, this serene Pacific, once beheld, must ever after be the sea of his adoption. It rolls the midmost waters of the world, the Indian ocean and Atlantic being but its arms. The same waves wash the moles of the new-built California towns, but yesterday planted by the recentest race of men, and lave the faded but still gorgeous skirts of Asiatic lands, older than Abraham; while all between float milky-ways of coral isles, and low-lying, endless, unknown Archipelagoes, and impenetrable Japans.

Melville first saw the Pacific from the New Bedford whaler *Acushnet* in 1841. In July 1842 he deserted at Nuku Hiva in the Marquesas, lived for a month in the valley of the Typees (in his book he made it four months), escaped to a decrepit Australian whaler, was briefly jailed at Tahiti as a mutineer, escaped to Hawaii, worked at odd jobs in Honolulu before enlisting in the U.S. Navy to return to Boston in 1844. Melville's extraordinary initiation, his epochal voyage of almost four years, never left his mind. In book after book, even in his posthumous masterpiece *Billy Budd*, Melville wrote *the* imaginative history of his countrymen's ever more frenzied wandering and their confrontation with the elemental in Nature, the primitive in society, the violence of the human heart.

The "happy valley" Melville described in *Typee* (1846) with both rapture and fear is in the South Seas. But with its gorges, nearly impenetrable jungles, wild beaches and (for all their hospitality) unpredictable savages, it is Nature as the American saw it—all too raw, spellbinding, delusive and terrible, fundamentally the frontier as the great "unknown." Melville said he was just having a "peep" at island life in Polynesia. As an admirer (up to a point) of the natives in their natural state, he was scornful of the French impersonating imperial power and the Anglo-Saxon missionaries playing God. Melville called the "white civilized man . . . the most ferocious animal on the face of the earth." But in the idyllic descriptions of scenes that Melville, just before Gauguin, was among the first white men to picture, we see ourselves, as Columbus did watching the Orinoco drop its awesome force into the Atlantic, back to the morning of creation, back to the innocent world rising out of the sea.

In *Typee* Melville is carried on a native's back to a stream where his mysteriously wounded leg may be healed. There he sees a woman

sitting upon a rock in the midst of the current, and watching with the liveliest interest the gambols of something, which at first I took to be an uncommonly large species of frog that was sporting in the water near her. . . . I could hardly credit the evidence of my senses when I beheld a little infant, the period of whose birth could not have extended back many days, paddling about as if it had just risen to the surface, after

Yosemite Valley (*Thomas Hill, 1876, detail*).

being hatched into existence at the bottom. Occasionally the delighted parent reached out her hands toward it, when the little thing, uttering a faint cry, and striking out its tiny limbs, would sidle for the rock, and at the next moment be clasped to its mother's bosom. This was repeated again and again, the baby remaining in the stream about a minute at a time. . . .

Unlike his countrymen at war with the Indians, Melville came to the firm conclusion that it was "better for what we call the barbarous part of the world to remain unchanged." Before he was done, Melville was to incorporate into his work everything he had ever seen, from those islands that seem lost in the Pacific like the stars in the Milky Way, to the Pyramids and the view of Jerusalem, stony and broken, from the graves atop the Mount of Olives. Melville certainly covered the world, as only an American wanderer could. And in the end all these "versions of pastoral" were the versions not only of his own hungrily encompassing mind, but of an America forever discovering that it was half-savage.

Henry Adams's passing observation that he had never seen a finished landscape in America would have been a point of pride in California. California as the promised land, the ultimate experience for many Americans, was defiantly unfinished in the writing of Californians from Frank Norris in *The Octopus* to John Steinbeck in *The Grapes of Wrath*. The extraordinary physicality of California, this "country of the new," made for a classic cycle of temptation and disillusionment. The climate was usually benign; its main features, as the old handbooks said in some wonder, were few and bold. There was a mountain fringe along the ocean, another mountain system along the east border. Between them, closed in at both ends by their junction, was a splendid valley of imperial extent. Outside all this, a great area of barren, arid lands. Mark Twain in *Roughing It*, describing his delight at Lake Tahoe, could not get over the way the lake burst into sight after weary mountain climbs—"a noble sheet of blue water lifted six thousand three hundred feet above the level of the sea, and walled in by a rim of snow-clad mountain peaks that towered aloft full three thousand feet higher!"

Observers fresh in from the Nevada desert were sure that the Sierra Nevada was the finest mountain system in the country. Then the overpowering redwoods in the north, Mount Whitney, the highest summit of the "lower 48," the rough country where the coastal ranges and Sierras unite, the eastern half of this country covered chiefly with volcanic plains, very dry and barren, the western half magnificently timbered. California had the highest and lowest land in the United States: Death Valley far below sea level, yet the mountains about it high and bare and brilliant with varied colors. Early on, there were points in Southern California where one could actually look from sea to desert and from snow to orange groves. In the Bay area near San Francisco, the vast fields, meadows, groves owned by Leland Stanford and donated to the university he established in memory of his son still astonish us by their range and beauty. In the country of the greatest atom smashers, here, still, is the pastoral California that existed until 1848, the Mexican war, the gold rush. And ever since the Franciscans introduced vines from Spain in 1771, California proved positively Mediterranean; an early census report boasted that "The state has such a variety of soil, slope, elevation, temperature and climatic conditions as to reproduce, somewhere within its borders, any wine now manufactured."

The extraordinary beauty of Yosemite, on the western slope of the Sierra Nevada, only seven miles long and in many places only half a mile wide, came under the protection of the Federal government thanks to the Scottish immigrant John Muir. California drove

Much of the vast Southwest still remains open and desolate, as this contemporary photograph of Arizona shows.

LAKE TAHOE (or BIGLER)
Van Wagener's Hotel, and Fishery, at the South Shore of the Lake. (Aug. 30, 1861.)

Lake Tahoe, 1861. Mark Twain in Roughing It *was delighted by the lake's sudden appearance after long mountain climbs.*

Muir to ecstasy. It made him a useful field scientist, while allowing him to remain a pilgrim who had no trouble finding God in Nature. *The Mountains of California* (1894), his first and best book, is a classic in the literary discovery of California. Muir was to become famous for "walking a thousand miles to the Gulf" and for taking the high and mighty personages of his time camping at his favorite places. But on California he excelled himself because *here* was the world of wonders he constantly prayed to see. Everything in the very approach to Yosemite showed "the hand of the creator."

> All my first day was pure pleasure; simply mountaineering indulgence, crossing the dry pathways of the ancient glaciers, tracing happy streams, and learning the habits of the birds and marmots in the groves and rocks. Before I had gone a mile from the camp, I came to the foot of a white cascade that beats its way down a rugged gorge in the cannon wall, from a height of about nine hundred feet, and pours its throbbing waters into the Tuolumne. I was acquainted with its fountains, which, fortunately, lay in my course. What a fine traveling companion it proved to be, what songs it sang, and how passionately it told the mountain's own joy. . . .
>
> Climbing higher, higher, new beauty came on the sight: painted meadows, late blooming gardens, peaks of rare architecture, lakes here and there, shining like silver, and glimpses of the forested middle region and the yellow lowlands far in the west. Beyond the range I saw the so-called Mono desert, lying dreamily silent in thick purple light—a desert of heavy sun-glare beheld from a desert of ice-burnished granite. Here the waters divide, shouting in glorious enthusiasm, and falling eastward

to vanish in the volcanic sands and dry sky of the Great Basin, or westward in the Great Valley of California, and thence through the Bay of San Francisco and the Golden Gate to the sea.

The abundance California produced in "the era of wheat" inspired Frank Norris to plan a trilogy based on the San Joaquin Valley. The first volume was *The Octopus* (1901), which deals with the struggle over land prices and freight rates between the valley's "land-farmers" and the all-powerful Southern Pacific Railroad. Like all major railroads in the era of expansion, the Southern Pacific had been given enormous tracts of land on both sides of its tracks. With his exact contemporaries Theodore Dreiser and Stephen Crane, Norris saw the social enmities of America in the 1890s as a reflection of the all-pervading struggle for existence.

But Norris was a Californian excited by the natural opulence of his surroundings. Jack London had seen cosmic cruelty in the contrast between the beauty of the San Francisco Bay area and the deprivations of working men. Norris, like John Steinbeck after him, was a native bewitched; there was some pagan sexuality in the struggle between man and "the mystical, unassailable, eternal power of the wheat-giving earth." The planting scene in *The Octopus* can remind us of the gusty emotions evoked by rural scenes in Thomas Hardy and D.H. Lawrence:

The day was fine. Since the first rain of the season, there had been no other. Now the sky was without a cloud, pale blue, delicate, luminous, scintillating with morning. The great brown earth turned a huge flank to it, exhaling the moisture of the early dew. The atmosphere, washed clean of dust and mist, was translucent as crystal. Far off to the east, the hills on the other side of Broderson Creek stood out against the pallid saffron of the horizon as flat and as sharply outlined as if pasted on the sky. . . . All about between the horizons, the carpet of the land unrolled itself to infinity. But now it was no longer parched with heat, cracked and warped by a merciless sun, powdered with dust. The rain had done its work; not a clod that was not swollen with fertility, not a fissure that did not exhale the sense of fecundity. One could not take a dozen steps upon the ranches without the brusque sensation that underfoot the land was alive; aroused at last from its sleep. . . .

The ploughing, now in full swing, enveloped Vanamee in a vague, slow-moving whirl of things. Underneath him was the jarring, jolting, trembling machine; not a clod was turned, not an obstacle encountered, that he did not receive the swift impression of it through all his body, the very friction of the damp soil, sliding incessantly from the shiny surface of the shears, seemed to reproduce itself in his finger-tips and along the back of his head. He heard the horsehoofs by the myriads crushing down easily, deeply, into the loam, the prolonged clinking of trace-chains, the working of the smooth brown flanks in the harness, the clatter of wooden hames, the champing of bits, the click of iron shoes against pebbles, the brittle stubble of the surface ground crackling and snapping as the furrows turned, the sonorous, steady breaths wrenched from the deep, labouring chests, strap-bound, shining with sweat, and all along the line the voices of the men talking to the horses. Everywhere there were visions of glossy brown backs, straining, heaving, swollen with muscle; harness streaked with specks of froth, broad, cup-shaped hoofs, heavy with brown loam . . .—

and stronger and more penetrating than everything else, the heavy, enervating odor of the upturned, living earth.

Almost forty years later, John Steinbeck's most famous novel, *The Grapes of Wrath* (1939), stamped on American minds an unforgettable image: "Okies" driven out of the dust bowl of the Middle West and permitted to enter California as virtual peons for seasonal labor. There was something awesome in the fact that the greatest evocation of America's stricken land in the 1930s should have come from a native of the fertile and beautiful Salinas Valley. No other writer of the period celebrated "Westering," the historic migration to California, as tellingly as Steinbeck did. He had a positive genius for identifying his characters entirely with their beloved valley. They moved into the landscape with an unconscious grace that showed just how deeply it pervaded them. In one of Steinbeck's best stories, "The Leader of the People," an elderly grandfather, forever repeating the epic story of how he led a "crossing" to California, desperately sums up for Jody, ten years old, "with hair like dusty yellow grass and with shy polite eyes":

> "I feel as though the crossing wasn't worth doing. . . . I tell these old stories, but they're not what I want to tell. I only know how I want people to feel when I tell them.
> "It wasn't Indians that were important, nor adventures, nor even getting out here. It was a whole bunch of people made into one big crawling beast. And I was the head. It was westering and westering. Every man wanted something for himself, but the big beast that was all of them wanted only westering. . . .
> "Under the little bushes the shadows were black at white noonday. When we saw the mountains at last, we cried—all of us. . . .
> "We carried life out here and set it down the way those ants carry eggs. And I was the leader. The westering was as big as God, and the slow steps that made the movement piled up and piled up until the continent was crossed."

Steinbeck had an almost professional interest in biology. For him history was really the life cycle "of mice and men." His profoundest instinct as a writer was for the rhythms inherent in all organic being. His best passages invariably give poignancy to the simplest interactions of man with nature. In "The Chrysanthemums" a farm woman planting the flowers surprises herself by telling a stranger

> "It's the budding that takes the most care," she said hesitantly. "I don't know how to tell you . . . I'll try to tell you. Did you ever hear of planting hands?"
> "Can't say I have, ma'am."
> "Well, I can only tell you what it feels like. It's when you're picking off the buds you don't want. Everything goes right down into your fingertips. You watch your fingers work. They do it themselves. You can feel how it is. They pick and pick the buds. They never make a mistake. They're with the plant. Do you see? Your fingers and the plant. You can feel that, right up your arm. They know. They never make a mistake. You can feel it. When you're like that you can't do anything wrong."

Even in his shattering tale of the Okies crawling out of the side roads onto the great cross-country highway—"in the daylight they scuttled like bugs to the westward; and as the dark caught them, they clustered like bugs near to shelter and to water"—Steinbeck found the perfect symbol for their refusal to give up. It was a turtle taking forever to crawl up the concrete highway. The highway

was edged with a mat of tangled, broken, dry grass, and the grass heads were heavy with oat beards to catch on a dog's coat, and foxtails to rangle in a horse's fetlocks, and clover burrs to fasten in sheep's wool; sleeping life waiting to be spread and dispersed . . .

And over the grass at the roadside a land turtle crawled, turning aside for nothing, dragging his high-domed shell over the grass. His hard legs and yellow-nailed feet threshed slowly over the grass, not really walking, but boosting and dragging his shell along. The barley beards slid off his shell, and the clover burrs fell on him and rolled to the ground. His horny beak was partly open, and his fierce, humorous eyes, under brows like fingernails, stared straight ahead. He came over the grass leaving a beaten trail behind him, and the hill, which was the highway embankment, reared up ahead of him. For a moment he stopped, his head held high. He blinked and looked up and down. At last he started to climb the embankment.

California pea fields; the luckless migrants from the Midwest "dust bowl" movingly depicted in Steinbeck's The Grapes of Wrath. *Photograph by Dorothea Lange.*

California in the 1930s. Migrants in their jalopy. A photograph by Dorothea Lange, as evocative as Steinbeck's prose.

The stolid obstinacy of the turtle is an irresistible fact on cross-country Route 66. "And now a light truck appeared, and as it came near, the driver saw the turtle, and swerved to hit it." Steinbeck captured all the meanness of the depression period. No one else left such searing images of dispossession from the land, the long days and nights in the rattling old trucks and jalopies, the dwindling water, the unstopping anxiety and monotony of Highway 66:

> over the red lands and the gray lands, twisting up into the mountains, crossing the Divide and down into the bright and terrible desert, and across the desert to the mountains again, and into the rich California valleys.

66 is the path of a people in flight . . . and they come into 66 from the tributary side roads, from the wagon tracks and the rutted country roads. 66 is the mother road, the road of flight.

Clarksville and Ozark and Van Buren and Fort Smith on 64, and there's an end of Arkansas. And all the roads onto Oklahoma City, 66 down from Tulsa, 27 up from McAlester, 81 from Wichita Falls South, from Enid north . . . Shamrock and McLean, Conway and Amarillo, the yellow. Wildorado and Vega and Boise, and there's an end of Texas . . . there's the border of New Mexico.

And now the high mountains. . . . Then out of the broken sun-rotted mountains of Arizona to the Colorado, with green reeds on its banks, and that's the end of Arizona. There's California just across the river, and a pretty town to start it. Needles, on the river. But the river is a stranger in this place. Up from Needles and over a burned range, and there's the desert. And 66 goes on over the terrible desert . . .

For all the barren harshness of the southwest, the positive resistance of human settlement, *The Grapes of Wrath* portrayed indelibly Steinbeck's characters' attachment to the American land as the nutriment of their being. Nothing in the most beautiful patriotic hymn, "America the Beautiful" (1893), has meant so much to Americans as the litany of the country's continental extent. It made up a world in itself, and one that to the many undergoing the famous "Westering" had seemed to need nothing but itself—plus a little help from the Almighty.

> O beautiful for spacious skies,
> For amber waves of grain,
> For purple mountain majesties
> Above the fruited plain!
> America! America!
> God shed his grace on thee
> And crown thy good with brotherhood
> From sea to shining sea!

This was the romantic nineteenth-century view. Was attachment to the land in a later age anything more than the need to wrest a living out of it? Just how profound and even desperate love for the American land could become in the twentieth century we know from the genius of Ernest Hemingway, the most deliberate native artist in landscape after Thoreau. The elusive connections between writing and painting in America were made tangible and even passionate by Hemingway. He was so deeply influenced by modern French masters, first at the Chicago Art Institute, then by Gertrude Stein's famous collection in the Rue de Fleurus, that he said he "wanted to do the country like Cézanne." "Cézanne" was another word for France itself—a country this free-wheeling American novelist, journalist, international sportsman could still choose. It was that *other* country American writers, in the 1920s particularly, chose as an exercise in imagination.

Each place Hemingway lived in became in its turn a story—with Hemingway the master stylist working up some different landscape. Hemingway inhabited the globe as only Americans do. He made his way season by season to Switzerland for the skiing, Key West and Cuba for the fishing, Venice in the marshes for bird shooting, Spain for the bullfights. He ended up in Idaho. Only an American free as air would so emblematically have chosen the emptiness and grim mountain landscape of Idaho, virtually the last of the old West. Hemingway's death in Idaho became the expected, the last great Hemingway story.

The complete story began with the earth under young Hemingway's feet in upper Michigan. This was still primitive when he was growing up, North Woods country, known from earliest time for its abundance of forest and furred animals. The Hemingways were from the respectable Chicago suburb of Oak Park, "where the saloons end and the churches begin." They summered in upper Michigan, making a ritual of it as they made their way north. The contrast between the Victorian propriety and the freedom open to an adventurous boy "up in Michigan" established forever Hemingway's passion for wild landscape. It was not just getting away from a Chicago suburb that made the summer's wilderness so important to him. His was a genuinely, fiercely out-of-doors imagination. Landscape fired him, gave him a "feel" for weather, a love of every risk out in the open. It committed him to an elaborately plain style, the only one suitable to a view of life that he made to seem totally external. It was a style that could magnify every moment of exertion and danger.

In Hemingway's story "Big Two-Hearted River," a soldier back from the First World War, seeking on a fishing trip to empty his troubled mind, becomes obsessively concerned with every detail as he makes camp in a section of burned land. This was artistically Hemingway's particular triumph of style, an unnervingly close way of seeing.

> Nick sat smoking, looking out over the country. He did not need to get his map out. He knew where he was from the position of the river.
>
> As he smoked, his legs stretched out in front of him, he noticed a grasshopper walk along the ground and up onto his woolen sock. The grasshopper was black. As he had walked along the road, climbing, he had started many grasshoppers from the dust. They were all black. They were not the big grasshoppers with yellow and black or red and black wings whirring out from their black wing sheathing as they fly up. . . . Now as he watched the black hopper that was nibbling at the wool of his sock with its fourway lip, he realized that they had all turned black from living in the burned-over land. He realized that the fire must have come the year before, but the grasshoppers were all black now.

Through the ritual of making camp, fishing, then setting the fish between ferns, Nick's uneasy mind throws its shadow on the field his body is working.

> On the left, where the meadow ended and the woods began, a great elm tree was uprooted. Gone over in a storm, it lay back into the woods, its roots clotted with dirt, grass growing in them, rising a solid bank beside the stream. The river cut to the edge of the uprooted tree. From where Nick stood he could see deep channels, like ruts, cut in the shallow bed of the stream by the flow of the current. Pebbly where he stood and pebbly and full of boulders beyond; where it curved near the tree roots, the bed of the stream was marly and between the ruts of deep water green weed frond swung in the current. . . . Ahead the river narrowed and went into a swamp. The river became smooth and deep and the swamp looked solid with cedar trees, their trunks close together, their branches solid. It would not be possible to walk through a swamp like that. The branches grew so low. You would have to keep almost level with the ground

to move at all. You could not crash through the branches. That must be why the animals that lived in swamps were built the way they were, Nick thought.

The repetitions can be disturbing; what Hemingway wanted in his manipulative way. "In the swamp the banks were bare, the big cedars came together overhead, the sun did not come through, except in patches; in the fast deep water, in the half light, the fishing would be tragic. In the swamp fishing was a tragic adventure." But the overlying sense of the wild country as "tragic adventure" should not distract us from the piercing love that Hemingway, beyond anyone else of his time and place, brought to Nature in America. Nature was his first, his last, his only enduring love. As a man of sixty, "all across Iowa Nebraska Wyoming he counted and identified every bird he saw and kept a running record of the wild animals." His political resentments and his ideals for writing came to the same point. He wrote in one letter: "No unit larger than the village can function justly." In an essay "On Writing," he said that he used what he got from the country "to do people with."

Hemingway was so deeply attached to place as an element correlative with himself that the sensations he learned in upper Michigan woods he duplicated in the bullfights in Spain, on a street in Paris, in the Italian countryside of *A Farewell to Arms*. There the opening ("In the bed of the river there were pebbles and boulders, dry and white in the sun, and the water was clear and swiftly moving and blue in the channels") justifies Ford Madox Ford's perfect praise—"Hemingway's words strike you, each one, as if they were pebbles fetched fresh from a brook. They live and shine, each in its place. So one of his pages has the effect of a brook-bottom into which you look down through the floating water." The right assemblage of details would make a "true sentence": the right assemblage in Nature could pacify the heart weary of itself. In "Big Two-Hearted River," Nick Adams fishing for trout was magnetized by the intense clarity, light and dark, stillness and motion, of the movement in the water. "He felt he had left everything behind, the need for thinking, the need to write, other needs. It was all back of him."

Hemingway was the greatest influence on American prose in his time. It extended even to poetry. However, his way of magnifying details and repeating them in love for the terrain was not taken up by later writers like Norman Mailer, who was spellbound by the conquest of space rather than by the tired old earth itself.

Richard Henry Dana regarded California as the great unknown, the primitive coast. Nathanael West in Hollywood saw California as an end. In his bitterly satiric novel, *The Day of the Locust* (1939), he described the crowd of recent arrivals at a Hollywood opening exuberantly violent, taking on everything in sight:

> It was a mistake to think them harmless curiosity seekers. They were savage and bitter, especially the middle-aged and the old, and had been made so by boredom and disappointment.
>
> All their lives they had slaved at some kind of dull, heavy labor . . . saving their pennies and dreaming of the leisure that would be theirs when they had enough. . . . Where else should they go but California, the land of sunshine and oranges?
>
> Once there, they discover that sunshine isn't enough. They get tired of oranges, even of avocado pears and passion fruit. Nothing happens. They don't know what to do with their time. . . . They watch the waves come in at Venice. There wasn't any ocean where most of them came from, but after you've seen one wave, you've seen them all. . . .

Their boredom becomes more and more terrible. They realize that they've been tricked and burn with resentment. Every day of their lives they read the newspapers and went to the movies. Both fed them on lynchings, murder, sex crimes, explosions, wrecks, love nests, fires, miracles, revolutions, war. This daily diet made sophisticates of them. The sun is a joke. Oranges can't titillate their jaded palates. Nothing can ever be violent enough to make taut their slack minds and bodies. They have been cheated and betrayed. They have slaved and saved for nothing.

Hollywood as the "dream factory," manufacturing illusions for the rest of the world, became the arch symbol of California as pseudo-Nature, mere appearance, "sets," costuming and pretense. In *The Day of the Locust*, in John Dos Passos's *The Big Money*, F. Scott Fitzgerald's *The Last Tycoon*, Mailer's *The Deer Park*, Joan Didion's *Play It as It Lays*, Hollywood was pictured as America's most flamboyant manufacturing center, the apex of artificiality, dominated by what S.J. Perelman called (after a stay in the place writing the Marx Brothers comedies) "hoodlums of immense wealth." It would seem that no good writer worked for the studios without ending up in a rage.

Primitive California in the Mexican era had merged into "romantic" California at the dawn of the twentieth century. Romantic California was typified even by the geologist explorer of the Sierra Nevada, Clarence King, head of the U.S. Geological Survey, who in *Mountaineering in the Sierra Nevada* (1872) had created out of scientific exploration a work of inspiration. The romantic spirit was typified for the world at large by Isadora Duncan from San Francisco, who thought of early, sea-lined California as Greece. "By the side of the Pacific," wrote one of her adoring observers, "on California shores, Isadora Duncan wed her classic Grecian beauty to the wild rhythm rolling westward across the nation's heartland and pounding in its ocean surface, and for a moment, in the barefoot abandon of her variegated dance, America moved in graceful freedom like a butterfly golden in the morning sun."

By contrast, the "Hollywood novel" and the "private eye" detective stories by Raymond Chandler, Dashiell Hammett and Ross MacDonald emphasized serpents in the garden. The Hollywood novel had to be more lurid, the scene more evil than evil elsewhere. Hollywood felt itself watched, the Klieg lights on. There was always some enticing moral corruption behind the golden appearance. An historian of California, Kevin Starr, says that its real history was "inventing the dream." The last frontier, the final edge of things, had promised the pioneers that they could start life over again.

Southern California was the most favored example of California's special good fortune. It was the American Eden before orange trees and arroyo cabins transformed it into a vast suburban wasteland of shopping malls and freeways. California as the Land of Oz, a magic kingdom of film makers and film stars, was pictured as inventing America's dreams, then preying upon it. California turned into Sodom and Gomorrah, said Kevin Starr, "a modern Babylon where Middle Western values and old-fashioned pieties turned rancid in the tropical air." He wanted to show how "the California of fact and the California of imagination shape and reshape each other," and portrayed the epic struggles over land and water and politics between the great magnates like Leland Stanford, William Randolph Hearst, the *Los Angeles Times* publisher Harrison Gray Otis, the wine maker Paul Masson, the movie moguls.

Southern California came to embody America's stupendous acceleration. *El Pueblo de Nuestra Señora La Reina de Los Angeles de Porcinuncula* evolved from a random collection of adobe huts into America's second largest city and boasted that it would soon be first. Southern California could once be held up as a symbol of a youthful country's sense of dislocation, its innocence of history. That itself attracted some extraordinarily wilful individuals—from cattle barons to aspiring movie stars to religious eccentrics intent on remaking their lives—and everyone else's—there on the sunny coast.

The producer Monroe Stahr in Scott Fitzgerald's unfinished novel *The Last Tycoon* (posthumously published 1941) has taste and humor, and is not unwilling to take on a project sure to lose money. He in fact becomes, like Fitzgerald's "great" Gatsby, a tragic hero of sorts. He had gone up very high, said Fitzgerald; he stood for something real in an unreal world that made 90 percent of the world's movies, the nation's largest industry. Everyone thought Stahr "dazzling"; to Fitzgerald he truly was a hero. Since Monroe Stahr is a man of the keenest perceptions, he is doomed.

Tod Hackett, the painter and scene designer in Nathanael West's *The Day of the Locust*, is surrounded by Hollywood small fry, grotesques. There are also Eskimos. "The Gingos were Eskimos who had been brought to Hollywood to make retouches for a picture about polar exploration. Although it had been released long ago, they refused to return to Alaska. They liked Hollywood." A hotel bookkeeper from the Midwest, Homer Simpson, has come out to Southern California to recover his health and rents a cottage in Pinyon Canyon. "Homer is just barely attached to his surroundings; they do not exactly *include* him. Homer is somehow pasted onto Southern California, like so many settlers there who never cease to feel transient." Everything is as make-believe as the movies. The successful script-writer Claude Estee lives in an imitation of Southern colonial architecture, teeters back and forth on his heels like a Civil War colonel, addresses his Chinese servant "Here, you black rascal!" and keeps in his pool the life-size, realistic reproduction of a dead horse. This earns him respect.

So much artificiality, boredom, vacancy, meaninglessness at the heart of the "dream" Nathanael West saw as a portent. The "cheated," in their dismay, would turn to the violence that is a feature of American life. The riot at the Hollywood opening that ends the book has its real-life counterpart in California's earthquakes and fires, the stormy Pacific eroding the shore. Tod Hackett dreams of painting "the burning of Los Angeles"—*at high noon.*

For its best novelists Hollywood was a mirror reproducing the central anxieties of American society. Norman Mailer in *The Deer Park* (1955) saw in Hollywood's favorite pleasure place, Palm Springs, nothing but frightened movie people enmeshed in the McCarthyite hysteria. The evil, sour-smelling "Herman Teppis" extracts sexual favors from starlets under contract; he is a caricature of a famous super-patriot movie mogul allied with William Randolph Hearst and the most reactionary forces in California. During the reign of the "black list" in Hollywood, Teppis virtuously tells Mailer's protagonist Eytel (and he *will* "tell" on his old buddies in order to get work), "I wouldn't even want to breathe the air a subversive breathes."

The most publicized of recent Hollywood novels, Joan Didion's *Play It as It Lays* (1970), portrays everything through the eyes of an actress suffering a nervous breakdown. She is obsessed with evil, sees nothing in her immediate surroundings but unbearable moral intricacy. "For days during the rain she did not speak out loud or read a newspaper. She could not read newspapers because certain stories leapt at her from the page: the four-year olds in the abandoned refrigerator, the tea party with Purex, the infant in the driveway, rattlesnake in the playpen, the peril, unspeakable peril, in the everyday." The

219

OVERLEAF: *Hollywood, Los Angeles, a make-believe city that was to inspire Fitzgerald, Mailer, West, and Didion.*

everlasting sunniness of the sky, the splendid houses and gleaming swimming pools, the insistence on perfect health and beauty at every age, are contrasted with a shiftiness in people and constant demand for sexual novelty. It all seems somewhat pointless, but this is Hollywood, where existential *nada* is more *nada* than elsewhere. A decadent producer and his masseur are pictured with "bodies gleaming, unlined, as if they had an arrangement with mortality." The heroine drives the five-lane freeways, madly shifting from lane to lane as if she were playing Russian roulette . . . "she imagined herself driving . . . driving straight into the hard white empty core of the world."

Every detail is heightened, luridly emphasized, by cutting out anything that does not spring to an effect. In *Slouching towards Bethlehem* (1968), her chronicle of the drug and hippy scene in San Francisco, and in her reflections on living in Malibu overlooking the Pacific, Didion has described how, when the Malibu hills were on fire, the young surfers in the water would look up at the fires raging overhead and go on with their surfing. Hell as Southern California. Didion herself writes a prose theatrically restrained, as if her style in all things is to keep the world from eating her up. She describes her surroundings in terms of fire, rattlesnakes, cave-ins, earthquakes, civic indifference to other people's disasters, the terrible wind called the Santa Ana.

> The city burning is LA's deepest image of itself; Nathanael West perceived that, in *The Day of the Locust*; and at the time of the 1965 Watts riots what struck the imagination most indelibly were the fires. For days one could drive the Harbor Freeway and see the city on fire, just as we had always known it would be in the end. Los Angeles weather is the weather of catastrophe, of apocalypse . . . the violence and the unpredictability of the Santa Ana affect the entire quality of life in Los Angeles, accentuate its impermanence, its unreliability. The wind shows us how close to the edge we are.
>
> ("Los Angeles Notebook")

For all this, California could still remind writers unencumbered by too much fashionable baggage of America's pure beginnings. To travel Route 1 north of San Francisco up to Russian River—taking in Muir Woods, Point Reyes, the old stockades built by Russian settlers, a place on the map actually called Eureka—was to rejoice in the beauty and undiminished solitude of coastal California. Robinson Jeffers in Carmel saw life entirely as coastal landscape. No other California writer had such a love of the spare rocky coast. Jeffers even displaced "self-centered man" in favor of brute Nature. In *The Tower beyond Tragedy*, his own version of the Orestes-Electra relationship, Orestes finds salvation from the madness of humanity by "falling in love outward" with his non-human surroundings. In his most famous expression of political rejection, "Shine, Perishing Republic," Jeffers advises his sons to "be in nothing so moderate as in love of man." In "The Women at Point Sur" the preacher in the California coast town ends up, after all the violence, starving to death in the hills, where he thinks "on the nothing/Outside the stars, the other shore of me, there's peace."

Jeffers was sure that there was a "wild God of the world, intemperate and savage, beautiful and wild." In his posthumous volume *The End and the Beginning* he declaimed against his favorite setting of granite cliffs, surf-beaten shore, towering redwoods, "Cut humanity out of my being, that is the wound that festers. . . . Solace will come to the earth only when it has attained a white and most clean, colorless quietness." War and any other negative force could be considered good in that it cleansed civilization and led back to "the primal and the latter silences."

For Jeffers the coast on which he lived in the stone tower he built himself was the dividing line between himself and an intolerable world.

> Here the human past is dim and feeble and alien to us
> Our ghosts draw from the crowded future. . . .
> The inhuman years to be accomplished,
> The inhuman powers, the service cunning under pressure,
> In a land grown old, heavy and crowded

The mythification of California as primal land, the world in all the purity of its barely known beginnings, began in Jeffers's work as soon as he moved to Carmel during the First World War and built his house and studio tower of native stone. There, said the Pittsburgh-born poet, he found his own way and discovered a meaningful setting for his poetry in the surrounding region. "For the first time in my life I could see people living—amid magnificent unspoiled scenery—essentially as they did in the Idylls or the Sagas, or in Homer's Ithaca. Here life was purged of its ephemeral accretions. Men were plowing the headland, hovered by sea-gulls, as they have done for thousands of years."

Carmel is as picturesque as anybody could desire, but for some time has catered more to the tourist trade than to plowing the headland in the style of Homer's Ithaca. But Jeffers's sense of the region as peculiarly his kind of country—rugged, stony, fiercely isolated—made for a California mythology: the bard of the simple, natural life who did not need anything else. The rest of America could always be condemned for uselessly carrying on the burden of modern civilization. "Shine, Perishing Republic," Jeffers wrote in 1925,

> While this America settles in the mold of its vulgarity, heavily thickening to
>   empire,
> And protest, only a bubble in the molten mass, pops and sighs out, and the
>   mass hardens,
>
> I sadly smiling remember that the flower fades to make fruit, the fruit rots to
>   make earth.
> Out of the mother; and through the spring exultances, ripeness and decadence;
>   and home to the mother. . . .
>
> But for my children, I would have them keep their distance from the thickening
>   center; corruption
> Never has been compulsory, when the cities lie at the monster's feet there are
>   left the mountains.

Such total rejections became all too familiar in Jeffers's work. He described himself as forever looking out to sea, his back turned to the rest of the continent. But his coastal landscapes showed an awesome sense of the world in its beginnings, unmarred by progress. In "Phenomena" (1925) he caught

> The airplane dipping over the hill; hawks hovering
> The white grass of the headland; cormorants roosting upon the guano-

223

Whitened skerries; pelicans awind; sea-slime
Shining at night in the wave-stir like drowned men's langerhans; smugglers
    signalling
A cargo to land; or the old Point Piños lighthouse
Lawfully winking over dark water; the flight of the twilight herons,
Lonely wings and a cry; or with motor-vibrations
That hum in the rock like a new storm-tone of the ocean's to turn eyes
    westward

Jeffers had the long view that so struck the Irish poet "A.E." (George Russell). "You Americans," he told Averell Harriman in the 1920s, "have a vision about this planet that no other nation has ever had." But it was the immediate thing forever moving and gleaming, glinting with flashes of light, that seemed to *root* Jeffers's being as he looked out from his famous stone tower on the headland. Hawks were a preoccupation, especially when they were hurt but still proud, minding only their "incapacity" (Jeffers tended in profile to resemble a hawk)—

The broken pillar of the wing jags from the clotted shoulder,
The wing trails like a banner in defeat,
No more to use the sky forever but live with famine
And pain a few days: . . .

. . . no one but death the redeemer will humble that head,
The intrepid readiness, the terrible eyes.
The wild God of the world is sometimes merciful to those
That ask mercy, not often to the arrogant.
You do not know him, you communal people, or you have forgotten him;
Intemperate and savage, the hawk remembers him;
Beautiful and wild, the hawks, and men that are dying, remember him. . . .

. . . I gave him the lead gift in the twilight. What fell was relaxed.
Owl-downy, soft feminine feathers; but what
Soared: the fierce rush: the night-herons by the flooded river cried fear at its
    rising
Before it was quite unsheathed from reality.

("Hurt Hawks")

The "soaring" Robinson Jeffers admired so much in hawks was actually a thing of the past as America moved into the space age. The rockets, satellites, missiles, super-speed planes usually started from land long disused, very close indeed to wilderness areas in the most agreeable climates—California and Florida. The "sun belt" beckoned to millions of Americans moving, forever moving in the great migration that expresses American history. Far north Alaska, the forty-ninth state, the first not in the continental United States, had its devotees. It was the largest state, huge beyond anything known in the "lower forty-eight." Homesteading dreams were being fulfilled in Alaska for the first time since the Homestead Act was passed during the Civil War in order to draw respectable farm families to the wild West. Tracts of land were awarded in an annual homestead lottery—40-acre and 160-acre tracts. There were good writers to follow suit—

224

John McPhee, Edward Hoagland, Norman Mailer in the opening hunting chapters of *Why Are We in Vietnam?*

McPhee specialized in American landscapes that truly were "last frontier" and were experienced as "suspect terrain." Describing a game warden who inspected the great uninhabited empty stretches of Maine from a plane with the most modern maps and equipment, McPhee made clear the attraction of such areas: they called for the ultimate in know-how. "Nature" could always come up with something unexpected. It might not be "news that stayed news," Ezra Pound's demand of literature, but it was certainly news that could give a writer an edge as he flew over Maine's emptiness with the game warden.

> In certain lakes and ponds—McKennan Lake, Fourth Pelletier Pond—there were large dark patches, roseate bruises in the water. He said they were "boiling" springs. Trout hung around them in crowds. Deer in the woods looked like Dobermans, and he would be counting ten, eleven, twelve before I could separate one from its background. Cow moose, up to their knees in water, stood motionless, like equestrian statues with missing riders.

Bears were everywhere. Bull moose walked through the water trailing mud-blue herons in white pines. Flying under 50-foot ceilings, "scud running," the warden knew "the way the land lays," knew "most of the trees," but in snow could not see ahead. "To the unaccustomed eye, severe clarity could be just as misleading as low scud." Along the Allagash (a prominent feature of Thoreau's book on the Maine Woods) it seemed as if time had stood still. People were poling, *standing* in their canoes. The North Maine woods were being advertised as "the last Eastern frontier." Nowhere else in the United States below Alaska was there such a large forest, with virtually no structures except a few cabins and some logging camps. But the unstoppable logging, virtually Maine's most important industry, with logs assembled by diesel-powered machines, could provoke "a variety of perspectives":

> If you rest against the thwarts of a canoe, the woods are much the same as ever. If you climb Allagash Mountains, you look across a broadloom of hundreds of square miles of trees—and if you have come from the megalopolis, you cannot help being impressed. If you sit in a Super Cub, however, and criss cross the forest, you may suffer recurrent attacks of myocardial ambivalence. As you look to the horizons, the vastness of the evergreen forest—the great volume of unpopulated space—has lost none of its effect.
>
> To look down, though, at the patchwork landscape is to see and to sense something else. While the warden pilot has the most comprehensive view of his beloved backcountry, it is also in some respects the least encouraging.

So much cutting made the terrain look like an old badly tanned pelt, the big "clear cuts on their way to becoming as numerous as the obsolescent lakes."

The back country was obviously not being left behind. The Adirondack preserve in New York State was the largest protected area in the country, and had been kept "Forever Wild" under a stringent amendment of the New York State Constitution since the nineteenth century. But the big news about landscape in America seemed to be in the air and about the air. Early twentieth-century writers had already had the intuition, as Edmund Wilson wrote to Vladimir Nabokov in 1942, that "Everything around me seems of an emptiness that opens right out on the interstellar spaces. I think that airplanes in changing our point of view on the permanence and authority of human habitations are also changing our intellectual and imaginative constructions." Gertrude Stein, always quick to absorb any novelty, had seen on her first trip by air

> all the lines of cubism made at the time when not any painter had ever gone up in an airplane . . . the twentieth century is a century which sees the earth as no one has ever seen it, the earth has a splendor that it never has had . . . the twentieth century has a splendor which is its own . . . that strange quality of an earth that one has never seen and of things destroyed as they have never been destroyed.

What fascinated Norman Mailer in his documentary on the lunar landings, *Of a Fire on the Moon* (1970), was the new order of magnitude that the great rockets presented as they waited in their super-large hangars. Standing in the largest possible construction, the Vehicle Assembly Plant at Cape Kennedy, Mailer recognized that

> he was standing at last in the first cathedral of the age of technology and he might well recognize that the world would change, that the world *had* changed. . . . And it had changed in ways he did not recognize, had never anticipated, and could possibly not comprehend now. The change was mightier than he had counted on. The full brawn of the rocket came over him in this cavernous womb of an immensity, this giant cathedral of a machine designed to put together another machine which would voyage through space. Yes, the emergence of a ship to travel the ether was no event he could measure by any philosophy he had been able to put together in his brain.

Winslow Homer's An Adirondack Guide *(1894, detail). One wilderness that has remained "Forever Wild." The urge to escape from civilization, to live the life of a primitive hunter or fisher, was a part of the American literary tradition up to Hemingway and beyond.*

Only Americans chose to put a man on the moon. Russians landed a radio-controlled moon-buggy, which automatically transmitted observations about the lunar surface. It even sent back to earth samples of lunar rock. President Kennedy's science advisers opposed the Apollo man-on-the-moon project, argued that the cost was incommensurate with its possible scientific value. Kennedy decided that it was necessary for political prestige. But of course the man-landing (there were to be six) was of a piece with Americans feeling that space was their natural element. As the poet Charles Olson said in describing *Moby-Dick*, Americans "rode on space."

Never was there such a people for wandering *en masse*. In the last decades of the twentieth century, five million Americans moved to the new State each year. Everything past seemed a perch from which to move farther and farther, and what was once most distant and improbable was now right at home on the television screen. Looking at the first moon landings on television in 1969, scholars at an American "think tank" on the shores of Lake Como, surrounded by pines and exquisite gardens that had existed since Roman times, could well admit, as the world bitterly charged, that Americans were too much everywhere. Despite their country's pugnacious concern with space, rocketry, the wild blue yonder, they were able to appreciate the terraces that Italian peasants had lovingly preserved over the centuries.

American poets had reason to complain that "unlimited growth" was a hindrance to the peaceful fostering of imagination. Adrienne Rich asked in *Ghazals* (1968): "How did we get caught up fighting this forest fire,/we, who were only looking for a still place in the woods?" "Texas" became a symbol of the obsession with riches; in a novel of that name by the most successful author in America, James Michener, the author nervelessly listed statistics where an old-fashioned novelist would have introduced characters The obsession with size, power, movement for movement's sake, had enthralled European writers reading Americans' accounts of themselves. After World War II, when the American novel exerted its force on an exhausted Europe, Jean-Paul Sartre wrote

What fascinated us all really—petty bourgeois that we were, sons of peasants securely attached to the earth of our farms, intellectuals entrenched in Paris for life—was the constant flow of men across a whole continent, the exodus of an entire village to the orchards of California, the homeless wanderings of the hero in *Light in August*, and of the uprooted people who drifted along at the mercy of the storm in *The 42nd Parallel*, the dark murderous fury which sometimes swept through an entire city. . . .

But now American writers themselves felt that their famous *Wanderlust* was all too much. The exquisitely intelligent poet Elizabeth Bishop wrote in "Questions of Travel," about her life between Canada, the United States, Brazil,

> "Continent, city, country, society:
> the choice is never wide and never free.
> And here, or there . . . No. Should we have stayed at home,
> wherever that may be?"

In truth, Americans did not know what to make of nature as "a diminished thing." The *New Yorker* writer Thomas Powers, in a harrowing meditation on the world facing "Nuclear Winter," described how he "took an air taxi down the length of Long Island toward New York City and watched the sun set through the yellow and purple and violent streaks of gunk suspended over the city. It seemed hard to believe that living creatures could breathe that livid stew. A lot of what we think of as nature is really the work of man." E.B. White, when he moved from New York City to a still empty Maine, spoke for a whole generation alarmingly suspicious of civilization. He said he was "homesick for loneliness."

A century before, Thomas Carlyle had accused Walt Whitman of thinking himself a big poet "because he lived in a big country." There is no question that Whitman, like so many of his countrymen, adored progress. In the great poem of his old age, "Passage to India," Whitman celebrated simultaneously the completion of the Suez Canal, the railroad route to the Pacific, and the successful laying of the Atlantic cable. Of this poem Whitman, half-paralyzed and poor as ever in a rundown house in Camden on the Delaware River, had said to Horace Traubel: "There's more of me, the essential ultimate me, in that than in any of the poems . . . the burden of it is evolution—the one thing escaping the other—the unfolding of cosmic purposes."

> Lands found and nations born, thou born America,
> For purpose vast, man's long probation fill'd,
> Thou rondure of the world at last accomplish'd.

Hector St. John Crèvecoeur in his *Letters from an American Farmer* had said of his new countrymen: "They will finish the great circle." The "cosmic purpose" Whitman boasted of was Columbus's dream of reaching Asia directly from Europe—anticipating, Whitman said, the eventual, necessary unity of the world. Which would justify America in all its history across the continent as nothing else could. The "marriage of continents" was in Whitman's "Passage to India," along with the "facts of modern science," the "myths and fables of eld, . . ./The deep diving bibles and legends," which would unify the world. The process would be carried on "not for trade or transportation only,/But in God's name, and for thy sake O soul."

The long history of mankind, from Oriental antiquity to the present culture of the West would be *justified* in America only when "the poet, worthy of that name,/The true son of God shall come singing his songs." The passage of the soul must be "to more than India." "Cosmic purposes" or not, the real thrust of Whitman's "passage" was not in such transcendental longings to reach beyond America's shores, but in man's happiness with Nature, in the real details of his minute involvement with Nature. Whitman's dream was not in the cosmic but in his hope that

> The whole earth, this cold, impassive, voiceless Earth, shall be completely
>   justified, . . .
> Nature and Man Shall be disjoin'd and diffused no more.

Here, nearing his end, Whitman put his finger on the key problem that his people, once a "wilderness people," now faced beyond any other. As he said when "Facing West from California Shores," accurately describing himself as always alone, a solitary singer—

> But where is what I started for so long ago?
> And why is it yet unfound?

PERSONAL ACKNOWLEDGMENTS

This book was made possible, long before it was actually thought of, by many farflung experiences of the American landscape. Thanks to assignments from American magazines, to benevolent American colleges, universities and foundations, I have covered a lot of American territory from my native New York to Death Valley in California, from Black Mountain and the Outer Banks of North Carolina to Russian River north of San Francisco, from the dunes of Cape Cod to the dunes (and steel mills) of Lake Michigan. For companionship and instruction on more recent journeys during the writing of *A Writer's America*, I owe much to my wife Judith Dunford.

ACKNOWLEDGMENTS

Permission to use copyright material is gratefully acknowledged to the following:

For permission to reprint from the works of Robert Frost: to The Estate of Robert Frost, Edward Connery Lathem, editor of *The Poetry of Robert Frost*, and to Jonathan Cape Ltd. Poems by Robert Frost copyright 1930, 1934, 1939, © 1969 by Holt, Rinehart and Winston. Copyright © 1958, 1962 by Robert Frost. Copyright © 1967 by Lesley Frost Ballantine. Reprinted from THE POETRY OF ROBERT FROST edited by Edward Connery Lathem, by permission of Henry Holt and Company, Inc.

Selection from Robert Lowell reprinted by permission of Faber and Faber Ltd from FOR THE UNION DEAD by Robert Lowell. Excerpt from "For the Union Dead" from FOR THE UNION DEAD by Robert Lowell. Copyright © 1956, 1960, 1961, 1962, 1963, 1964 by Robert Lowell. Reprinted by permission of Farrar, Straus and Giroux, Inc.

Quotation from "Chicago" in CHICAGO POEMS by Carl Sandburg, copyright 1916 by Holt, Rinehart and Winston, Inc.; renewed 1944 by Carl Sandburg. Reprinted by permission of Harcourt Brace Jovanovich, Inc.

Excerpts from THE SELECTED POETRY OF ROBINSON JEFFERS by Robinson Jeffers. Copyright 1938 and renewed 1966 by Donnan Jeffers and Garth Jeffers. Reprinted by permission of Random House, Inc.

BIBLIOGRAPHY

AUDUBON, John James, *The Birds of America*, New York, N.Y., 1953
————, *Delineations of American Scene and Character*, New York, N.Y., 1926
BARTRAM, William, *Travels through North and South Carolina, Georgia, East and West Florida, the Cherokee Country, the Extensive Territories of the Muscogulges, or Creek Confederacy, and the Country of the Chactaws: Containing an Account of the Soil and Natural Productions of these Regions, together with Observations on the Manners of the Indians*, Philadelphia, Pa., 1791
BERGON, Frank, ed., *The Wilderness Reader*, New York, N.Y., 1980
BERRY, Wendell, *The Unsettling of America: Culture and Agriculture*, New York, N.Y., 1977
BILLINGTON, R. A., *Westward Expansion: A History of the American Frontier*, New York, N.Y., 1949
BREBNER, Bartlett J., *The Explorers of North America, 1492–1806*, New York, N.Y., 1933
CADDELL, Harry, *Night Comes to the Cumberlands*, Boston, Mass., 1962
CARSON, Rachel, *Silent Spring*, New York, N.Y., 1966
CARVER, Jonathan, *Three Years Travels through the Interior Parts of North America*, London, 1778
CONNELL, Evan S., *Son of the Morning Star*, San Francisco, Calif., 1984
CONRON, John R., ed., *The American Landscape*, New York, N.Y., 1973
CRÈVECOEUR, Hector St. John De, *Letters from an American Farmer*, London, 1912
CRONON, William, *Changes in the Land*, New York, N.Y., 1983
DELORIA, Jr., Vine, *Custer Died for Your Sins*, New York, N.Y., 1970
DE TOCQUEVILLE, Alexis, *Democracy in America*, New York, N.Y., 1969
DE VOTO, Bernard, ed., *The Journals of Lewis and Clark*, Boston, Mass., 1953
————, *The Course of Empire*, Boston, Mass., 1952
EDMISTON, Susan, and Cirino, Linda D., *Literary New York: A History and Guide*, New York, N.Y., 1976
FEDERAL Writers Project, *New York Panorama*, New York, N.Y., 1984
FLEXNER, James Thomas, *First Flowers of our Wilderness*, New York, N.Y., 1947
FREMONT, John C., *Narratives of Exploration and Adventure*, ed. Allan Nevins, New York, N.Y., 1947
HONOUR, Hugh, *The New Golden Land: European Images of America from the Discoveries to the Present Time*, New York, N.Y., 1976
JACOBS, Jane, *The Death and Life of Great American Cities*, New York, N.Y., 1961
JACKSON, John Brinckerhoff, *Discovering the Vernacular Landscape*, New Haven, Conn., 1984
JAMES, Henry, *The Art of Travel*, ed. Morton Dauwen Zabel, New York, N.Y., 1948
————, *The American Scene*, New York, N.Y., 1946

KELLY, Lawrence C., *Navajo Indians and Federal Indian Policy, 1900–1935*, Tucson, Ariz., 1968

KING, Clarence, *Mountaineering in the Sierra Nevada*, Boston, Mass., 1872

KOLODNY, Annette, *The Land before Her: Fantasy and Experience of the American Frontiers (1630–1860)*, Chapel Hill, N.C., 1983

KLUCKHOHN, Clyde, and Leighton, Dorothea, *The Navaho*, Cambridge, Mass., 1974

LEYDA, Jay, ed., *The Melville Log*, New York, N.Y., 1951

———, *The Years and Hours of Emily Dickinson*, New Haven, Conn., 1960

LORCA, Federico García, *The Poet in New York*, New York, N.Y., 1955

McCULLOGH, David, *The Great Bridge*, New York, N.Y., 1972

McPHEE, John, *Coming into the Country*, New York, N.Y., 1977

MARX, Leo, *The Machine in the Garden: Technology and the Pastoral Ideal*, New York, N.Y., 1964

MATTHIESSEN, Peter, *Wild Life in America*, New York, N.Y., 1950

MAXIMILIAN OF WIED, Prince, *Travels in the Interior of North America*, Cleveland, Ohio, 1905

MILLER, Perry, *Nature's Nation*, Cambridge, Mass., 1967

MITCHELL, Lee Clark, *Witness to a Changing America*, Princeton, N.J., 1981

MUIR, John, *My First Summer in the Sierra*, New York, N.Y., 1987

NASH, Roderick, *Wilderness and the American Mind*, New Haven, Conn., 1967

NABOKOV, Vladimir, *Lolita*, New York, N.Y., 1958

PISANO, Ronald G., *Long Island Landscape Painting, 1820–1920*, Boston, Mass., 1985

POWELL, John Wesley, *Exploration of the Colorado River of the West and its Tributaries*, New York, N.Y., 1987

REINGOLD, Nathan, ed., *Science in Nineteenth-Century America*, New York, N.Y., 1964

RISCHIN, Moses, *The Promised City*, Cambridge, Mass., 1964

ROURKE, Constance, *American Humor: A Study of the National Character*, New York, N.Y., 1931

SEELYE, John, *Prophetic Waters*, New York, N.Y., 1977

SMITH, Henry Nash, *Virgin Land: The American West as Symbol and Myth*, Cambridge, Mass., 1950

STARR, Kevin, *Americans and the California Dream, 1850–1915*, New York, N.Y., 1973

STEWART, George R., *American Place Names*, New York, N.Y., 1970

TERRIE, Philip G., *Forever Wild*, Philadelphia, Pa., 1985

THOMAS, Keith, *Man and the Natural World*, New York, N.Y., 1984

TRAFZER, Clifford, *The Kit Carson Campaign*, Norman, Okla., 1982

VAN DYKE, John C., *The Desert*, Salt Lake City, Nev., 1980

WALLACE, David Rains, *The Klamath Knot*, San Francisco, Calif., 1983

WATERS, Frank, *Book of the Hopi*, New York, N.Y., 1977

WHITEHEAD, Alfred North, *Science and the Modern World*, New York, N.Y., 1967

WILSON, Edmund, ed., *The Shock of Recognition*, New York, N.Y., 1967

LIST OF ILLUSTRATIONS

BLACK & WHITE

Pages

2–3   View on the Sweetwater, with burial place of soldier, 1862, Fremont Co., Wyoming, photo William Henry Jackson. National Archives, Washington

10   Aerial View of Monticello, Charlottesville, Virginia. Photo Rieley and Associates

13   *The Natural Bridge of Virginia*, painting by David Johnson, 1860. Jo Ann and Julian Ganz, Jr., Collection

21   *Solitude*, lithograph by Thomas Moran, 1869

26   Bull Alligators, St. John's River, Florida, sketch by William Bartram, 1773

29   *River in the Catskills*, detail of painting by Thomas Cole (1801–48). Museum of Fine Arts, Boston

31   Passenger pigeons, drawing. University of Wisconsin

38   *The Lewis and Clark Expedition*, painting by Thomas Mickell Burnham, *c.* 1850. Courtesy Buffalo Bill Historical Center, Cody, Wyoming

39   Frontispiece of a journal of the Lewis and Clark expedition. Library of Congress, Washington

       Buffalo Chase in Winter, Indians on Snowshoes, painting by George Catlin, *c.* 1832. National Museum of American Art, Smithsonian Institution, Washington

42   *Fort Laramie*, detail of painting by Alfred J. Miller, 1851. The Thomas Gilcrease Institute of American History and Art, Tulsa, Oklahoma

43   *Caravan en Route*, American Fur Company Expedition, 1837, painting by Alfred Jacob Miller, *c.* 1845. Boatmen's National Bank of St. Louis

46   The Old Manse, Concord, photo by Alice Moulton

49   *Philosophers' Camp in the Adirondacks*, painting by W.J. Stillman, *c.* 1857–58. Free Public Library, Concord

51   New England, photo by Ian Pleeth

56   *Cape Cod, Evening*, painting by Edward Hopper, 1939. National Gallery of Art, Washington

59   Henry Thoreau's Cabin, from a sketch by Thoreau's sister Sophie, first edition of *Walden*, 1854

65   *Capture of a Sperm Whale*, lithograph, *c.* 1850, after painting by Ambroise Louis Garneray. Shelburne Museum, Shelburne, Vermont

68   *Hiawatha*, illustration by Frederic Remington in Longfellow's *Song of Hiawatha*, 1891 edition

77   *Looking over the Sand Dunes — East Hampton*, etching by Thomas Moran, 1880. Print Collection, New York Public Library

       City of Brooklyn, Long Island, lithograph by John Barnet, 1855. Print Collection, New York Public Library

79   Burying the Dead, Cold Harbor, Virginia, detail of photo by J. Reekie and A. Gardner, 1865

82   *Crossing the Plains*, painting by Charles Christian Nahl, 1856. Stanford University Museum of Art, Stanford, California

85   *The Old Stagecoach of the Plains*, painting by Frederic Remington, 1901. Amon Carter Museum, Fort Worth, Texas

86–87   Devil's Gate, Wyoming, photo by William Henry Jackson, *c.* 1871. National Archives, Geological Survey, Washington

93   Illustration from *Life on the Mississippi* (1863) by Mark Twain, 1914 edition

94   *Fishing on the Mississippi*, painting by George Caleb Bingham, 1851. Nelson-Atkins Museum of Art, Kansas City

95   *St. Louis from the River Below*, painting by George Catlin, *c.* 1832. National Museum of American Art, Washington

97   Clearing a Homestead, *c.* 1900. National Archives, Washington

98   Landscape scene from *The Last of the Mohicans*, painting by Thomas Cole, 1827. New York State Historical Association, Cooperstown

100   Theodore Roosevelt on a Hunting Trip in Colorado, 1905. Theodore Roosevelt Collection, Harvard College Library
        Snowsheds on the Central Pacific Railroad in the Sierra Nevada Mountains, painting by Joseph Becker, 1869. The Thomas Gilcrease Institute of American History and Art, Tulsa, Oklahoma

103   A member of the Pioneer Automobile party, at rim of Grand Canyon, Arizona. Photo by Aultman, *c.* 1902. Library of Congress, Washington
        The Grand Canyon of the Yellowstone, painting by Thomas Moran, 1872. US Department of the Interior

110   Immigrants entering South Loop Valley, Custer County, Nebraska, 1886. Solomon D. Butcher Collection, Nebraska State Historical Society

113   *Robidoux Pass, White Mountains of New Mexico*, watercolor by Richard H. Kern, 1848. Amon Carter Museum, Fort Worth, Texas

114   *I Feed You All*, poster, 1876. Library of Congress, Washington

115   Henry George. California Historical Society, San Francisco

118   Jack London. California Historical Society, San Francisco

120   Oregon Trail, Wyoming, photo by William Henry Jackson, *c.* 1875

122   The Dickinson Homestead, Amherst, lithograph by J. Batchelder, 1858

127   Dickinson Gravesite, West Cemetery, Amherst. The Jones Library, Amherst, Mass.

131   *Boston Common at Twilight*, detail of painting by Childe Hassam, 1885–6. Museum of Fine Arts, Boston

132   Grand Union Hotel, Saratoga, stereoscopic view by Baker and Record, *c.* 1875

134   The Drive, Newport, *Harper's New Monthly Magazine*, 1874

135   *Beach at Newport, Rhode Island*, painting by John Frederick Kensett, 1869/72. National Gallery of Art, Washington

137   *Maine Cliffs*, watercolor over charcoal by Winslow Homer, 1883. The Brooklyn Museum, New York

141   Stone Wall in New England, photo by Ian Pleeth

145   *Ruin Rising Gaunt*, Mississippi. Photo by Walker Evans, *c.* 1948. Courtesy of estate of Walker Evans

149   *Roasting Ears*, painting by Thomas Benton (1889–1975). Metropolitan Museum, New York

153   *Sunset, West 23rd Street, New York*, detail of painting by John Sloan, 1905–6. The Joslyn Art Museum, Omaha, Nebraska

154   *Washington Arch, Spring*, painting by Childe Hassam, 1890. The Phillips Collection, Washington D.C.
Washington Square Park, lithograph, *c.* 1880. New York Public Library

157   *The Battery, New York*, detail of painting by Samuel B. Waugh, *c.* 1855. Museum of the City of New York

159   Maiden Lane, New York, lithograph by J.J. Fogerty, *c.* 1885. New York Public Library

160   Row of brownstones

163   The Building of Brooklyn Bridge, illustration from *Harper's Weekly*, 1877

164   *Looking through Brooklyn Bridge*, drypoint by C.R.W. Nevinson (1919–20). Museum of Modern Art, New York

167   Brooklyn Bridge, detail of photo by the Wittemann Brothers, *c.* 1900. Library of Congress, Washington

169   *Bird's Eye View of Central Park*, drawing by John Bachman, *c.* 1870. Courtesy of New York Historical Society

170   *Central Park*, watercolor by Maurice Prendergast, 1901. Whitney Museum of American Art, New York

171   Orchard Street, New York, photo by Byron, *c.* 1900

174   Plaza Hotel, illustration in *Vanity Fair*, 1922. Periodical Division, Library of Congress, Washington

175   Manhattan, New York

176   Christ Church, built 1723, Boston, Mass. Photo Sandak

180   Colonel Robert Gould Shaw Memorial by Augustus Saint-Gaudens (1848–1907). Courtesy Bostonian Society

181   Chicago stockyard. Library of Congress, Washington

182   World Columbian Exposition, Court of Honor, 1893

183   View in Little Poland, Chicago, 1903. Chicago Historical Society

187   The El on the South Side, Chicago, photo by Russell Lee, 1941. Library of Congress, Washington

192   Construction of the Washington Monument, Washington, photo by M. Brady, 1879. National Archives, Washington

194   Adams Memorial, Rock Creek Cemetery, Washington, D.C., by Augustus Saint-Gaudens, 1886–91. Library of Congress, Washington

196   Catching Grasshoppers, detail from *Hutchings Californian Scenes*, California Historical Society, San Francisco

197   Santa Barbara Mission, drawing by William Rich Hutton, 1852. Henry E. Huntington Library, San Marino, California
San Joaquin County, California Historical Society, San Francisco

198   Cypress Point, Monterey, California. California Historical Society, San Francisco

199   West Coast View, lithograph. California Historical Society
Old Whaling Station at Carmel Bay, lithograph. California Society, San Francisco

200   San Francisco in 1847, drawing by William Rich Hutton, 1852. Henry Huntingdon Library, San Marino, California

201   *Panning Gold, California*, detail of watercolor by W. McIlvaina (1813–67). Museum of Fine Arts, Boston

203   San Francisco General View, 1856. California Historical Society, San Francisco
Map of San Francisco. California Historical Society, San Francisco

204   Bret Harte. California Historical Society, San Francisco

210   Lake Tahoe, Van Wagener's Hotel and Fishery, drawing by E.Vischer, 1861.

California Historical Society, San Francisco

213   Migrant family, 1935, F.S.A. photo by Dorothea Lange. F.D.R. Library, Washington

214   Migrant workers, F.S.A. photo by Dorothea Lange. Library of Congress, Washington

200–1   Los Angeles, Hollywood, and forty other towns. Photo Mount Wilson and Palomar Observatories, California

226   *The Adirondack Guide*, watercolor by Winslow Homer, 1894. Museum of Fine Arts, Boston

COLOR

pages

17   *In Nature's Wonderland*, detail of painting by Thomas Doughty, 1835. Detroit Institute of Arts, Founders Society Purchase, Gibbs-Williams Fund

18   "Franklinia," colored drawing by William Bartram (1756–88). British Museum (Natural History), London

35   *St. John's River, Florida*, painting by Hermann Herzog (1832–1932). Courtesy Messrs Sotheby's, New York

36   *Indians Hunting the Bison*, detail of illustration by Karl Bodmer from *Wied-Neuwied's Travels . . .*, 1844. Rare Book Division, New York Public Library

53   *The Peaceable Kingdom*, detail of painting by Edward Hicks, c. 1848. Albright-Knox Art Gallery, Buffalo, New York, James G. Forsyth Fund

54   *Twilight in the Wilderness*, detail of painting by Frederic Church, 1860. The Cleveland Museum of Art, Mr. and Mrs. William H. Marlatt Fund

71   *The Much-Resounding Sea*, detail of painting by Thomas Moran, 1884. National Gallery of Art, Washington, gift of the Avalon Foundation

72   *Walden Pond*, photograph by Ivan Massar, Concord, Massachusetts

89   *Raftsmen Playing Cards*, painting by George Caleb Bingham, 1847. The St. Louis Art Museum, Ezra H. Linley Fund

90   *Overland Trail*, detail of painting by Albert Bierstadt (1830–1902). Photo by J.O. Milmoe. Courtesy of Auschutz Collection, Colorado

107   *Prairie Burial*, detail of painting by William Ranney (1813–57). Photo by J.O. Milmoe. Courtesy of Auschutz Collection, Colorado

108   *Turn Him Loose, Bill*, detail of painting by Frederic Remington (1861–1909). Photo by J.O. Milmoe. Courtesy of Auschutz Collection, Colorado

189   *Washington View Looking West with Imaginative Rendering of the Capitol*, detail of lithograph by E. Sachse and Co., 1852. Prints and Photographs Division, Library of Congress, Washington D.C.

190   *California Stage Coach Halt*, detail of painting by C.W. Hahn, 1875. Photo by J.O. Milmoe. Courtesy of Auschutz Collection, Colorado

207   *Yosemite Valley*, detail of painting by Thomas Hill, 1876. The Oakland Museum, California

108   Arizona Landscape, photo by Gerd Kittel

INDEX

Page numbers in italics refer to illustrations.
Books are listed under the author's name.

A

aborigines, American 16, 19
Adams, Henry 88, 156, 184–6, 191, 193–4;
  Democracy 191, 193; *The Education of
  Henry Adams* 178, 182, 188, 191
Adams, John (2nd US President 1797–1801)
  188
Adams, John Quincy (6th US President 1825–
  29) 188
Adirondack preserve (N.Y. state) 7, *49*, 225,
  226
Alaska 75, 224
Algren, Nelson, on Chicago 183
Altgeld, John Peter (governor of Chicago) 184
"America the Beautiful" (hymn) 215
Anderson, Margaret: *The Little Review* 184
Anderson, Sherwood 105, 182
Arizona *209*
Ashbery, John 173
Auden, W.H. 155, 162, 173
Audubon, John James 30–1

B

Baldwin, James 155; *The Fire Next Time*
  173; *Go Tell It on the Mountain* 173
Balzac, Honoré de 128, 183
Baudelaire, Charles 161
Barnet, John: *Brooklyn, Long Island* 77
Bartram, John 30; *Journal of the Five
  Nations and Lake Ontario* 22
Bartram, William 8, 30; *Travels* 23–8, 40
Belker, Joseph: *The Central Pacific Railroad
  in the Sierra Nevada* 100
Bellow, Saul 8, 105, 183, 155, 185; "Looking
  for Mr. Green" 186; *Seize the Day* 173;
  The Victim 173
Benton, Thomas: *Roasting Ears* 149
Berkeley, Bishop: *On the Prospect of
  Planting Arts and Learning in America* 12
Bierstadt, Albert 88; *Overland Trail* 90
Bingham, George Caleb: *Fishing on the
  Mississippi* 94; *Raftsmen Playing Cards* 89
Bishop, Elizabeth 173; "Questions of Travel"
  227
Blue Ridge Mountains (Virginia) 11, 12, 14
Bodmer, Karl: *Indians Hunting the Bison*
  36

Boone, Daniel (pioneer) 8
Boston 19–20, 128–9, 136, 174–80
Braddock, General 42–4
Bradford, William: *History of Plymouth
  Plantation* 19
Brooklyn, New York 77, 91
Brooklyn Bridge, New York 161, *163*, *164*,
  165–6, *167*, 168, 172
Brown, John (abolitionist) 12, 50
Bryan, William Jennings (candidate for
  Presidency 1896) 112, *112*
Bryant, William Cullen 168
Buffon, Count (naturalist) 15–16
Burnham, Thomas Mickell: *The Lewis and
  Clark Expedition* 38
Byron, George Gordon 28

C

California 195–228; *197*, *198*, *199*, *213*, *214*;
  Mexican influence 115, 195–6, 200, 202;
  John Steinbeck on 212–15
Campbell, Thomas 28
Camus, Albert 147
Canada 28, 42, 102
Cape Cod, Massachusetts 55–6, 59
Capote, Truman: *Breakfast at Tiffany's* 173
Carlyle, Thomas 25, 52, 57, 75, 228
Carson, Kit (trapper and guide) 112
Catlin, George: *Buffalo Chase in Winter,
  Indians in Snowshoes* 39; *St. Louis from
  the River Below* 95
Cather, Willa 81, 105, 110, 155; *My Ántonia*
  105–6, 109; *Death Comes for the
  Archbishop* 111–12; *A Lost Lady* 110–11;
  The Professor's House 109–10
Central Park, New York 168, *169*, 170–1
Chandler, Raymond 218
Chapman, John Jay 112
Charles II (1630–85), King of England,
  Scotland and Ireland 14
Cheever, John 19; "The Enormous Radio"
  173
Chicago 181–6, *187*
Chicago World's Fair (1893) 184
Church, Frederic: *Twilight in the Wilderness*
  54
Civil War, American (1861–65) 40–1, 75, 78,
  79, 80, 81, 130, 144
Clark, Captain William (explorer) 9, 33–4,
  37–8, *39*
Clemens, Orion (Secretary of Nevada
  Territory) 81, 83

Clemens, Samuel Langhorne. *See* Twain, Mark
Cole, Thomas: *River in the Catskills* 29
Coleridge, Samuel Taylor 23–5, 28, 50; *Kubla Khan* 24
Collinson, Peter (Quaker) 22
Columbus, Christopher 228
Concord, Massachusetts 45–6, 48
Coney Island, New York 76, 78
Connell, Evan S.: *Son of the Morning Star* 102
Connolly, Cyril, on New York 173
conservation. *See under* wilderness
Cooper, James Fenimore 30, 99; *The Last of the Mohicans* 98; *The Prairie* 96, 98
Cowley, Malcolm 147
Crane, Hart 155; *The Bridge* 165–6
Crane, Stephen 116–17, 155, 211; *Maggie: A Girl of the Streets* 172
De Crèvecoeur, Hector St. John: *Letters from an American Farmer* 28–33
Cummings, E.E. 155, 173
Custer, General George Armstrong: *My Life on the Plains* 102

D

Dana, Richard Henry *197, 217*; *Two Years before the Mast* 195–6, 198, 200, 202
Dangerfield, George 88
Declaration of Independence 11, 30, 50
Dewey, John 184
Dickens, Charles, on America 155, 188
Dickinson, Austin (brother of Emily) 121, 122–3
Dickinson, Edward (father of Emily) 121
Dickinson, Emily 8, 19, 121–7, *122*; "Because I Could Not Stop for Death" 126–7
Didion, Joan: *Play It as It Lays* 218, 219, 222; *Slouching Towards Bethlehem* 222
Donne, John 30
Dos Passos, John 74, 155; *The Big Money* 173, 177; *U.S.A.* 74
Doughty, Thomas: *In Nature's Wonderland* 17
Dreiser, Theodore 105, 155; *An American Tragedy* 183; *Dawn* 183; *Sister Carrie* 172, 182, 183
Duncan, Isadora 218

E

Edel, Leon: biography of Henry James 129, 183
Eliot, George 128
Eliot, T.S. 184; *Four Quartets* 92; "The Love-Song of J. Alfred Prufrock" 177–8; *Preludes* 178
Ellison, Ralph 8, 155; *Invisible Man* 173
Emerson, Ralph Waldo 8, 40, 48–57, 58, 64, 70, 148; on California 195; on cities 191; *Concord Hymn* 45; *Nature* 45, 47–8, 49–50; "Two Rivers" 46
L'Enfant, Prosper (architect) 188

F

Farrell, James T. 181, 183, 185; *Young Lonigan* 186; *Studs Lonigan* 181
Faulkner, William 8, 11, 15, 144–50; "The Bear" 148–9; *Light in August* 144–7; *Sanctuary* 146; *The Sound and the Fury* 147
Ferber, Edna: *Saratoga Trunk* 130
Fitzgerald, F. Scott: *The Great Gatsby* 7, 105, 173, 182; *The Last Tycoon* 219
Florida 23, 24–8, 35, 40
Ford, Ford Madox: on Hemingway 217
Forster, E.M. 168
Fothergill, Dr. John (botanist) 23, 25
Frank, Waldo 165
Fremont, John C. (explorer) 202
frontiers 82–3, 206
Frost, Robert 138–43; *A Boy's Will* 138, 139–40; "The Death of the Hired Man" 142–3; "The Gift Outright" 20; "Mending Wall" 140, 142; *North of Boston* 138–9, 140
Fuentes, Carlos, on Old World and New World 14
Fuller, Henry Blake: *With the Procession* 182, 183

G

Galsworthy, John 194
Garland, Hamlin 182
Garneray, Ambroise Louis: *Capture of a Sperm Whale* 65
Gass, William 84–5, 105
George III (King of England 1760–1820) 22
George, Henry: *Progress and Poverty* 115, 116
Gilded Age, the 74, 128, 130–5, 161
gold rush: California (1849) 115–16, 202, 204; Klondyke (1897–9) 119–20; Nevada 88, 115–16
Gone With the Wind (Margaret Mitchell) 150
Grand Canyon 102, *103*
Gray, John Chipman (jurist) 129
Greeley, Horace (editor, *New York Tribune*) 63

H

Hahn, C.W.: *California Stage Coach Halt* 190
Hammett, Dashiell 218
Hardwick, Elizabeth, on Boston 174
Hardy, Thomas 211
Harpers Ferry, Virginia 12
Harte, Bret *204*
Hartley, Marsden 156
Hassam, Childe: *Boston Common at Twilight* 131; *Washington Arch, Spring* 154
Hawthorne, Nathaniel 8, 46, 130; *Mosses from an Old Manse* 45, 47, 48; *The Scarlet Letter* 19, 177; "Young Goodman Brown" 8, 20
Hay, John (Secretary of State) 191

Hazlitt, William 28
Hearst, George 202
Hearst, William Randolph 218
Hecht, Ben and Charles MacArthur: *The Front Page* 184
Hegel, Georg 168
Hemingway, Ernest 41, 105, 144, 215–17; "Big Two-Hearted River" 216–17; *A Farewell to Arms* 217
Herbst, Josephine 105, 106
Herrick, Robert 183, 184
Herzog, Hermann: *St. John's River, Florida* 35
Hicks, Edward 28, 60; *The Peaceable Kingdom* 53
Higginson, Thomas Wentworth 125
Hill, Thomas: *Yosemite Valley* 207
Hoagland, Edward 225
Holmes, Oliver Wendell 64, 136, 176–7
Hollywood 218–19, *220–1*, 222
Homer, Winslow: *An Adirondack Guide* 226; *Maine Cliffs* 137
Hopper, Edward: *Cape Cod Evening* 56
Horgan, Paul 88
Howells, William Dean 82, 150, 155, 176–7; *A Hazard of New Fortunes* 172
Huckleberry Finn. See under Twain, Mark
Hutchins, Robert Maynard (President, University of Chicago) 185

I

Independence, Declaration of 11, 30, 50
Independence, American War of 9, 45
Indians: in California 196; and Custer 102; and explorers 22, 25, 26, 34; Melville's view of 206, 209; on Nantucket 32; observed by Parkman (*q.v.*) 44; Twain's view of 85; wars against 101–2
Irving, Washington 30

J

Jackson, Andrew (US President 1828–37) 88, 191
James, Henry 127–8; 130, 152, 172–3, 183; *The American Scene* 130, 155–6, 171–2; "The Art of Fiction" 128; *The Bostonians* 129, 178; *The Europeans* 128–9; "Pandora" 191; *A Small Boy and Others* 172–3
James, Henry, Sr. (father of Henry James) 128, 130, 133
James, William 129, 139, 177
Jeffers, Robinson: *The End and the Beginning* 222–3; "Hurt Hawks" 224; "Phenomena" 223–4; "Shine, Perishing Republic" 222, 223; *The Tower Beyond Tragedy* 222
Jefferson, Thomas 8, 9–22, 30, 38, 44, 75, 116; and exploration of Florida 9, 32; on virtue 191
Jewett, Sarah Orne: *The Country of the Pointed Firs* 136–8
Johnson, Lyndon (US President 1963–9) 193

K

Kafka, Franz, on Whitman 74
Kalm, Peter (Swedish botanist) 22
King, Clarence: *Mountaineering in the Sierra Nevada* 218
Kennedy, John F. (US President 1961–3) 179, 227
Kensett, John Frederick: *Beach at Newport, Rhode Island* 134
Kern, Richard H.: *Robidoux Pass* 113

L

Lawrence, D.H., on American literature 8, 22, 60, 211
Lazarus, Emma: "The New Colossus" 156
Levin, Meyer 183
Lewis, Captain Meriwether (explorer) 9, 33–4, 37–8, 39
Lewis, Sinclair 105
Lincoln, Abraham (US President 1861–5) 11, 19, 41, 67, 82, 88, 184
Lindsay, Vachel 105, 112, 114–15; "The Eagle that is Forgotten" 182; *Three Poems about Mark Twain* 95
Locke, John 14, 30, 33
London, Jack 64, 117, *118*, 119–20, 211; *John Barleycorn* 118–19; "Love of Life" 120
Longfellow, Henry Wadsworth: *Evangeline* 67; *The Song of Hiawatha* 68–9
Longworth, Alice Roosevelt, on Washington 193
Lorca, Federico García 155; *Brooklyn Bridge Nocturne* 166, 168
Los Angeles 196, 218–19
Louisiana Territory 33
Lovett, Robert Morss (liberal) 184
Lowell, James Russell 55, 173, 176–7
Lowell, Robert 174; *For the Union Dead* 179–80
Lux, Charles (land speculator) 116

M

McCullough, David (Theodore Roosevelt's biographer) 102
MacDonald, Ross 218
McIlvaina, William: *Panning Gold* 201
Mackay, John W. (prospector) 202
McPhee, John 8; "frontier" landscapes 225
Madson, John: *Where the Sky Began* 105
Mailer, Norman 217; *An American Dream* 173; *The Deer Park* 218, 219; *Of a Fire on the Moon* 226; *Why Are We in Vietnam?* 225
Maine, forests of 63, 225
Malamud, Bernard: *The Tenants* 152
Malone, Dumas (Jefferson's biographer) 11, 15
Marin, John 156
Marquand, John: *The Late George Apley* 178; *The Proper Bostonians* 178
Masson, Paul 218

Mayakovsky, Vladimir 166
Mead, George Herbert 184
Melville, Herman 8, 19, 64, 126–7, 152–6,
    161, 204–9; *Billy Budd* 206; "The
    Encantadas" 205; "The House-top" 160–1;
    Moby Dick 14, 22, 44, 64–6, 157–8, 204–6;
    The Piazza Tales 156; *Pierre* 156; *Redburn*
    156–7; *Typee* 206, 209
Mencken, H.L. 177
Menuhin, Yehudi 155
Michener, James: *Texas* 227
Millay, Edna St. Vincent 173
Miller, Alfred J.: *Fort Laramie 42–3*
Miller, Henry (land speculator) 116
Miller, Perry, on Puritanism 20
Mississippi river 56–7, 81, 82, 92
Moby Dick. See under Melville, Herman
Monroe, Harriet: *Poetry: A Magazine of
    Verse* 184
Monticello (Jefferson's home) 9, *10*, 11
Moody, William Vaughan 184
Moore, Marianne 155, 173
Moran, Thomas: *The Grand Canyon of the
    Yellowstone 103; Looking over the Sand
    Dunes – East Hampton 77; The Much-
    Resounding Sea 71; Solitude 21*
Mormons 85, 106, 119
Morris, Wright 105
Mozart, Leopold 7
Muir, John 209: *The Mountains of California*
    210–11
Mumford, Lewis: *The Brown Decades* 161
myth; America as 7, 14–15, 19, 30, 222–4, 228

N

Nahl, Charles Christian: *Crossing the Plains*
    82
Nantucket, Massachusetts 32, 55
Nature 22, 67–70; relationship to man 30–3,
    63–4, 70, 73–80, 217; Romantic attitude to
    24–5, 50, 57, 80, 215; *see also*
    transcendentalism; wilderness
Natural Bridge, the (Virginia) 12, *13*, 14
Nebraska 105–6, 109, 116
Nevada 81, 83, 88
Nevinson, C.R.W.: *Looking through Brooklyn
    Bridge* 164
New England 19–20, 121–42; Emily
    Dickinson on 121–7; Robert Frost on 138–
    43; Henry James on 128–35; as
    'picturesque' 136–8
New York 152, 155–73
New Yorker magazine 173, 227
Newport, Rhode Island 133, *134*, *135*
Norris, Frank 197; *The Octopus* 209, 211–12
Norton, Charles Eliot, on Central Park 171

O

O'Connor, Flannery 150–1; *A Good Man is
    Hard to Find* 150; "Greenleaf" 151; "The
    Misfit" 150–1
O'Hara, Frank 173
O'Hara, John: *Butterfield 8* 173

O'Keeffe, Georgia 156
Olmsted, Frederick Law (designer of Central
    Park) 161, *169*, 170–1
O'Neill, Eugene 55, 155; *The Iceman
    Cometh* 173
Oregon Trail 2–3, *90*, 202
Oregon Trail, The (Francis Parkman) 41–2
Orwell, George 74
Otis, Harrison Gray (publisher) 218

P

Paine, Thomas 9, 155, 172
Palladio 9
Parker, Dorothy: "Big Blonde" 173
Parkman, Francis 30; "History of the
    American Forest" 40–4; *Montcalm and
    Wolfe 42–4; The Oregon Trail 41–2*
Paumanok (Long Island) 75–6
Peabody, Sophia (wife of Nathaniel
    Hawthorne) 45, 47
Pennsylvania 22
Petre, Lord (botanist) 22
Poe, Edgar Allan 8, 66–7, 155; "The Gold-
    Bug" 66; "MS Found in Battle" 67; "The
    Mystery of Marie Roget" 161; "The
    Philosophy of Composition" 67; "A Tale of
    the Ragged Mountains" 66–7
Porter, Katherine Anne 173
Portland, Duchess of 23
Potomac river 11, 12
Powers, Thomas: *Nuclear Winter* 227–8
Pound, Ezra 19, 139, 184, 225
Prendergast, Maurice. *Central Park 170*
Proust, Marcel 20, 40, 122
Puritanism 19–20, 176–77

Q

Quakers 22, 25–6, 80, 133

R

Ranney, William: *Prairie Burial 107*
Reagan, Ronald (US President 1981-date) 194
Reed, John (journalist) 155
Remington, Frederic 104; *The Old
    Stagecoach of the Plains 85; Turn Him
    Loose, Bill 108*
Revere, Paul 133
Richardson, Henry Hobson (architect) 191
Rich, Adrienne: *Ghazala* 227
Riis, Jacob: *How the Other Half Lives* 172
Rilke, Rainer Maria 126
Ripley, Ezra (Puritan minister) 45
Roebling, John Augustus (designer of
    Brooklyn Bridge) 161, 165; *The Condition
    of the United States Reviewed by the
    Higher Law 168*
Roebling, Washington 165
Rolle, Mr. (English settler described by
    William Bartram, *q.v.*) 27
Roosevelt, Theodore (US President 1901–9)
    99, *100*, *102*, 104; *Autobiography 101; The
    Winning of the West 101*

Rosenfeld, Paul: *Port of New York* 156
Rousseau, Jean-Jacques 33
Russell, George (A.E.) 224

S

Sacco and Vanzetti case 177, 178
Saint-Gaudens, Augustus: memorial to Mrs.
  Henry Adams *194*; memorial to Col.
  Robert Shaw *180*
Salinger, J.D.: *The Catcher in the Rye* 173
San Francisco *200, 202, 203*
Sandburg, Carl 105; "Chicago" 181, 184
Santayana, George: *The Last Puritan* 179
Saratoga Springs (New York state) 130–4, *132*
Sartre, Jean-Paul, on American wanderlust
  227
Scarlet Letter, The. See under Hawthorne,
  Nathaniel
Schlesinger, Arthur M., Sr. 135
Sewall, Samuel: record of early
  Massachusetts 20
Shaw, Quincy Adams (cousin of Francis
  Parkman, *q.v.*) 41
Shaw, Col. Robert, memorial to 179–80, *180*
Shenandoah river 11, 12
Sheridan, General Phil 101–2
Sinclair, Upton: *Boston* 178
Singer, Isaac Bashevis 155
Sloan, John: *Sunset, West 23rd Street, New
  York 153*
South, American, representation of 143–4; by
  Faulkner 144–9; by Flannery O'Connor
  150–1
Southey, Robert 23, 28
space, conquest of 225–7
Stafford, Jean: *Boston Adventure* 178
Stanford, Leland (founder of Stanford
  University) 209, 218
Starr, Kevin 218
Stein, Gertrude 215, 226
Steinbeck, John 211; "The Chrysanthemums"
  212; *The Grapes of Wrath* 209, 212–15;
  "The Leader of the People" 212
Stevens, Wallace 155, 184
Stieglitz, Alfred 156
Stillman, W.J.: *Philosophers' Camp in the
  Adirondacks* 49
Sullivan, Louis (architect) 184

T

Tahoe, Lake (California) 209, *210*
de Tocqueville, Alexis: *Democracy in
  America* 16, 19
Tate, Allen 155
Temple, Minnie (cousin of Henry James) 129
Tennyson, Alfred, Lord 57
Thoreau, Henry David 8, 14, 25, 45–8, 52, 55,
  70; *The Maine Woods* 63, 225; *Walden* 14,
  57–62; "Walking" 63; *A Week on the
  Concord and Merrimack Rivers* 46
transcendentalism 46, 48–50, 52, 55, 57–66
Turgenev, Ivan 128
Turner, Frederick Jackson, on 'end of the
  frontier' 83, 112
Twain, Mark (Samuel Clemens) 14, 41, 58,
  74, 80, 152; *The Gilded Age* 128;
  Huckleberry Finn 61, 92, 95–6, 99;
  "Jumping Frog" story 204; *Life on the
  Mississippi* 81, 92–4; *Roughing It* 83–5, 88,
  91–2, 209

V

Vaux, Calvin (landscape architect) 170
Veblen, Thorstein 184; *The Theory of the
  Leisure Class* 182
De Voto, Bernard (editor of Lewis & Clark
  expedition journal) 34

W

Walden. See under Thoreau
Walden Pond 52
Wallace, David Rains (naturalist) 24
Washington, George (US President 1789–97)
  25, 40, 43, 44, 188; memorial *192*
Washington, D.C. 11, 186–94
West, Nathanael: *The Day of the Locust*
  217–18, *219*, 222
West, American: symbol of virility 98–9
Wharton, Edith 152, *160*; *A Backward
  Glance* 130, 161; *The Buccaneers* 130; *The
  House of Mirth* 172
White, E.B. 228
Whitman, Walt 8, 48, 73, 91–2, 127, 171;
  Calamus 70; "Crossing Brooklyn Ferry"
  162; on California 195; *Democratic Vistas*
  74, 127, 128; "Earth My Likeness" 70, 92;
  "Facing West from California Shores" 228;
  Leaves of Grass 14, 20, 74–5, 152, 162;
  "Out of the Cradle Endlessly Rocking" 75–
  6; "Passage to India" 228; "Slang in
  America" 74; *Song of Myself* 15, 73–4, 78,
  80; *Specimen Days* 76, 78, 79, 80, 105
Whittier, John Greenleaf 64; *Snow-Bound*
  69–70
wilderness: love of 40–4, 57, 96, 98; New
  World as 19–20; preservation of 7, 102,
  104, 209, 225
Wilderness Society 57
Williams, Roger (founder of Rhode Island) 20
Wilson, Alexander: *Ornithology* 23
Wilson, Edmund 55, 155, 176, 184; on space
  225–6
Winthrop, Governor John (Puritan leader)
  176
Wister, Owen: *The Virginian* 104–5
Wolfe, Thomas 155; *Of Time and the River*
  173
Wordsworth, William 23, 25, 50
Wright, Frank Lloyd 184
Wright, Richard 8, 183; *Native Son* 181,
  185–6

Y

"Yoknapatawpha County" (in Faulkner's
  novels) 15, 147